Fodor's

KAUAI

WELCOME TO KAUAI

Hawaii's ultimate tropical paradise, Kauai has amazing natural wonders to explore, from the velvety green, accordion-folded cliffs of Napali Coast to the multicolor vistas of Waimea Canyon. Sun seekers choose favorites from more than 50 miles of beaches, while hikers and kayakers have abundant options in unspoiled beauty. Best of all, laid-back Kauai is one of the state's least-crowded islands, with low-key resorts and mellow former plantation villages. Places like the North Shore's Hanalei Bay, with its turquoise water, are perfect for simply relaxing.

TOP REASONS TO GO

★ **Beaches:** Pristine strips of sand and palm-fringed shores make vacation dreams real.

★ **Napali Coast:** Its towering cliffs astonish all who see them from land, sea, or air.

★ **Outdoor Fun:** Kauai offers great surfing and snorkeling, plus top-notch golf and hiking.

★ **Charming Towns:** Artsy Hanapepe, colorful Hanalei, historic Koloa, and more.

★ **Kayaking:** Paddling on a river is a tranquil way to discover the island's allure.

★ **Scenic Drives:** The North Shore's Highway 560, the West Side's Waimea Canyon Drive.

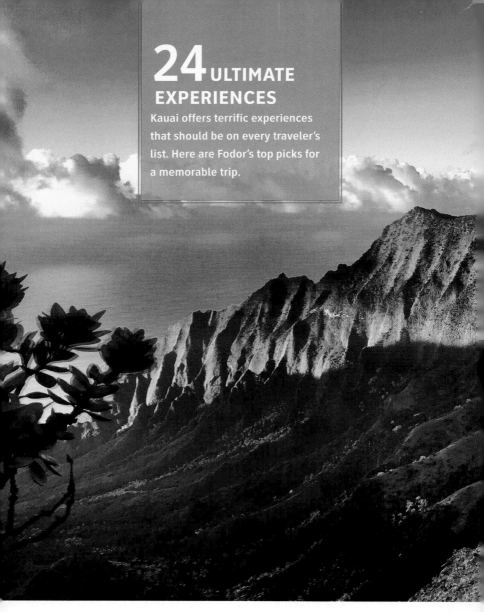

24 ULTIMATE EXPERIENCES

Kauai offers terrific experiences that should be on every traveler's list. Here are Fodor's top picks for a memorable trip.

1 Hike the Kalalau Trail

Winding 11 taxing miles along rugged Napali Coast, this is one of the world's most outrageous hikes. The first 2 miles to Hanakapiai Beach is fairly moderate; the two- to three-day round-trip hike includes camping along the way (permit required). *(Ch. 9)*

2 Coastal Sunset Sail

Kauai sunsets are sublime, and perhaps the best way to experience that magical hour of the day is by boat, facing stunning Napali Coast. *(Ch. 8)*

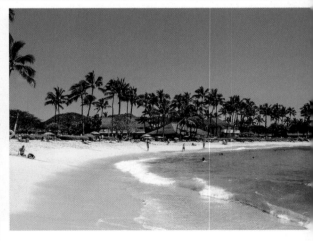

3 Relax on Poipu Beach

Popular with tourists and locals, uncrowded Poipu Beach has calm waters ideal for snorkeling, and you might just spot an endangered Hawaiian monk seal. *(Ch. 3)*

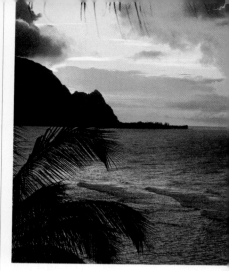

4 Mountain Tubing

A century ago, Lihue Plantation dug waterways to irrigate it's fields. Now you can take a tubing tour via the waterways for a glimpse of Kauai's hidden interior. *(Ch. 9)*

5 Sunrise on the Royal Coast

Kauai's Royal Coconut Coast—Lydgate State Park and the Ke Ala Hele Makalae biking/walking path are great vantage points—is the perfect place to watch the sunrise. *(Ch. 3, 9)*

6 Seak out the Menehune

The mythical Menehune are said to be descendants of the island's first settlers. Their "work" is found throughout Kauai, including Alekoko Fishpond near Lihue. *(Ch. 2)*

7 Learn Island History

The island's most important receptacle of island culture and history, Kauai Museum covers topics like geological formation and Hawaiian kings. *(Ch. 2, 7)*

8 Admire the Spouting Horn

Shooting water as high as 50 feet, Kauai's version of Old Faithful was once guarded by a lizard. Today, you can still hear her roar. *(Ch. 2)*

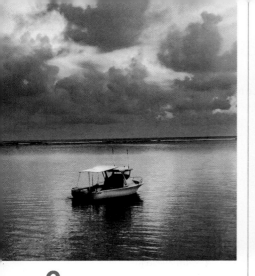

9 Go Deep Sea Fishing

The deep Pacific waters surrounding Kauai are teaming with fish. Charters, most of which depart from Lihue, visit the best spots and provide all the gear. *(Ch. 8)*

10 Hanalei Valley Views

In a land of stellar vistas, the North Shore's Hanalei Valley stands out; head to the viewpoint on Highway 56 just outside the town of Hanalei. *(Ch. 2)*

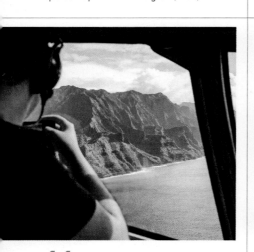

11 Helicopter Vistas

Kauai's interior is best seen via helicopter. Tours give access to breathtaking scenery like Waimea Canyon and Waialeale Crater. *(Ch. 9)*

12 Visit Sacred Heiaus

Remains of sacred structures of the Kauai kingdom are found in Wailua along Route 580 between the mouth of the Wailua River and Mount Waialeale. *(Ch. 2)*

13 Plunge into the Queen's Bath

It takes dexterity to get to this large tidal pool, but you can dawdle like a royal, emerging only to climb the rocks to dive back in. *(Ch. 2)*

14 Eat Shave Ice

The Hawaiian version of a snow cone—shave (never shaved) ice topped with a sugary syrup and condensed milk—is found throughout Kauai. *(Ch. 4)*

15 Sun-Kissed Farmers Markets

Known as the Garden Isle, Kauai's numerous farmers' markets have the freshest fruits. *(Ch. 2, 7)*

16 Cocktails Overlooking Bali Hai

Order a tropical cocktail at the Happy Talk Lounge and enjoy an enchanting sunset over Hanalei Bay. *(Ch. 6)*

17 Bird- and Whale-Watching

The northernmost point of the inhabited Hawaiian Isles, Kilauea Point has stunning ocean and coast views and amazing opportunites for bird- and whale- watching. *(Ch. 2, 8)*

18 Waimea Canyon Dazzles

A vast canyon on the island's west side, this geologic wonder measures a mile wide, more than 10 miles long, and 3,567 feet deep. *(Ch. 2, 9)*

19 Attend a Luau

Guests are treated to Hawaiian-style storytelling, complete with hula dancing, traditional knife dancing, and fire poi ball throwing at traditional luaus. *(Ch. 1, 6)*

20 Old Koloa Town

In 1835 Koloa's first sugar mill ushered in Hawaii's era of sugar production. Today, many of these historic buildings are shops and restaurants. *(Ch. 2)*

21 Art in Hanapepe

Established over a century ago, Hanapepe is filled with bougainvillea-draped, plantation-style buildings that contain restaurants, boutiques, and art galleries. *(Ch. 2)*

22 World-Class Golf

Breathtaking beauty, quality, and a vast number of thrilling, heart-stopping holes helps Kauai remain one of Hawaii's top golf destinations. *(Ch. 9)*

23 Kayaking to Secret Falls

One of Hawaii's few navigable rivers, kayaking Wailua River leads you into a mystical realm of lush rain forests, velvety green mountains, and secret, crystal-clear waterfalls. *(Ch. 2, 8)*

24 Snorkel at Kee Beach

Kauai has many fabulous snorkeling beaches, but Kee Beach is one of the best, especially for beginners and kids. Expect spectacled parrotfish, unicornfish, and green sea turtles. *(Ch. 3, 8)*

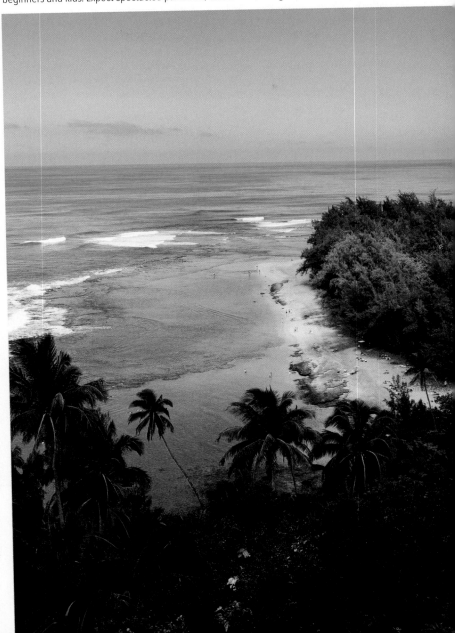

Fodor's KAUAI

Editorial: Douglas Stallings, *Editorial Director*; Margaret Kelly, Jacinta O'Halloran, *Senior Editors*; Kayla Becker, Alexis Kelly, Amanda Sadlowski, *Editors*; Teddy Minford, *Content Editor*; Rachael Roth, *Content Manager*

Design: Tina Malaney, *Design and Production Director;* Jessica Gonzalez, *Production Designer*

Photography: Jennifer Arnow, *Senior Photo Editor*

Maps: Rebecca Baer, *Senior Map Editor*; Mark Stroud and Henry Colomb (Moon Street Cartography), David Lindroth, *Cartographers*

Production: Jennifer DePrima, *Editorial Production Manager*; Carrie Parker, *Senior Production Editor*; Elyse Rozelle, *Production Editor*

Business & Operations: Chuck Hoover, *Chief Marketing Officer*; Joy Lai, *Vice President and General Manager*; Stephen Horowitz, *Director of Business Development and Revenue Operations;* Tara McCrillis, *Director of Publishing Operations;* Eliza D. Aceves, *Content Operations Manager and Strategist*

Public Relations and Marketing: Joe Ewaskiw, *Manager;* Esther Su, *Marketing Manager*

Writers: Joan Conrow, Charles E. Roessler

Editor: Alexis Kelly

Production Editor: Elyse Rozelle

7th Edition

ISBN 978-1-64097-058-8

ISSN 1934–550X

All details in this book are based on information supplied to us at press time. Always confirm information when it matters, especially if you're making a detour to visit a specific place. Fodor's expressly disclaims any liability, loss, or risk, personal or otherwise, that is incurred as a consequence of the use of any of the contents of this book.

SPECIAL SALES

This book is available at special discounts for bulk purchases for sales promotions or premiums. For more information, e-mail SpecialMarkets@fodors.com.

PRINTED IN THE UNITED STATES OF AMERICA

10 9 8 7 6 5 4 3 2 1

CONTENTS

CONTENTS

ABOUT THIS GUIDE

Fodor's Recommendations

Everything in this guide is worth doing—we don't cover what isn't—but exceptional sights, hotels, and restaurants are recognized with additional accolades. Fodor's Choice★ indicates our top recommendations. Care to nominate a new place? Visit Fodors.com/contact-us.

Trip Costs

We list prices wherever possible to help you budget well. Hotel and restaurant price categories from $ to $$$$ are noted alongside each recommendation. For hotels, we include the lowest cost of a standard double room in high season. For restaurants, we cite the average price of a main course at dinner or, if dinner isn't served, at lunch. For attractions, we always list adult admission fees; discounts are usually available for children, students, and senior citizens.

Hotels

Our local writers vet every hotel to recommend the best overnights in each price category, from budget to expensive. Unless otherwise specified, you can expect private bath, phone, and TV in your room. For expanded hotel reviews visit, Fodors.com.

Top Picks		Hotels & Restaurants	
★	Fodor's Choice	🏨	Hotel
		➯	Number of rooms
Listings		🍽	Meal plans
✉	Address	✗	Restaurant
✉	Branch address	⌣	Reservations
☎	Telephone	👔	Dress code
🖷	Fax	▭	No credit cards
⊕	Website	$	Price
✍	E-mail		
🖃	Admission fee	**Other**	
⊙	Open/closed times	⇨	See also
Ⓜ	Subway	☞	Take note
⊹	Directions or Map coordinates	🏌	Golf facilities

Restaurants

Unless we state otherwise, restaurants are open for lunch and dinner daily. We mention dress code only when there's a specific requirement and reservations only when they're essential or not accepted. For expanded restaurant reviews, visit Fodors.com.

Credit Cards

The hotels and restaurants in this guide typically accept credit cards. If not, we'll say so.

EUGENE FODOR

Hungarian-born Eugene Fodor (1905–91) began his travel career as an interpreter on a French cruise ship. The experience inspired him to write *On the Continent* (1936), the first guidebook to receive annual updates and discuss a country's way of life as well as its sights. Fodor later joined the U.S. Army and worked for the OSS in World War II. After the war, he kept up his intelligence work while expanding his guidebook series. During the Cold War, many guides were written by fellow agents who understood the value of insider information. Today's guides continue Fodor's legacy by providing travelers with timely coverage, insider tips, and cultural context.

EXPERIENCE KAUAI

WHAT'S WHERE

1 North Shore. Dreamy beaches, verdant mountains, breathtaking scenery, and abundant rain, waterfalls, and rainbows characterize the North Shore, which includes Kilauea, Princeville, Hanalei, and Haena.

2 East Side. This is Kauai's commercial and residential hub, dominated by the island's largest town, Kapaa. The airport, main harbor, and government offices are found in the county seat of Lihue.

3 South Shore. Peaceful landscapes, sunny weather, and beaches that rank among the best in the world make the South Shore the resort capital of Kauai. The Poipu resort area is here, along with the main towns of Koloa, Lawai, and Kalaheo.

4 West Side. Dry, sunny, and sleepy, the West Side includes the historic towns of Hanapepe, Waimea, and Kekaha. The area's ideal for outdoor adventurers as it's the entryway to the Waimea Canyon and Kokee State Park, and the departure point for most Napali Coast boat trips.

■ TIP→ On Kauai, the directions "mauka" (toward the mountains) and "makai" (toward the ocean) are often used. Locals tend to refer to highways by name rather than by number.

NAPALI COAST

Kokee State Park

550

WAIMEA CANYON

WEST SIDE
4

552

550

50

Kekaha

Waimea

Kaulakahi Channel

← TO NIIHAU

50

Hanapepe

Eleele

Hanapepe Bay

KAUAI PLANNER

When You Arrive

All commercial and cargo flights use the Lihue Airport, 2 miles east of the town of Lihue. It has just two baggage-claim areas, each with a visitor information center.

A rental car is the best way to get to your hotel, though taxis and some hotel shuttles are available. From the airport it will take you about 15 to 25 minutes to drive to Wailua or Kapaa, 30 to 40 minutes to reach Poipu, and 45 minutes to an hour to get to Princeville or Hanalei.

Visitor Information

Information Hawaii Beach Safety. ☎ *808/245–3971* ⊕ *www.kauaiexplorer. com.* **Hawaii Department of Land and Natural Resources.** ⊕ *hawaiistateparks.org.* **Kauai Vacation Explorer.** ⊕ *www.kauaiexplorer.com.* **Kauai Visitors Bureau.** ✉ *4334 Rice St., Suite 101, Lihue* ☎ *808/245–3971, 800/262–1400* ⊕ *www.gohawaii. com/kauai.* **Poipu Beach Resort Association.** ☎ *808/742–7444* ⊕ *www.poipubeach. org.*

Getting Here and Around

Unless you plan to stay strictly at a resort or do all of your sightseeing as part of guided tours, you'll need a rental car. There is bus service on the island, but the bumpy buses tend to run limited hours.

You most likely won't need a four-wheel-drive vehicle anywhere on the island, so save yourself the money. And although convertibles look like fun, the frequent, intermittent rain showers and intense tropical sun make hardtops a better (and cheaper) choice.

If possible, avoid the "rush" hours when the local workers go to and from their jobs. Kauai has some of the highest gas prices in the Islands. ⇨ *See "Travel Smart Kauai" for more information on renting a car and driving.*

Island Driving Times

It might not seem as if driving from the North Shore to the West Side, say, would take much time, as Kauai is smaller than Oahu, Maui, and certainly the Big Island. But it will take longer than you'd expect, and Kauai roads are subject to some heavy traffic, especially going through Kapaa and Lihue.

Haena to Hanalei	5 miles/15 mins
Hanalei to Princeville	4 miles/10 mins
Princeville to Kilauea	5 miles/10 mins
Kilauea to Anahola	8 miles/12 mins
Anahola to Kapaa	5 miles/10 mins
Kapaa to Lihue	10 miles/20 mins
Lihue to Poipu	13 miles/25 mins
Poipu to Kalaheo	8 miles/15 mins
Kalaheo to Hanapepe	4 miles/8 mins
Hanapepe to Waimea	7 miles/10 mins

Money-Saving Tips

There are ways to travel to paradise even on a budget. Pick up free publications at the airport and at racks all over the island; many of them are filled with money-saving coupons. Access to beaches and most hiking trails on the island is free to the public. Grocery stores and Walmart generally stock postcards and souvenirs; they can be less expensive here than at hotel gift shops. For inexpensive fresh fruit and produce, check out farmers' markets and farm stands along the road.

Choose high-end restaurants for lunch rather than dinner (check hours). Lunch is often less expensive. Early evening happy hour deals are a great way to save money while sampling the chef's specialties. If you're staying in a condo, eat in or pack a picnic when you can.

Dining and Lodging on Kauai

Hawaii is a melting pot of cultures, and nowhere is this more apparent than in its cuisine. From luau and "plate lunch" to sushi and steak, there's no shortage of interesting flavors and presentations.

There are several top-notch resorts on Kauai, as well as a wide variety of condos, vacation rentals, and bed-and-breakfasts to choose from. Selecting vacation lodging is a tough decision, but fret not—our expert writers and editors have done most of the legwork.

Looking for a tropical forest retreat, a big resort, or a private vacation rental? We'll give you all the details you need to book a place that suits your style. Quick tips: Reserve your room far in advance. Be sure to ask about discounts and special packages (hotel websites often have Internet-only deals).

Seeing Napali

Let's put this in perspective: even if you had only one day on Kauai, we'd still recommend heading to Napali Coast on Kauai's northwest side. Once you're there, you'll soon realize why no road traverses this series of folding-fan cliffs. That leaves three ways to experience the coastline—by air, by water, or on foot. We recommend all three, in this order: air, water, foot. Each one gets progressively more sensory.

Napali Coast runs 15 miles from Kee Beach, one of Kauai's more popular snorkeling spots, on the island's North Shore to Polihale State Park, the longest stretch of beach in the state, on the West Side of the island.

If you can't squeeze in all three methods—air, water, and foot—or you can't afford all three, we recommend the helicopter tour for those strapped for time and the hiking for those with a low budget. The boat tours are great for family fun.

When to Go

Kauai is beautiful in every season, but if you must have good beach weather, you should plan to visit between June and October. The rainy season runs from November through February, with the windward or east and north areas of the island receiving most of the rainfall. Nights can be chilly from November through March. Rain is possible throughout the year, of course, but it rarely rains everywhere on the island at once. If it's raining where you are, the best thing to do is head to another side of the island, usually south or west.

If you're a beach lover, keep in mind that big surf can make many North Shore beaches unswimmable during winter months, while the South Shore gets its large swells in summer. If you want to see the humpback whales, February is the best month, though they arrive as early as October and a few may still be around in early April. In winter, Napali Coast boat tours can be rerouted due to high seas, the Kalalau Trail can become very wet and muddy or, at times, impassable, and sea kayaking is not an option. If you have your heart set on visiting Kauai's famed coast, you may want to visit in the drier, warmer months (May–September).

KAUAI TODAY

Hawaiian culture and tradition here have experienced a renaissance over the last few decades. There's a real effort to revive traditions and to respect history as the Islands go through major changes. New developments often have a Hawaiian cultural expert on staff to ensure cultural sensitivity and to educate newcomers. Kauai public, private, and charter schools now offer full-time course work in the Hawaiian language.

Nonetheless, development remains a huge issue for all Islanders—land prices are still skyrocketing, putting many areas out of reach for locals. Approximately 45% of recent new housing on Kauai is bought by off-island purchasers, often as second homes. Traffic is also a major problem on aging Kauai roads that were not designed to accommodate all the new drivers as well as the surge in tourism. Plus, the Islands' limited natural resources are being seriously tapped.

Sustainability

Although sustainability is an effective buzzword and authentic direction for the Islands' dining establishments, 90% of Hawaii's food and energy is imported, though solar power is making a major inroad in power production. On some sunny days, for a few hours, the Kauai electric grid is more than 95% powered by alternative-energy sources. In fact, Kauai leads the state in alternative energy solutions, including hydro.

Most of the land was used for mono-cropping of pineapple or sugarcane, both of which have all but vanished. Sugarcane is now a memory, while pineapple production has dropped precipitously. Dole, once the largest pineapple company in Hawaii, closed its plants in 1991, and after 90 years, Del Monte stopped pineapple production in 2008. But the Islands have perfected a sugar pineapple that is way less acidic than the usual ones. Although the imports have negatively affected market share, they have also set the stage for great agricultural change to be explored.

Back-to-Basics Agriculture

Emulating how the Hawaiian ancestors lived and returning to their simple ways of growing and sharing a variety of foods have become statewide initiatives. Many Kauai locals buy all their fruit and produce from the numerous farmers' markets, which often feature exotic in-season crops at reasonable costs.

The seed of this movement is thriving with various farmers' markets and partnerships between restaurants and local farmers. Localized efforts such as the Hawaii Farm Bureau Federation are collectively aiding the organic and sustainable agricultural renaissance. From home-cooked meals to casual plate lunches or fine-dining cuisine, these sustainable trailblazers enrich Kauai's culinary tapestry. The recent "explosion" of food trucks offering various cuisines also uplifts the overall quality of life.

Tourism and the Economy

The $17 billion tourism industry represents more than a third of Hawaii's state income. Naturally, this dependency caused economic hardship when the 2008 financial meltdown affected tourists' ability to visit and spend, but the tourism industry has bounced back stronger than ever.

One way the industry has changed has been to adopt more eco-conscious practices, as many Kauai residents feel that development shouldn't happen without regard for impact to local communities and their natural environment.

The belief that an industry based on the Hawaiians' *aloha* should protect, promote, and empower local culture and provide more entrepreneurial opportunities for local people has become more important to tourism businesses. More companies are incorporating authentic Hawaiiana in their programs and aim not only to provide a commercially viable tour but also to ensure that the visitor leaves feeling connected to his or her host.

The concept of *kuleana,* a word denoting both privilege and responsibility, is a traditional value. Having the privilege to live in such a sublime place comes with the responsibility to protect it.

Sovereignty

Political issues of sovereignty continue to divide Native Hawaiians, who have formed myriad organizations, each operating with a separate agenda and lacking one collectively defined goal. Ranging from achieving complete independence to solidifying a nation within a nation, existing sovereignty models remain fractured and their future unresolved.

The introduction of the Native Hawaiian Government Reorganization Act of 2009 attempts to set up a legal framework in which Native Hawaiians can attain federal recognition and coexist as a self-governed entity, similar to Native American status. Also known as the Akaka Bill, after former Senator Daniel Akaka of Hawaii, this bill has been presented before Congress and is still pending.

Rise of Hawaiian Pride

After the overthrow of the monarchy in 1893, a process of Americanization began. Traditions were duly silenced in the name of citizenship. Teaching the Hawaiian language was banned from schools, and children were distanced from their local customs.

But Hawaiians are resilient people, and with the rise of the civil rights movement they began to reflect on their own national identity, bringing an astonishing renaissance of the Hawaiian culture to fruition.

The people rediscovered language, hula, chanting, and even the traditional Polynesian arts of canoe building and wayfinding (navigation by the stars without use of instruments). This cultural resurrection is now firmly established in today's Hawaiian culture, with a palpable pride that exudes from Hawaiians young and old.

The election of former President Barack Obama increased Hawaiian pride. The president's strong connection and commitment to Hawaiian values of diversity, spirituality, family, and conservation have restored confidence that Hawaii can inspire a more peaceful, tolerant, and environmentally conscious world.

GREAT ITINERARIES

Kauai is small, but its major byways generally circumnavigate the island with no through roads, so it can take more time than you expect to get around. Hiking Kalalau Trail, kayaking Wailua River, showering in a waterfall, watching whales at Kilauea Lighthouse, shopping for gifts at Koloa Town shops, et cetera: there's so much to see and do. Rather than trying to check everything off your list in one fell swoop, choose your favorites and devote a full day to the experiences.

Day 1: Settle in on the East Side
The East Side of the island is a convenient area to make a home base. Stay here and you'll have the easiest access to most of the island's top attractions. Fresh off a long flight, you'll likely just want to relax by the pool at your hotel/condo or hit **Kealia Beach** just north of funky Kapaa town. The far end near the rock jetty is for safe swimming and easy bodysurfing. There are plenty of welcoming dining options around Kapaa, such as the **Lemongrass Grill** or **Restaurant Kintaro** for a fantastic first meal.

Logistics: Wailua/Kapaa traffic can be a nightmare so avoid rush and midday times. It's 10 miles from the airport to Kapaa but drive times can vary from 15 to 35 minutes. Kealia Beach is three minutes outside Kapaa and has plenty of parking.

Day 2: Take It All In
For an incredible, and literal, overview of Kauai's beaches, forests, canyons, waterfalls, and ocean, take a morning helicopter trip with **Blue Hawaiian Helicopters** or **Jack Harter** out of Lihue. Images of the rolling verdant carpet far below will linger long in your memory. Afternoon is free for beach time or laid-back shopping in Kapaa Town. Or have lunch in Lihue and lounge on **Kalapaki Beach.**

Logistics: Lihue Airport to Kalapaki Bay is five minutes south of Lihue.

Day 3: East Side Offerings
Check out the Kapaa/Wailua area, which has a little something for everyone. Rent a bike at **Kauai Cycle** and coast along the Kauai Path (Ke Ala Hele Makalae), enjoying the ocean views and invigorating fresh air. Or take a moderate, 2-mile hike on the **Sleeping Giant Trail** for panoramic vistas of the entire East Side. Then get back on the main road for a few-minutes' drive up to **Opaekaa Falls,** one of the Wailua River's mightiest displays.

Logistics: From mid-Kapaa to the starting point of the Sleeping Giant Trail is 3 miles; just avoid rush hours.

Day 4: South Side Sights
Start with a hike on the **Mahalepu Heritage Trail** for wondrous ocean-side views of pristine beaches and craggy ledges. A quick dip at **Poipu Beach Park** will refresh your limbs after your hike. Drive down Lawai Road to spot the **Spouting Horn,** Kauai's version of Old Faithful. Right next door is the **National Tropical Botanical Garden,** where you can tour beautiful grounds of exotic flora and learn about the biodiversity in Hawaii and the Pacific.

Logistics: The Mahalepu Trail is about 10 minutes from Koloa Town. From there to Spouting Horn is about another 10-minute drive.

Day 5: At Sea on Napali Coast
Choose your preferred watercraft (Zodiac for adventure rafting or catamaran for pleasure cruising) and depart from the boat harbor in Eleele for an unforgettable journey up breathtakingly scenic Napali Coast. Most trips are about four hours and usually include a light snack; some include drinks. Don't schedule anything too demanding afterwards, as you'll likely

be tired and you'll want to savor the memories of the sights you just beheld.

Day 6: Explore the Other Kauai

In the mountains of Kokee on the West Side, you'll enjoy the splendor of the mountains, the ocean, the sunlight, and the crisper air. Stop along the way at the scenic overlooks of **Waimea Canyon** and be dazzled by the interplay of light and shadow as the sun moves across this spectacular landscape. Hike the relatively short Canyon Trail to a divine waterfall. Have lunch at the **Kokee Lodge,** check out the **Kokee Museum** next door, and continue another 5 miles or so to the Kalalau Lookout.

Logistics: Drive up from Waimea and come down on the Kekaha side, which is more gradual. It's about 30 minutes straight up to the lodge, but scenic spots stretch it out.

Day 7: North Shore Playground

The North Shore's plentiful sights and activities include swimming, surfing, golf, tennis, botanical gardens, zip-lining, hiking, and horseback riding. Visit **Limahuli Garden** in Haena, which features an ancient Hawaiian layout of a typical self-sufficient community, or **Na Aina Kai** with its artistic and working-farm focus. At the **Kilauea Lighthouse** behold the cliffs, exotic birds, and magnificent coastal view. Spend the rest of your day at **Hanalei Bay,** swimming, taking a surf lesson, or just walking the 2-mile jewel of a crescent-shape beach. For the family, a round of golf at **Kauai Mini-Golf** can be joyful and instructive as the 18-hole layout reveals Hawaii's story through its landscaping.

Logistics: Limahuli is about a 10-minute drive past Hanalei. From there back to Kilauea is about a 20-minute drive on the main road.

Day 8: Hike the Kalalau Trail

You've taken in magnificent Napali Coast from the sea, now experience it from land. This moderate trek offers incredible views peering straight down over the deep blue sea, a visit to a lovely beach, and a hike up a stream to a 300-foot waterfall. You won't be taking the arduous 11-mile journey of the entire coastal Kalalau Trail, so take your time and enjoy Kauai's scenery. Get up early to secure (of all things) a parking spot before hitting the trail.

Logistics: It's 2 miles in to Hanakapiai Beach. Allow an hour. The hike up the valley is also 2 miles—but plan on 90 minutes each way, as the trail cuts through jungle.

TOP 5 KAUAI BEACHES

With more than 50 miles of sandy shores—more than any other Hawaiian island—Kauai is a beach bum's dream. It's easy to give in to "Hawaii time" and spend your trip relaxing on the sand. Here are some of our top places to park your beach towel.

Haena Beach Park (Tunnels Beach)

Even if all you do is sit on the beach, you'll leave here happy. The scenic beauty is unsurpassed, with verdant mountains serving as a backdrop to the turquoise ocean. Snorkeling here is the best on the island during the calm summer months. When the winter's waves arrive, surfers line up on the outside break.

Hanalei Bay Beach Park

When you dream of Hawaii, this is what comes to mind: a vast bay rimmed by a wide beach and waterfalls draping distant mountains. Everyone finds something to do here—surf, kayak, swim, sail, sunbathe, walk, and celebrity-watch. Like most North Shore beaches in Hawaii, Hanalei switches from calm waters in summer to big waves in winter.

Mahaulepu Beach

You'll have to drive through private property to reach this gem, though the beach—like all in Hawaii—is public. The 2-mile stretch is unlike anything else you'll find on Kauai. The land is rugged, with limestone cliffs, caves, and sand dunes. Although swimming here isn't always recommended, it's a great spot to wander around or take a hike along the Mahaulepu Heritage Trail, a beautiful coastal path.

Poipu Beach Park

The *keiki* (children's) swimming hole makes Poipu a great family beach, but it's also popular with snorkelers and moderate-to-experienced surfers. And although Poipu is considered a tourist destination, Kauai residents come out on the weekends, adding a local flavor. Watch for the endangered Hawaiian monk seals; they like it here, too.

Polihale State Park

If you're looking for remote, if you're looking for guaranteed sun, if you're thinking of camping on the beach (permit required), drive down the bumpy 5-mile-long road to the westernmost point of Kauai. Be sure to stay for the sunset. Unless you're an experienced water person, we advise staying out of the water due to a steep onshore break. You can walk for miles along this beach, the longest in Hawaii.

KIDS AND FAMILIES

Choosing a Place to Stay

Resorts: On the North Shore the best bet is the St. Regis Princeville Resort, where kids can spend the day (without their parents) exploring local sea life with a marine biologist. The Kauai Marriott Resort is a good choice on the East Side, and on the South Shore both the Grand Hyatt Kauai and Sheraton Kauai Resort have kids' programs.

Condos: Condo rentals are a fantastic value for families vacationing in Hawaii. On the North Shore, there are numerous condo resort choices in Princeville, including Hanalei Bay Resort with eight tennis courts and two pools. On the South Shore, Outrigger Kiahuna Plantation is a family favorite, with an excellent location that includes a swimmable beach adjacent to a grassy field great for picnics.

Transit Vacation Rentals (TVRs): The new kids on the block are rentals in homelike dwellings that are licensed for such activity. These rentals, and others that are "under the table," have in essence created another resort area along the North Shore—think private home with exclusive beach access. Make sure your renter is operating legally before plunking down your plastic.

Ocean Activities

On the Beach: There are several beaches in Kauai that are nearly as safe as a pool— Anini Beach and Hanalei Bay Beach Park on the North Shore, Lydgate State Park and Kalapaki Beach on the East Side, Poipu Beach Park on the South Shore, and Salt Pond Beach Park on the West Side.

On the Waves: Surf lessons are a great idea for older kids, especially if Mom and Dad want a little quiet time. The Blue Seas Surfing School is best for beginners, and you can book your kids a 1½-hour lesson for $75.

The Underwater World: If your kids are ready to try snorkeling, Kauai is a great place to introduce them to the underwater world. Get your kids used to the basics at Lydgate State Park on the island's East Side, where there's no threat of a current. On its guided snorkel tours, SeaFun Kauai will show kids of all ages how to identify marine life and gives great beginner instruction.

Land Activities

On the North Shore, kids will love Na Aina Kai, a garden with a 16-foot-tall Jack and the Beanstalk bronze sculpture, gecko maze, tree house, kid-size train, and tropical jungle, and on the East Side is Smith's Tropical Paradise, a 30-acre botanical garden.

Horseback riding is a popular family activity, and most of the tours on Kauai move slowly, so no riding experience is required.

ATV tours are the activity of choice when it rains. Try Kauai ATV Tours, which has two-passenger "Mud Bugs" to accommodate families with kids ages five and older.

After Dark

At night, younger kids get a kick out of luau, and many of the shows incorporate young audience members. The older kids might find it all a bit lame, but there are a handful of new shows in the Islands that are more modern, incorporating acrobatics, lively music, and fire dancers. If you're planning on hitting a luau with a teen in tow, we highly recommend going the modern route—try Luau Kalamaku in Lihue. The best luau for young kids on Kauai is Smith's Tropical Paradise, in Wailua. A tram tour takes families through the botanical garden before dinner, and the show starts with some high-tech pyrotechnics.

WEDDINGS AND HONEYMOONS

There's no question that Hawaii is one of the country's foremost honeymoon destinations. Romance is in the air here, and the white, sandy beaches, turquoise water, swaying palm trees, balmy tropical breezes, and perpetual sunshine put people in the mood for love. So it goes without saying, that Kauai has also become a popular wedding destination, especially as new resorts and hotels entice visitors, and same-sex marriage is legal. Once the knot is tied, why not stay for the honeymoon?

The Big Day

Choosing the Perfect Place. You really have two choices to make: the ceremony location and where to have the reception. For the former, Kauai boasts stunning beaches, sea-hugging bluffs, gardens, private residences, resort lawns, and, of course, places of worship. As for the reception, there are these same choices, as well as restaurants and even a luau. If you decide to go outdoors, make sure to have a backup plan for inclement weather.

Finding a Wedding Planner. If you're planning to invite more than an officiant and your loved one to your wedding ceremony, seriously consider a Kauai wedding planner who can help select a location, design the floral scheme, and recommend a florist and photographer. They can also plan the menu and choose a restaurant, caterer, or resort, and suggest any Hawaiian traditions to incorporate into your ceremony.

Getting Your License. There's no waiting period in Hawaii, no residency or citizenship requirements, and no required blood test or shots. You can apply and pay the fee online; however, both the bride and groom must appear together in person before a marriage-license agent to receive the marriage license (the permit to get married) at the State Department of Health

in Lihue. You'll need proof of age—the legal age to marry is 18. Upon approval, a marriage license is immediately issued and costs $60. After the ceremony, your officiant will mail the marriage certificate to the state. Approximately four months later, you will receive a copy in the mail. For more detailed information, visit ⊕ *marriage.ehawaii.gov*.

Also—this is important—the person performing your wedding must be licensed by the Hawaii Department of Health, even if he or she is a licensed officiant. Be sure to ask.

Wedding Attire. In Hawaii, basically anything goes, from long, formal dresses with trains to white bikinis. For men, a pair of solid-colored slacks with a nice aloha shirt is appropriate. If you're planning a wedding on the beach, barefoot is the way to go.

Local Customs. The most obvious traditional Hawaiian wedding custom is the lei exchange in which the bride and groom take turns placing a lei around the neck of the other—with a kiss. Bridal lei are usually floral, whereas the groom's is typically made of *maile*, a green leafy garland that drapes the neck. Brides often also wear a *lei poo*—a circular floral headpiece.

The Honeymoon

Do you want Champagne and strawberries delivered to your room each morning? A breathtaking swimming pool in which to float? A five-star restaurant in which to dine? Then a resort is the way to go. A small inn is also good if you're on a tight budget or don't plan to spend much time in your room. The lodging accommodations are almost as plentiful as the beaches.

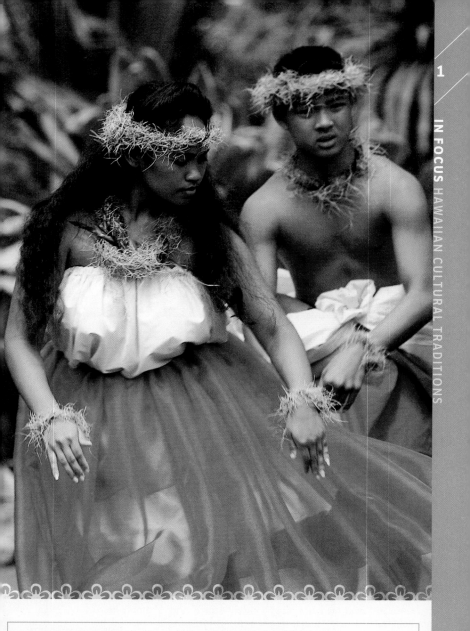

HAWAIIAN CULTURAL TRADITIONS HULA, LEI, AND LUAU

HULA: MORE THAN A FOLK DANCE

Hula has been called "the heartbeat of the Hawaiian people" and also "the world's best-known, most misunderstood dance." Both are true. Hula isn't just dance. It is storytelling.

Chanter Edith McKinzie calls it "an extension of a piece of poetry." In its adornments, implements, and customs, hula integrates every important Hawaiian cultural practice: poetry, history, genealogy, craft, plant cultivation, martial arts, religion, protocol. So when 19th-century Christian missionaries sought to eradicate a practice they considered depraved, they threatened more than just a folk dance.

With public performance outlawed and private hula practice discouraged, hula went underground for a generation. The fragile verbal link by which culture was transmitted from teacher to student hung by a thread. Even increasing literacy did not help because hula's practitioners were a secretive and protected circle.

As if that weren't bad enough, vaudeville, Broadway, and Hollywood got hold of the hula, giving it the glitz treatment in

an unbroken line from "Oh, How She Could Wicky Wacky Woo" to "Rock-A-Hula Baby." Hula became shorthand for paradise: fragrant flowers, lazy hours. Ironically, this development assured that hundreds of Hawaiians could make a living performing and teaching hula. Many danced *auana* (modern form) in performance; but taught *kahiko* (traditional), quietly, at home or in hula schools.

Today, decades after the cultural revival known as the Hawaiian Renaissance, language immersion programs have assured a new generation of proficient—and even eloquent—chanters, songwriters, and translators. Visitors can see more, and more authentic, traditional hula than at any other time in the last 200 years.

Like the culture of which it is the beating heart, hula has survived.

Lei *poo*. Head lei. In *kahiko*, greenery only. In *auana*, flowers.

Face emotes appropriate expression. Dancer should not be a smiling automaton.

Shoulders remain relaxed and still, never hunched, even with arms raised. No bouncing.

Eyes always follow leading hand.

Lei. Hula is rarely performed without a shoulder lei.

Arms and hands remain loose, relaxed, below shoulder level—except as required by interpretive movements.

Traditional hula skirt is loose fabric, smocked and gathered at the waist.

Hip is canted over weight-bearing foot.

Knees are always slightly bent, accentuating hip sway.

Kupee. Ankle bracelet of flowers, shells, or foliage.

In kahiko, feet are flat. In auana, they may be more arched, but not tiptoes or bouncing.

BASIC MOTIONS

Speak or Sing

Moon or Sun

Grass Shack or House

Mountains or Heights

Love or Caress

At backyard parties, hula is performed in bare feet and street clothes, but in performance, adornments play a key role, as do rhythm-keeping implements such as the pahu drum and the *ipu* (gourd).

In hula *kahiko* (traditional style), the usual dress is multiple layers of stiff fabric (often with a pellom lining, which most closely resembles *kapa*, (the paperlike bark cloth of the Hawaiians). These wrap tightly around the bosom but flare below the waist to form a skirt. In pre-contact times, dancers wore only kapa skirts. Men traditionally wear loincloths.

Monarchy-period hula is performed in voluminous muumuu or high-necked muslin blouses and gathered skirts. Men wear white or gingham shirts and black pants.

In hula *auana* (modern), dress for women can range from grass skirts and strapless tops to contemporary tea-length dresses. Men generally wear aloha shirts, but sometimes grass skirts over pants or even everyday gear.

SURPRISING HULA FACTS

■ Grass skirts are not traditional; workers from Kiribati (the Gilbert Islands) brought this custom to Hawaii.

■ In olden-day Hawaii, *mele* (songs) for hula were composed for every occasion—name songs for babies, dirges for funerals, welcome songs for visitors, celebrations of favorite pursuits.

■ Hula *mai* is a traditional hula form in praise of a noble's genitals; the power of the *alii* (royalty) to procreate gave *mana* (spiritual power) to the entire culture.

■ Hula students in old Hawaii adhered to high standards: scrupulous cleanliness, no sex, daily cleansing rituals, certain food prohibitions, and no contact with the dead. They were fined if they broke the rules.

WHERE TO WATCH

If you're interested in "the real thing," there are annual hula festivals on each island. Check the individual island visitors' bureaus websites at ⊕ *www.gohawaii.com*.

If you can't make it to a festival, there are plenty of other hula shows—at most resorts, many lounges, and even at certain shopping centers. Ask your hotel concierge for performance information.

ALL ABOUT LEI

Lei brighten every occasion in Hawaii, from birthdays to bar mitzvahs to baptisms. Creative artisans weave nature's bounty—flowers, ferns, vines, and seeds—into gorgeous creations that convey an array of heartfelt messages: "Welcome," "Congratulations," "Good luck," "Farewell," "Thank you," "I love you." When it's difficult to find the right words, a lei expresses exactly the right sentiment.

WHERE TO BUY THE BEST LEI

Most airports in Hawaii have lei stands where you can buy a fragrant garland upon arrival. Every florist shop in the Islands sells lei; you can also treat yourself to a lei while shopping for provisions at any supermarket or box store. And you'll always find lei sellers at crafts fairs and outdoor festivals.

LEI ETIQUETTE

■ To wear a closed lei, drape it over your shoulders, half in front and half in back. Open lei are worn around the neck, with the ends draped over the front in equal lengths.

■ Pikake, ginger, and other sweet, delicate blossoms are "feminine" lei. Men opt for cigar, crown flower, and ti leaf lei, which are sturdier and don't emit as much fragrance.

■ Lei are always presented with a kiss, a custom that supposedly dates back to World War II when a hula dancer fancied an officer at a U.S.O. show. Taking a dare from members of her troupe, she took off her lei, placed it around his neck, and kissed him on the cheek.

■ It has become a custom for visitors to toss their lei into the ocean before leaving to ensure a return trip, but this poses an entanglement risk to marine life. Instead, cut the lei string and remove the flowers so they can be loosely scattered into the water.

ORCHID

Growing wild on every continent except Antarctica, orchids—which range in color from yellow to green to purple—comprise the largest family of plants in the world. There are more than 20,000 species of orchids, but only three are native to Hawaii—and they are very rare. The pretty lavender vanda you see hanging by the dozens at local lei stands has probably been imported from Thailand.

MAILE

Maile, an endemic twining vine with a heady aroma, is sacred to Laka, goddess of the hula. In ancient times, dancers wore maile and decorated hula altars with it to honor Laka. Today, "open" maile lei usually are given to men. Instead of ribbon, interwoven lengths of maile are used at dedications of new businesses. The maile is untied, never snipped, for doing so would symbolically "cut" the company's success.

ILIMA

Designated by Hawaii's Territorial Legislature in 1923 as the official flower of the island of Oahu, the golden ilima is so delicate it lasts for just a day. Five to seven hundred blossoms are needed to make one garland. Queen Emma, wife of King Kamehameha IV, preferred ilima over all other lei, which may have led to the incorrect belief that they were reserved only for royalty.

PLUMERIA

This ubiquitous flower is named after Charles Plumier, the noted French botanist who discovered it in Central America in the late 1600s. Plumeria ranks among the most popular lei in Hawaii because it's fragrant, hardy, plentiful, inexpensive, and requires very little care. Although yellow is the most common color, you'll also find plumeria lei in shades of pink, red, orange, and "rainbow" blends.

PIKAKE

Favored for its fragile beauty and sweet scent, pikake was introduced from India. In lieu of pearls, many brides in Hawaii adorn themselves with long, multiple strands of white pikake. Princess Kaiulani enjoyed showing guests her beloved pikake and peacocks at Ainahau, her Waikiki home. Interestingly, pikake is the Hawaiian word for both the bird and the blossom.

KUKUI

The kukui (candlenut) is Hawaii's state tree. Early Hawaiians strung kukui nuts (which are quite oily) together and burned them for light; mixed burned nuts with oil to make an indelible dye; and mashed roasted nuts to consume as a laxative. Kukui nut lei may not have been made until after Western contact, when the Hawaiians saw black beads from Europe and wanted to imitate them.

LUAU: A TASTE OF HAWAII

The best place to sample Hawaiian food is at a backyard luau. Aunts and uncles are cooking, the pig is from a cousin's farm, and the fish is from a brother's boat.

But even locals have to angle for invitations to those rare occasions. So your choice is most likely between a commercial luau and a Hawaiian restaurant.

Some commercial luau are less authentic; they offer little of the traditional diet and are more about umbrella drinks, spectacle, and fun.

For greater culinary authenticity, folksy experiences, and rock-bottom prices, visit a Hawaiian restaurant (most are in anonymous storefronts in residential neighborhoods). Expect rough edges and some effort negotiating the menu.

In either case, much of what is known today as Hawaiian food would be as foreign to a 16th-century Hawaiian as risotto or chow mien. The pre-contact diet was simple and healthy—mainly raw and steamed seafood and vegetables. Early Hawaiians used earth ovens and heated stones to cook seafood, taro, sweet potatoes, and breadfruit and seasoned their food with sea salt and ground kukui nuts. Seaweed, fern shoots, sweet potato vines, coconut, banana, sugarcane, and select greens and roots rounded out the diet.

Successive waves of immigrants added their favorites to the ti leaf–lined table. So it is that foods as disparate as salt salmon and chicken long rice are now Hawaiian—even though there is no salmon in Hawaiian waters and long rice (cellophane noodles) is Chinese.

AT THE LUAU: KALUA PORK

The heart of any luau is the *imu*, the earth oven in which a whole pig is roasted. The preparation of an imu is an arduous affair for most families, who tackle it only once a year or so, for a baby's first birthday or at Thanksgiving, when many Islanders prefer to imu their turkeys. Commercial luau operations have it down to a science, however.

THE ART OF THE STONE

The key to a proper imu is the *pohaku*, the stones. Imu cook by means of long, slow, moist heat released by special stones that can withstand a hot fire without exploding. Many Hawaiian families treasure their imu stones, keeping them in a pile in the back-yard and passing them on through generations.

PIT COOKING

The imu makers first dig a pit about the size of a re-frigerator, then lay down *kiawe* (mesquite) wood and stones, and build a white-hot fire that is allowed to burn itself out. The ashes are raked away, and the hot stones covered with banana and ti leaves. Well-wrapped in ti or banana leaves and a net of chicken wire, the pig is lowered onto the leaf-covered stones. *Laulau* (leaf-wrapped bundles of meats, fish, and taro leaves) may also be placed inside. Leaves—ti, banana, even ginger—cover the pig followed by wet burlap sacks (to create steam). The whole is topped with a canvas tarp and left to steam for the better part of a day.

OPENING THE IMU

This is the moment everyone waits for: The imu is unwrapped like a giant present and the imu keep-ers gingerly wrestle out the steaming pig. When it's unwrapped, the meat falls moist and smoky-flavored from the bone, looking just like Southern-style pulled pork, but without the barbecue sauce.

WHICH LUAU?

Most resort hotels have luau on their grounds that include hula, music, and, of course, lots of food and drink. Each island also has at least one "authentic" luau. For lists of the best luau on each island, visit the Hawaii Visitors and Convention Bureau website at ⊕ *www.gohawaii.com.*

MEA AI ONO: GOOD THINGS TO EAT.

LAULAU

Steamed meats, fish, and taro leaf in ti-leaf bundles: fork-tender, a medley of flavors; the taro resembles spinach.

Laulau

LOMI LOMI SALMON

Salt salmon in a piquant salad or relish with onions and tomatoes.

POI

Poi, a paste made of pounded taro root, may be an acquired taste, but it's a must-try during your visit.

Consider: The Hawaiian Adam is descended from *kalo* (taro). Young taro plants are called "keiki"–children. Poi is the first food after mother's milk for many Islanders. Ai, the word for food, is synonymous with poi in many contexts.

Lomi Lomi Salmon

Not only that, we love it. "There is no meat that doesn't taste good with poi," the old Hawaiians said.

But you have to know how to eat it: with something rich or powerfully flavored. "It is salt that makes the poi go in," is another adage. When you're served poi, try it with a mouthful of smoky kalua pork or salty lomi lomi salmon. Its slightly sour blandness cleanses the palate. And if you don't like it, smile and say something polite. (And slide that bowl over to a local.)

Poi

E HELE MAI AI! COME AND EAT!

Local-style Hawaiian restaurants tend to be inconveniently located in well-worn storefronts with little or no parking, outfitted with battered tables and clattering Melmac dishes, but they personify aloha, invariably run by local families who welcome tourists who take the trouble to find them.

Many are cash-only operations and combination plates, known as "plate lunch," are a standard feature: one or two entrées, two scoops of steamed rice, one scoop of macaroni salad, and—if the place is really old-style—a tiny portion of coarse Hawaiian salt and some raw onions for relish.

Most serve some foods that aren't, strictly speaking, Hawaiian, but are beloved of ka-

maaina, such as salt meat with watercress (preserved meat in a tasty broth), or *akubone* (skipjack tuna fried in a tangy vinegar sauce).

MENU GUIDE

Much of the Hawaiian language encountered during a stay in the Islands will appear on restaurant menus and lists of luau fare. Here's a quick primer.

ahi: *yellowfin tuna.*

aku: *skipjack, bonito tuna.*

amaama: *mullet; it's hard to get but tasty.*

bento: *a box lunch.*

chicken luau: *a stew made from chicken, taro leaves, and coconut milk.*

haupia: *a light, pudding-like sweet made from coconut.*

imu: *the underground oven in which pigs are roasted for luau.*

kalua: *to bake underground.*

kimchee: *Korean dish of fermented cabbage made with garlic, hot peppers, and other spices.*

Kona coffee: *coffee grown in the Kona district of the Big Island.*

laulau: *literally, a bundle. Laulau are morsels of pork, chicken, butterfish, or other ingredients wrapped with young taro leaves and then bundled in ti leaves for steaming.*

lilikoi: *passion fruit, a tart, seedy yellow fruit that makes delicious desserts, juice, and jellies.*

lomi lomi: *to rub or massage; also a type of massage. Lomi lomi salmon is fish that has been rubbed with onions and herbs; commonly served with minced onions and tomatoes.*

luau: *a Hawaiian feast; also the leaf of the taro plant used in preparing such a feast.*

luau leaves: *cooked taro tops with a taste similar to spinach.*

mahimahi: *mild-flavored dolphinfish, not the marine mammal.*

mai tai: *potent rum drink with orange liqueurs and pineapple juice, from the Tahitian word for "good."*

malasada: *a Portuguese deep-fried doughnut without a hole, dipped in sugar.*

manapua: *steamed Chinese buns filled with pork, chicken, or other fillings.*

niu: *coconut.*

onaga: *pink or red snapper.*

ono: *a long, slender mackerel-like fish; also called wahoo.*

ono: *delicious; also hungry.*

opihi: *a tiny limpet found on rocks.*

papio: *a young ulua or jack fish.*

poha: *Cape gooseberry. Tasting a bit like honey, the poha berry is often used in jams and desserts.*

poi: *a paste made from pounded taro root, a staple of the Hawaiian diet.*

poke: *cubed raw tuna or other fish, tossed with seaweed and seasonings.*

pupu: *appetizers or small plates.*

saimin: *long thin noodles and vegetables in broth, often garnished with small pieces of fish cake, scrambled egg, luncheon meat, and green onion.*

sashimi: *raw fish thinly sliced and usually eaten with soy sauce.*

ti leaves: *a member of the agave family. The leaves are used to wrap food while cooking and removed before eating.*

uku: *deep-sea snapper.*

ulua: *a member of the jack family that also includes pompano and amberjack. Also called crevalle, jack fish, and jack crevalle.*

EXPLORING
KAUAI

Updated by
Charles E.
Roessler

Even a nickname like "The Garden Island" fails to do justice to Kauai's beauty. Verdant trees grow canopies over the few roads, and brooding mountains are framed by long, sandy beaches, coral reefs, and sheer sea cliffs. Pristine trade winds moderate warm daily temperatures while offering comfort for deep, refreshing sleep through gentle nights.

The main road tracing Kauai's perimeter takes you past much more scenery than would seem possible on one small island. Chiseled mountains, thundering waterfalls, misty hillsides, dreamy beaches, lush vegetation, and small towns make up the physical landscape. Perhaps the most stunning piece of scenery is a place no road will take you—breathtakingly beautiful Napali Coast, which runs along the northwest side of the island.

For adventure seekers, Kauai offers everything from difficult hikes to helicopter tours. The island has top-notch spas and golf courses, and its beaches are known to be some of the most beautiful in the world. Even after you've spent days lazing around drinking mai tais or kayaking your way down a river, there's still plenty to do, as well as see: plantation villages, a historic lighthouse, wildlife refuges, a fern grotto, a colorful canyon, and deep rivers are all easily explored.

■ TIP→ While exploring the island, try to take advantage of the many roadside scenic overlooks and pull over to take in the constantly changing view. Don't try to pack too much into one day. Kauai is small, but travel is slow. The island's sights are divided into four geographic areas, in clockwise order: the North Shore, the East Side, the South Shore, and the West Side.

GEOLOGY

Kauai is the oldest and northernmost of the main Hawaiian Islands. Five million years of wind and rain have worked their magic, sculpting fluted sea cliffs and whittling away at the cinder cones and caldera that prove its volcanic origin. Foremost among these is Waialeale, one of the wettest spots on Earth. Its approximate 450-inch annual rainfall feeds the mighty Wailua River, the only navigable waterway in Hawaii. The vast Alakai Swamp soaks up rain like a sponge, releasing it slowly into the watershed that gives Kauai its emerald sheen.

FLORA AND FAUNA

Kauai offers some of the best birding in the state, due in part to the absence of the mongoose. Many nene (the endangered Hawaiian state bird) reared in captivity have been successfully released here, along with an endangered forest bird called the puaiohi. The island is also home to a large colony of migratory nesting seabirds and has two refuges protecting endangered Hawaiian waterbirds. Kauai's most noticeable fowl, however, is the wild chicken. A cross between jungle fowl (*moa*) brought by the Polynesians and domestic chickens and fighting cocks that escaped during the last two hurricanes, they are everywhere, and the roosters crow when they feel like it, not just at dawn. Consider yourself warned.

HISTORY

Kauai's residents have had a reputation for independence since ancient times. Called "The Separate Kingdom," Kauai alone resisted King Kamehameha's charge to unite the Hawaiian Islands. In fact, it was only by kidnapping Kauai's king, Kaumualii, and forcing him to marry Kamehameha's widow that the Garden Isle was joined to the rest of Hawaii. That spirit lives on today as Kauai residents try to resist the lure of tourism dollars captivating the rest of the Islands. Local building tradition maintains that no structure be taller than a coconut tree, and Kauai's capital, Lihue, is still more small town than city.

TOURS

Guided tours are convenient; you don't have to worry about finding a parking spot or getting admission tickets. Certified tour guides have taken special classes in Hawaiian history and lore. On the other hand, you won't have the freedom to proceed at your own pace, nor will you have the ability to take a detour trip if something else catches your attention.

Aloha Kauai Tours. You get *way* off the beaten track on these four-wheel-drive van excursions. Choose from several options, including the half-day *Backroads Tour* covering mostly haul-cane roads behind the locked gates of Grove Farm Plantation, and the four-hour *Seafun Snorkeling Tour,* which takes you to a mellow bay where you'll get an up-close experience swimming with schools of multicolor ocean fish. ⊠ *3477A Weliweli Rd. (for check-in), Koloa* ☎ *808/245–6400* ⊕ *www.alohakauaitours.com.*

Roberts Hawaii Tours. The *Round-the-Island Tour*, sometimes called the *Waimea Canyon–Fern Grotto Tour,* gives a good overview of half the island, including Fort Elisabeth and Opaekaa Falls. Guests are transported in air-conditioned, 25-passenger minibuses. The $98 trip includes a boat ride up the Wailua River to the Fern Grotto and a visit to the lookouts above Waimea Canyon. They also offer a *Kauai Movie Tour* for $108. ⊠ *3-4567 Kuhio Hwy., Hanamaulu* ☎ *808/245–9101, 800/831–5541* ⊕ *www.robertshawaii.com/kauai/* ⌖ *From $98.*

Waimea Historic Walking Tour. Led by a *kupuna*, a respected Hawaiian elder, this two-hour tour begins promptly at 8:30 am every Monday

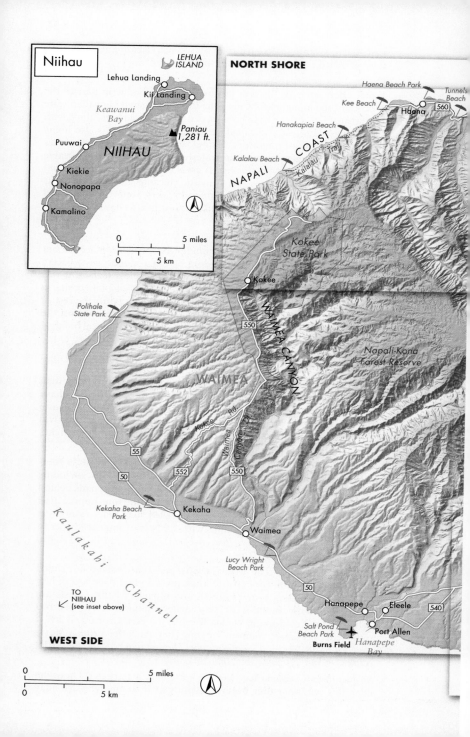

Niihau

LEHUA
ISLAND

Lehua Landing

Kii Landing

*Keawanui
Bay*

▲ Paniau
1,281 ft.

Puuwai

NIIHAU

Kiekie

Nonopapa

Kamalino

0   5 miles

0   5 km

Haena Beach Park

Tunnels
Beach

Kee Beach   Haena   560

Hanakapiai Beach

NAPALI   COAST

Kalalau Beach

Kalalau Trail

Kōkee
State Park

Kōkee

Polihale
State Park

550

WAIMEA CANYON

Napali-Kona
Forest Reserve

WAIMEA

Kōkee Rd.

Waimea Rd.

Canyon Dr.

55

50

552

550

Kaulakahi   Channel

Kekaha Beach
Park

Kekaha

Waimea

Lucy Wright
Beach Park

TO
NIIHAU
(see inset above)

50

Hanapepe   Eleele

540

Salt Pond
Beach Park

Port Allen

Burns Field   *Hanapepe
Bay*

0   5 miles

0   5 km

Kauai

Lumahai Beach
Hanalei Bay Beach Park
Hanalei Bay
Anini Beach Park
Kalihiwai Beach

Princeville

Hanalei

WAIPA VALLEY

Kilauea

Princeville Airport

56 Kuhio Hwy

HANALEI

EAST SIDE

Mamolahoa Halelea Forest Reserve

MAKALEHA MOUNTAINS

KAWAIHAU

Anahola Beach Park

Anahola

56

Donkey Beach

PACIFIC OCEAN

Waialeale 5,148 ft.

Lihue-Koloa Forest Reserve

Wailua River

581

Kealia

Kealia Beach

Kopaa

Waipouli

Wailua Beach

580

Wailua

Wailua Bay

Smith's Tropical Paradise

Lydgate State Park

LIHUE

583

56

Kilohana Crater 1,138 ft.

Hanamaulu

Lihue

Lihue Airport

Puhi

58

Kalapaki Beach

Nawiliwili Bay

TO OAHU →

KOLOA

50

Kalaheo

Lawai

520

530

Koloa

HAUPU RANGE

Huleia River

Mahaulepu Beach

Shipwreck Beach

Beach House

Poipu Beach Park

Brennecke Beach

Poipu

SOUTH SHORE

Kauai Channel

Elevation

feet	meters
5,148	1,569
3,600	1,100
3,280	1,000
2,950	900
2,620	800
2,300	700
1,970	600
1,640	500
1,310	400
980	300
660	200
330	100
feet	meters

Talk about remote: Beautiful Kalalau Beach is at the end of an 11-mile trail through the incredible Napali Coast State Wilderness.

at the West Kauai Visitor Center. While sharing her personal remembrances, Aletha Kaohi leads an easy walk that explains Waimea's distinction as a recipient of the 2006 National Trust for Historic Preservation Award. The tour is free, but a reservation is required. ⊠ *9565 Kaumualii Hwy., Waimea (Kauai County)* ☎ *808/338–1332* ⬚ *Free.*

VISITOR INFORMATION
For information about hiking and camping permits and rules and regulations for Napali Coast visit the Division of State Parks section of the ⊕ *hawaii.gov* website.

Contacts Division of State Parks. ⊠ *3060 Eiwa St., Suite 306, Lihue* ☎ *808/274–3444* ⊕ *dnlr.hawaii.gov.* **West Kauai Visitor Center.** ⊠ *West Kauai Technology and Visitor Center Building, 9565 Kaumualii Hwy, Waimea (Kauai County)* ☎ *808/338–1332* ⊕ *www.westkauaivisitorcenter.org.*

THE NORTH SHORE

The North Shore of Kauai includes the environs of Kilauea, Princeville, Hanalei, and Haena. Traveling north on Route 56 from the airport, the coastal highway crosses the Wailua River and the busy towns of Wailua and Kapaa before emerging into a decidedly rural and scenic landscape, with expansive views of the island's rugged interior mountains. As the two-lane highway turns west and narrows, it winds through spectacular scenery and passes the posh resort community of Princeville before dropping down into Hanalei Valley. Here it narrows further and becomes a federally recognized scenic roadway, replete with one-lane bridges (the local etiquette is for six or seven cars to cross at a time, before yielding to those on the other side), hairpin turns, and heart-stopping coastal vistas. The road ends at Kee, where the ethereal rain forests and fluted sea cliffs of Napali Coast Wilderness State Park begin.

In winter Kauai's North Shore receives more rainfall than other areas of the island. Don't let this deter you from visiting. The clouds drift over the mountains of Namolokama creating a mysterious mood and then, in a blink, disappear, rewarding you with mountains laced with a dozen waterfalls or more. The views of the mountain—as well as the sunsets over the ocean—from the St. Regis Bar, adjacent to the lobby of the St. Regis Princeville Resort, are fantastic.

The North Shore attracts all kinds—from celebrities to surfers. In fact, the late Andy Irons, three-time world surfing champion, along with his brother Bruce and legend Laird Hamilton grew up riding waves along the North Shore.

HANALEI, HAENA, AND WEST

Haena is 40 miles northwest of Lihue; Hanalei is 5 miles southeast of Haena.

Crossing the historic one-lane bridge into Hanalei reveals old-world Hawaii, including working taro farms, poi making, and evenings of throwing horseshoes at Black Pot Beach Park—found unmarked (as many places are on Kauai) at the east end of Hanalei Bay Beach Park. Although the current real-estate boom on Kauai has attracted mainland millionaires to build estate homes on the few remaining parcels of land in Hanalei, there's still plenty to see and do. It's *the* gathering place on the North Shore. Restaurants, shops, and people-watching here are among the best on the island, and you won't find a single brand name, chain, or big-box store around—unless you count surf brands like Quiksilver and Billabong.

The beach and river at Hanalei offer swimming, snorkeling, body boarding, surfing, and kayaking. Those hanging around at sunset often congregate at the Hanalei Pavilion, where a husband-and-wife-slack-key-guitar-playing combo makes impromptu appearances. There's an old rumor, since quashed by the local newspaper, the *Garden Island,* that says Hanalei was the inspiration for the song "Puff the Magic Dragon," performed by the 1960s singing sensation Peter, Paul & Mary. Even with the newspaper's clarification, some tours still point out the shape of the dragon carved into the mountains encircling the town.

Once you pass through Hanalei town, the road shrinks even more as you skirt the coast and pass through Haena. Blind corners, quick turns, and one-lane bridges force slow driving along this scenic stretch across the Lumahai and Wainiha valleys. ⚠ **Following extensive flooding in early 2018, areas of Haena, including the state park, are undergoing repairs. Please check before visiting to make sure places are open.**

GETTING HERE AND AROUND

There is only one road leading beyond Princeville to Kee Beach at the western end of the North Shore: Route 560. Hanalei's commercial stretch fronts this route, and you'll find parking at the shopping

The North Shore
and Napali Coast

PACIFIC OCEAN

NAPALI COAST

Kalalau Beach

Hanakapiai Beach

Kalalau Wilderness State Park

Kee Beach State Park

Waikapalae and Waikanaloa Wet Caves

Limahuli Garden

Haena Beach Park

Haena

Tunnels Beach

Maniniholo Dry Cave

560

Lumahai Beach

Hanalei Bay Beach Park

Queen's Bath

Princeville

Hanalei Bay

Hanalei Pier

Hanalei

Hanalei Bay

Waioli Huiia Church

Waioli Mission House

WAIPA VALLEY

Anini Beach Park

Hanalei Valley Overlook

56

Princeville National Airport

Hanalei National Wildlife Refuge

Hoopulapula Haraguchi Rice Mill

Hanalei River

HANALEI

Kalihiwai Beach

Kilauea Point National Wildlife Refuge and Kilauea Lighthouse

Na Aina Kai Botanical Gardens

Kilauea

56

Anaina Hou Mini Golf & Gardens

Kuhio Hwy

Moloaa Sunrise Fruit Stand

Anahola Beach Park

Donkey Beach

Anahola

56

Kealia Beach

Kealia

MAKALEHA MOUNTAINS

Mauaukahaa Halelea Forest Reserve

Kokee State Park

Kokee

550

2 mi

2 km

0

0

compounds on each side of the road. After Hanalei, parking is restricted to two main areas, Haena Beach Park and a new lot at Haena State Park, and there are few pullover areas along Route 560. Traffic and especially parking have become major concerns as the North Shore has gained popularity, so be prepared to be patient.

TOP ATTRACTIONS

Fodor's Choice
★
Hanalei Valley Overlook. Dramatic mountains and a patchwork of neat taro farms bisected by the wide Hanalei River make this one of Hawaii's loveliest sights. The fertile Hanalei Valley has been planted in taro since perhaps AD 700, save for a century-long foray into rice that ended in 1960. (The historic Haraguchi Rice Mill is all that remains of that era.) Many taro farmers lease land within the 900-acre Hanalei National Wildlife Refuge, helping to provide wetland habitat for four species of endangered Hawaiian waterbirds. ⊠ *Rte. 56, across from Foodland, Princeville.*

Limahuli Garden. Narrow Limahuli Valley, with its fluted mountain peaks and ancient stone taro terraces, creates an unparalleled setting for this botanical garden and nature preserve. Dedicated to protecting native plants and unusual varieties of taro, it represents the principles of conservation and stewardship held by its founder, Charles "Chipper" Wichman. Limahuli's primordial beauty and strong *mana* (spiritual power) eclipse the extensive botanical collection. It's one of the most gorgeous spots on Kauai and the crown jewel of the National Tropical Botanical Garden, which Wichman now heads. Call ahead to reserve a guided tour, or tour on your own. Be sure to check out the quality gift shop and revolutionary compost toilet, and be prepared to walk a somewhat steep hillside. ⊠ *5-8291 Kuhio Hwy., Haena* ☎ *808/826–1053* ⊕ *www.ntbg. org* ⊠ *Self-guided tour $20, guided tour $40 (reservations required).*

WORTH NOTING

Hanalei Pier. Built in 1892, the historic Hanalei Pier is a landmark seen from miles across the bay. It came to fame when it was featured in the award-winning 1957 movie *South Pacific.* Kids use it as a diving board, fishers fish, picnickers picnic. It's a great spot for a leisurely stroll and attracts a gathering every sunset. ⊠ *Weke Rd., Princeville.*

Hoopulapula Haraguchi Rice Mill. Rice grew in the taro fields of Hanalei Valley for almost 80 years—beginning in the 1880s and ending in the early 1960s. Today, this history is embodied in the Haraguchi family, whose ancestors threshed, hulled, polished, separated, graded, and bagged rice in their 3,500-square-foot rice mill, which was demolished once by fire and twice by hurricanes. Rebuilt to the exacting standards of the National Register of Historic Places, the mill—and neighboring taro fields—is now open for tours on a very limited schedule mainly due to endangered bird-nesting areas. The family still farms taro on the onetime rice paddies and also operates the Hanalei Taro & Juice kiosk in Hanalei town. Reservations are required for the tour, which currently runs on Wednesday at 10 am. ⊠ *5-5070 Kuhio Hwy., next to Kayak Kauai, Hanalei* ☎ *808/651–3399* ⊕ *haraguchiricemill.org* ⊠ *$87.*

Maniniholo Dry Cave. Kauai's North Shore caves echo an enchanting, almost haunting, alternative to sunny skies and deep blue seas. Steeped

Hanalei Bay attracts big-wave surfers in the winter and then becomes a calm haven for swimmers in the summer.

in legend, Maniniholo Dry Cave darkens and becomes more claustro-phobic as you glide across its sandy floor, hearing the drips down the walls and wondering at its past. Legend has it that Maniniholo was the head fisherman of the Menehune—Kauai's quasimythical first inhabit-ants. After gathering too much food to carry, his men stored the excess in the dry cave overnight. When he returned in the morning, the food had vanished and he blamed the imps living in the cracks of the cave. He and his men dug into the cliff to find and destroy the imps, leaving behind the cave. Across the highway from Maniniholo Dry Cave is Haena State Park. ⊠ *Rte. 560, Haena.*

Waikapalae and Waikanaloa Wet Caves. These wet caves are smaller (and wetter) than Maniniholo but are still visually worth a short jaunt. Said to have been dug by Pele, goddess of fire, these watering holes used to be clear, clean, and great for swimming. Now stagnant, they're nevertheless a photogenic example of the many haunting natural landmarks of Kauai's North Shore. Waikanaloa is visible right beside the highway, near the end of the road. Waikapalae is back a few hundred yards and is accessed by a five-minute uphill walk. ⊠ *Western end of Rte. 560, Haena.*

Waioli Huiia Church. Designated a National Historic Landmark, this little church—affiliated with the United Church of Christ—doesn't go unno-ticed right alongside Route 560 in downtown Hanalei, and its doors are often wide open (from 9 to 5, give or take) inviting inquisitive visitors in for a look around. Like the Waioli Mission House behind it, it's an exquisite representation of New England architecture crossed with Hawaiian thatched buildings. During Hurricane Iniki's visit in 1992, which brought sustained winds of 160 mph and wind gusts up to 220 mph, this little church was lifted off its foundation but, thankfully, lovingly restored. Services are held at 10 am on Sunday with many hymns sung in Hawaiian and often accompanied by piano and ukulele. ⊠ *5-5363A Kuhio Hwy., Hanalei* ☎ *808/826–6253* ⊕ *www. hanaleichurch.org.*

Waioli Mission House. This 1837 home was built by missionaries William and Mary Alexander. Its tidy New England architecture and formal koa-wood furnishings epitomize the prim and proper missionary influence, while the informative guided tours offer a fascinating peek into the private lives of Kauai's early white residents. Half-hour guided tours are available for a $10 requested donation on Tuesday, Thursday, and Saturday from 9 to 3. ■TIP→ **If no one is there when you arrive, don't despair; just ring the bell by the chimney.** ⊠ *Kuhio Hwy., Hanalei* ☎ *808/245–3202* ⊕ *www.grovefarm.org* ⊠ *$10.*

PRINCEVILLE AND KILAUEA

Princeville is 4 miles northeast of Hanalei; Kilauea is 5 miles east of Princeville.

Built on a bluff offering gorgeous sea and mountain vistas, including Hanalei Bay, Princeville is the creation of a 1970s resort development. The area is anchored by a few large hotels, world-class golf courses, and lots of condos and time-shares.

Five miles down Route 56, a former plantation town, Kilauea maintains its rural flavor in the midst of unrelenting gentrification encroaching all around it. Especially noteworthy are its historic lava-rock buildings, including **Christ Memorial Episcopal Church** on Kolo Road and, on Keneke and Kilauea Road (commonly known as Lighthouse Road), the Kong Lung Company, which is now an expensive shop.

GETTING HERE AND AROUND

There is only one main road through the Princeville resort area, so maneuvering a car here can be a nightmare. If you're trying to find a smaller lodging unit, be sure to get specific driving directions. Parking is available at the Princeville Shopping Center at the entrance to the resort. Kilauea is about 5 miles east on Route 56. There's a public parking lot in the town center as well as parking at the end of Kilauea Road for access to the lighthouse.

TOP ATTRACTIONS

Fodor's Choice ★ **Kilauea Point National Wildlife Refuge and Kilauea Lighthouse.** A beacon for sea traffic since it was built in 1913, this National Historic Landmark celebrated its centennial in 2013 and has the largest clamshell lens of any lighthouse in the world. It's within a national wildlife refuge, where thousands of seabirds soar on the trade winds and nest on the steep ocean cliffs. Seeing endangered nene geese, white- and red-tailed tropic birds, and more (all identifiable by educational signboards) as well as native plants, dolphins, humpback whales, huge winter surf, and gorgeous views of the North Shore are well worth the modest entry fee. The gift shop has a great selection of books about the island's natural history and an array of unique merchandise, with all proceeds benefiting education and preservation efforts. ⊠ *Kilauea Lighthouse Rd., Kilauea* ☏ *808/828–1413* ⊕ *www.kilaueapoint.org, www.fws.gov/kilaueapoint* ✉ *$5, under 15 free.*

Fodor'sChoice ★ **Na Aina Kai Botanical Gardens.** Joyce and Ed Doty's love for plants and art spans 240 acres and includes many different gardens, a hardwood plantation, an ahupua'a (a Hawaiian land division), a re-created Navaho compound and an Athabascan village, a Japanese teahouse, a hedge maze, a waterfall, and access to a sandy beach. Throughout are more than 200 bronze sculptures, one of the nation's largest collections. One popular feature is a children's garden with a 16-foot-tall Jack and the Beanstalk bronze sculpture, gecko maze, tree house, kid-size train, and, of course, a tropical jungle. Located in a residential neighborhood and hoping to maintain good neighborly relations, the Gardens, a nonprofit organization, limits tours (guided only). Tour lengths vary widely, from 1½ to 5 hours. Reservations are required. ⊠ *4101 Wailapa Rd., Kilauea* ☏ *808/828–0525* ⊕ *www.naainakai.org* ✉ *From $35.*

Fodor'sChoice ★ **Queen's Bath.** A tropical path tucked away in a North Shore neighborhood winds its way down to the oceanfront, where a large tide pool has been carved into the dark lava rock creating nature's version of an infinity pool. It takes some dexterity (and reef shoes) to get there, but once in you can dawdle like a regal queen, emerging only to scramble up the rocks for a short cliff dive back in. Every now and again a wave breaks the barrier, sending squealing bathers asunder. Be careful, though: October through May brings big surf, and people have been swept off the rocks and have drowned. ■ TIP→ **Look for green sea turtles swimming in the surf beyond the pool.** ⊠ *Kapiolani Rd., Princeville.*

WORTH NOTING

Anaina Hou Mini Golf & Gardens. The island's first miniature-golf course also has a small botanical garden and a new 300-seat theater/arts center. The 18-hole course was designed to be challenging, beautiful, and family-friendly. Replacing the typical clown's nose and spinning wheels are some water features and tropical tunnels. Surrounding each hole is plant life that walks players through different eras of Hawaiian history. A gift shop with local products and a concessions counter make it a fun activity for any time of day. On Saturday morning and Monday afternoon, a farmers' market is adjacent to the course with fresh Kauai produce and local goods. ⊠ *5-273 Kuhio Hwy., Kilauea* ☏ *808/828–2118* ⊕ *www.kauaiminigolf.com* ✉ *$18.*

Moloaa Sunrise Fruit Stand. Don't let the name fool you; they don't open at sunrise (more like 7:30 am, so come here after you watch the sun rise elsewhere). And it's not just a fruit stand. Breakfast is light and includes bagels, granola, smoothies, coffee, espresso, cappuccino, latte, and, of course, tropical-style fresh juices (pineapple, carrot, watermelon, guava, even sugarcane, in season). This is also a great spot to get out and stretch, take in the mountain view, and pick up sandwiches to go. Select local produce is available, although the variety is often not as good as at the island's farmers' markets. What makes this fruit stand different is the fresh, natural ingredients like multigrain breads and cold, homemade salads like potato or chicken curry that are perfect for a picnic. ⊠ *6011 Koolau Rd., at Kuhio Hwy., Kilauea* ☏ *808/822–1441.*

NAPALI COAST

Napali Coast is considered the jewel of Kauai, and for all its greenery, it would surely be an emerald. After seeing the coast, many are at a loss for words, because its beauty is so overwhelming. Others resort to poetry. Pulitzer Prize–winning poet W. S. Merwin wrote a book-length poem, *The Folding Cliffs*, based on a true story set in Napali. *Napali* means "the cliffs," and while it sounds like a simple name, it's quite an apt description. The coastline is cut by a series of small valleys, like fault lines, running to the interior, with the resulting cliffs seeming to bend back on themselves like an accordion-folded fan made of green velvet. More than 5 million years old, these sea cliffs rise thousands of feet above the Pacific, and every shade of green is represented in the vegetation that blankets their lush peaks and folds. At their base there are caves, secluded beaches, and waterfalls to explore.

Let's put this in perspective: even if you had only one day on Kauai, we'd still recommend heading to Napali Coast on Kauai's northwest side. Once you're there, you'll soon realize why no road traverses this series of folding-fan cliffs. That leaves three ways to experience the coastline—by air, by water, or on foot. We recommend all three, in this order: air, water, foot. Each one gets progressively more sensory.(⇨ *See the Napali feature in the chapter.*) A helicopter tour is your best bet if you're strapped for time. We recommend Jack Harter Helicopters or Safari Helicopters (⇨ *see Aerial Tours in the Golf, Hiking, and Outdoor Activities chapter for more information*). Boat tours are great for family fun; and hiking, of course, is the most budget-friendly option.

Whatever way you choose to visit Napali, you might want to keep this awe-inspiring fact in mind: at one time, thousands of Hawaiians lived self-sufficiently in these valleys. △ Following extensive flooding in early 2018, areas of the Napali Coast, including the Kalalau Trail, are undergoing repairs. Please check before visiting to make sure places are open.

GETTING HERE AND AROUND

Napali Coast runs 15 miles from Kee Beach, one of Kauai's more popular snorkeling spots, on the island's North Shore to Polihale State Park, the longest stretch of beach in the state, on the West Side of the island.

How do you explore this gorgeous stretch of coastline? You can't drive to it, through it, or around it. You can't see Napali from a scenic lookout. You can't even take a mule ride to it. The only way to experience its magic is from the sky, the ocean, or the trail. The Kalalau Trail can be hiked from the "end of the road" at Kee Beach where the trailhead begins in Haena State Park at the northwest end of Kuhio Highway (Route 56). There's no need to hike the entire 11 miles to get a full experience, especially if you just hike the first 2 miles into Hanakapiai Beach and another 2 miles up that valley. ⇨ *For information on Napali Coast tour operators, see the Boat Tours section in the Water Sports and Tours chapter and the Aerial Tours section in the Golf, Hiking, and Outdoor Activities chapter.*

TOP ATTRACTIONS

Kee Beach State Park. This stunning, and often extremely overcrowded, beach marks the start of majestic Napali Coast. The 11-mile **Kalalau Trail** begins near the parking lot, drawing day hikers and backpackers. Another path leads from the sand to a stone hula platform dedicated to **Laka,** the goddess of hula, which has been in use since ancient times. This is a sacred site that should be approached with respect; it's inappropriate for visitors to leave offerings at the altar, which is tended by students in a local hula *halau* (school). Local etiquette suggests observing from a distance. Most folks head straight for the sandy beach and its dreamy lagoon, which is great for snorkeling when the sea is calm. ✉ *Western end of Rte. 560, Haena.*

WORTH NOTING

Hanakapiai Beach. Hanakapiai Beach is a small jewel you'll discover after the first 2 miles of Napali Trail and crossing the stream. It's a beauty, with fine sand, a feeling of isolation, and a tropical stream valley to explore. Unfortunately, the beach is only swimmable in summer under the right conditions as there is often a dangerous shore break. And, at all times of the year, it's a sweep-away beach, since it is not protected as a bay would be. For relaxation, sunning, and as a solid refresher on your hiking journey, Hanakapiai offers a welcome and stunning respite. **Best for:** sunset; solitude. **Amenities:** toilets. ✉ *Hanalei ✛ Trailhead is at end of Rte. 560, 7 miles west of Hanalei.*

THE EAST SIDE

The East Side encompasses Lihue, Wailua, and Kapaa. It's also known as the Coconut Coast, as there was once a coconut plantation where today's aptly named Coconut Marketplace is located. A small grove still exists on both sides of the highway. *Mauka,* a fenced herd of goats keeps the grass tended; on the *makai* side, you can walk through the grove, although it's best not to walk directly under the trees—falling coconuts can be dangerous. Lihue is the county seat, and the whole East Side is the island's center of commerce, so early-morning and late-afternoon drive times (or rush hour) can get very congested. (Because there's only one main road, if there's a serious traffic accident the entire roadway may be closed, with no way around. Not to worry; it's a rarity.)

KAPAA AND WAILUA

Kapaa is 16 miles southeast of Kilauea; Wailua is 3 miles southwest of Kapaa.

Old Town Kapaa was once a plantation town, which is no surprise—most of the larger towns on Kauai once were. Old Town Kapaa is made up of a collection of wooden-front shops, some built by plantation workers and still run by their progeny today. Kapaa houses the two biggest grocery stores on the island, side by side: Foodland and Safeway. It also offers plenty of dining options for breakfast, lunch, and dinner, and gift shopping. If the timing is right, plan to cruise the town on the first Saturday evening of each month when the bands are playing and the town's wares are on display. To the south, Wailua comprises a few restaurants and shops, a few mid-range resorts along the coastline, and a housing community *mauka*. ⚠ **Following extensive flooding in early 2018, areas along the Wailua River, including the state park, are undergoing repairs. Please check before visiting to make sure places are open.**

GETTING HERE AND AROUND

Turn to the right out of the airport at Lihue for the road to Wailua. Careful, though—the zone between Lihue and Wailua has been the site of many car accidents. Two bridges—under which the very culturally significant Wailua River gently flows—mark the beginning of Wailua. It quickly blends into Kapaa; there's no real demarcation. Pay attention and drive carefully, always knowing where you are going and when to turn off.

TOP ATTRACTIONS

FAMILY **Opaekaa Falls.** The mighty Wailua River produces many dramatic waterfalls, and Opaekaa (pronounced oh-pie-kah-ah) is one of the best. It plunges hundreds of feet to the pool below and can be easily viewed from a scenic overlook with ample parking. Opaekaa means "rolling shrimp," which refers to tasty native crustaceans that were once so abundant they could be seen tumbling in the falls. Do not attempt to hike down to the pool. ■TIP➔ **Just before reaching the parking area for the waterfalls, turn left into a scenic pullout for great views of the Wailua River valley and its march to the sea.** ⊠ *Kuamoo Rd., Wailua (Kauai County)* ⊹ *From Rte. 56, turn mauka onto Kuamoo Rd. and drive 1½ miles.*

Fodor'sChoice
★ **Poliahu Heiau.** Storyboards near this ancient *heiau* (sacred site) recount the significance of the many sacred structures found along the Wailua River. It's unknown exactly how the ancient Hawaiians used Poliahu Heiau—one of the largest pre-Christian temples on the island—but legend says it was built by the Menehune because of the unusual stonework found in its walled enclosures. From this site, drive downhill toward the ocean to *pohaku hanau,* a two-piece birthing stone said to confer special blessings on all children born there, and *pohaku piko,* whose crevices were a repository for umbilical cords left by parents seeking a clue to their child's destiny, which reportedly was foretold by how the cord fared in the rock. Some Hawaiians feel these sacred stones shouldn't be viewed as tourist attractions, so always treat them with respect. Never stand or sit on the rocks or leave any offerings. ⊠ *Rte. 580, Kuamoo Rd., Wailua (Kauai County).*

FAMILY **Wailua Falls.** You may recognize this impressive cascade from the opening sequences of the *Fantasy Island* television series. Kauai has plenty of noteworthy waterfalls, but this one is especially gorgeous, easy to find, and easy to photograph. ⊠ *Maalo Rd., off Rte. 580, Lihue.*

WORTH NOTING

Fern Grotto. The Fern Grotto has a long history on Kauai, and though it's really not much to look at, visitors seem to like it. Perhaps it's the serenity of just cruising up and down the river accompanied by Hawaiian music. The grotto itself is nothing more than a yawning lava

Continued on page 64

NAPALI COAST: EMERALD QUEEN OF KAUAI

If you're coming to Kauai, Napali ("the cliffs" in Hawaiian) is a major must-see. More than 5 million years old, these sea cliffs rise thousands of feet above the Pacific, and every shade of green is represented in the vegetation that blankets their lush peaks and folds. At their base, there are caves, secluded beaches, and waterfalls to explore.

The big question is how to explore this gorgeous stretch of coastline. You can't drive to it, through it, or around it. You can't see Napali from a scenic lookout. You can't even take a mule ride to it. The only way to experience its magic is from the sky, the ocean, or the trail.

FROM THE SKY

If you've booked a helicopter tour of Napali, you might start wondering what you've gotten yourself into on the way to the airport. Will it feel like being on a small airplane? Will there be turbulence? Will it be worth all the money you just plunked down?

Your concerns will be assuaged on the helipad, once you see the faces of those who have just returned from their journey: Everyone looks totally blissed out. And now it's your turn.

Climb on board, strap on your headphones, and the next thing you know the helicopter gently lifts up, hovers for a moment, and floats away like a spider on the wind—no roaring engines, no rumbling down a runway. If you've chosen a flight with music, you'll feel as if you're inside your very own IMAX movie.

Pinch yourself if you must, because this is the real thing. Your pilot shares history, legend, and lore. If you miss something, speak up: pilots love to show off their island knowledge. You may snap a few pictures (not too many or you'll miss the eyes-on experience!), nudge a friend or spouse, and point at a whale breeching in the ocean, but mostly you stare, mouth agape. There is simply no other way to take in the immensity and greatness of Napali but from the air.

(left) The Napali Coast is a breathtaking stretch of Kauai coastline lined by sea cliffs rising thousands of feet into the sky. (bottom) Helicopter tour over Napali Coast

GOOD TO KNOW

Helicopter companies depart from the north, east, and west sides of the island. Most are based in Lihue, near the airport.

If you want more adventure—and air—choose one of the helicopter companies that flies with the doors off.

Some companies offer flights without music. Know the experience you want ahead of time. Some even sell a DVD of your flight, so you don't have to worry about taking pictures.

Wintertime rain grounds some flights; plan your trip early in your stay in case the flight gets rescheduled.

IS THIS FOR ME?

Taking a helicopter trip is the most expensive way to see Napali—as much as $300 for an hour-long tour.

Claustrophobic? Choose a boat tour or hike. It's a tight squeeze in the helicopter, especially in one of the middle seats.

Short on time? Taking a helicopter tour is a great way to see the island.

WHAT YOU MIGHT SEE

■ Nualolo Kai (an ancient Hawaiian fishing village) with its fringed reef

■ The 300-foot Hanakapiai Falls

■ A massive sea arch formed in the rock by erosion

■ The 11-mile Kalalau Trail threading its way along the coast

■ The amazing striations of aa and pahoehoe lava flows that helped push Kauai above the sea

FROM THE OCEAN

Napali from the ocean is two treats in one: spend a good part of the day on (or in) the water, and gaze up at majestic green sea cliffs rising thousands of feet above your head.

There are three ways to see it: a mellow pleasure-cruise catamaran allows you to kick back and sip a mai tai; an adventurous raft (Zodiac) tour will take you inside sea caves under waterfalls, and give you the option of snorkeling; and a daylong outing in a kayak is possible in the summer.

Any way you travel, you'll breathe ocean air, feel spray on your face, and see pods of spinner dolphins, green sea turtles, flying fish, and, if you're lucky, a rare Hawaiian monk seal.

Napali stretches from Kee Beach in the north to Polihale beach on the West Side. You'll be heading towards the lush Hanakapiai Valley, where within a few minutes, you'll see caves and waterfalls galore. About halfway down the coast just after the Kalalau Trail ends, you'll come to an immense arch—formed where the sea eroded the less dense basaltic rock—and a thundering 50-foot waterfall. And as the island curves near Nualolo State Park, you'll begin to notice less vegetation and more rocky outcroppings.

(left and top right) Kayaking on Napali Coast
(bottom right) Dolphin on Napali Coast

GOOD TO KNOW

If you want to snorkel, choose a morning rather than an afternoon tour—preferably during a summer visit—when seas are calmer.

If you're on a budget, choose a non-snorkeling tour.

If you want to see whales, take any tour, but be sure to plan your vacation for December through March.

You can only embark from the North Shore in summer. If you're staying on the South Shore, it might not be worth your time to drive to the north, so head to the West Side.

IS THIS FOR ME?

Boat tours are several hours long, so if you have only a short time on Kauai, a helicopter tour is a better alternative.

Even on a small boat, you won't get the individual attention and exclusivity of a helicopter tour.

Prone to seasickness? A large boat can be surprisingly rocky, so be prepared. Afternoon trips are rougher because the winds pick up.

WHAT YOU MIGHT SEE

■ Hawaii's state fish—the humuhumunukunukuapuaa—otherwise known as the reef triggerfish

■ Waiahuakua Sea Cave, with a waterfall coming through its roof

■ Tons of marine life, including dolphins, green sea turtles, flying fish, and humpback whales, especially in February and March

■ Waterfalls—especially if your trip is after a heavy rain

FROM THE TRAIL

If you want to be one with Napali—feeling the soft red earth beneath your feet, picnicking on the beaches, and touching the lush vegetation—hiking the Kalalau Trail is the way to do it.

Most people hike only the first 2 miles of the 11-mile trail and turn around at Hanakapiai. This 4-mile round-trip hike takes three to four hours. It starts at sea level and doesn't waste any time gaining elevation. (Take heart—the uphill lasts only a mile and tops out at 400 feet; then it's downhill all the way.) At the half-mile point, the trail curves west and the folds of Napali Coast unfurl.

Along the way you might share the trail with feral goats and wild pigs. Some of the vegetation is native; much is introduced.

After the 1-mile mark the trail begins its drop into Hanakapiai. You'll pass a couple of streams of water trickling across the trail, and maybe some banana, ginger, the native uluhe fern, and the Hawaiian ti plant. Finally the trail swings around the eastern ridge of Hanakapiai for your first glimpse of the valley and then switchbacks down the mountain. You'll have to boulder-hop across the stream to reach the beach. If you like, you can take a 4-mile, round-trip fairly strenuous side trip from this point to the gorgeous Hanakapiai Falls.

(left) Awaawapuhi mountain biker on razor-edge ridge
(top right) Feral goats in Kalalau Valley
(bottom right) Napali Coast

GOOD TO KNOW

Wear comfortable, amphibious shoes. Unless your feet require extra support, wear a self-bailing sort of shoe (for stream crossings) that doesn't mind mud. Don't wear heavy, waterproof hiking boots.

During winter the trail is often muddy, so be extra careful; sometimes it's completely inaccessible.

Don't hike after heavy rain—flash floods are common.

If you plan to hike the entire 11-mile trail (most people do the shorter hike described at left) you'll need a permit to go past Hanakapiai.

IS THIS FOR ME?

Of all the ways to see Napali (with the exception of kayaking the coast), this is the most active. You need to be in decent shape to hit the trail.

If you're vacationing in winter, this hike might not be an option due to flooding—whereas you can take a helicopter year-round.

WHAT YOU MIGHT SEE

■ Big dramatic surf right below your feet

■ Amazing vistas of the cool blue Pacific

■ The spectacular Hanakapiai Falls; if you have a permit don't miss Hanakoa Falls, less than 1/2 mile off the trail

■ Wildlife, including goats and pigs

■ Zany-looking hala trees, with aerial roots and long, skinny serrated leaves known as lau hala. Early Hawaiians used them to make mats, baskets, and canoe sails.

The East Side

Anahola
Beach Park

Anahola

Donkey Beach

Spalding
Monument

KAWAIHAU

56

Kealia Beach

Kealia

Steelgrass
Chocolate Farm

Kealia Scenic
Viewpoint

581

Keahua
Forestry
Arboretum

Kapaa

Baby Beach

Waipouli

56

Sleeping
Giant

Wailua Beach

Ōpaekaa
Falls

580

Wailua

Wailua Bay

Kamokila
Hawaiian
Village

Smith's
Tropical
Paradise

Poliahu Heiau

Wailua
Falls

Fern
Grotto

*Lydgate State
Beach Park*

Wailua River

56

583

Hanamaulu

Kapaia

LIHUE

Kauai
Museum

Lihue

✈ Lihue Airport

Kilohana
Plantation

50

56

Puhi

Grove Farm
Homestead

Nawiliwili

*Kalapaki
Beach*

Alekoko
(Menehune)
Fishpond

*Nawiliwili
Bay*

Huleia River

| 0 | | 2 mi |

| 0 | | 2 km |

tube swathed in lush fishtail ferns 3 miles up the Wailua River. Though it was significantly damaged after Hurricane Iniki in 1992 and again after heavy rains in 2006, the greenery has completely recovered. The Smith's Kauai tour group (⊕ *www. smithskauai.com*)is the only way to legally see the grotto. You can access the entrance with a kayak, but if boats are there, you may not be allowed to land. ⊠ *Rte. 56, just south of Wailua River, Kapaa* ☎ *808/821–6893* ⊕ *smithskauai. com* 🖃 *$25.*

ROADSIDE VENDORS

Lei. Tropical flowers. Corn. Rambutan. Avocados. Huli huli chicken. Kalua pig. It's not uncommon to run across individuals selling flowers, produce, and food on the side of the road. Some are local farmers trying to make a living; others are people fund-raising for the local canoe club. Don't be afraid to stop and buy. Most are friendly and enjoy chatting.

FAMILY **Kamokila Hawaiian Village.** The village is dramatically ensconced at the base of a steep, long, winding road right down to the Wailua River. In the days of King Kaumualii, it made the perfect hideout to tuck away his war canoes in this crook of the river. Today, there's a replica Hawaiian village in place of war canoes—numerous thatched-roof structures and abundant plant life along with traditional Hawaiian games. Yet, the lack of human activity here makes it seem abandoned, which may be why Hollywood found it an appealing location for the movie *Outbreak.* Visitors can rent canoes for the day and paddle up to the Fern Grotto or Secret Falls. ⊠ *5443 Kuamoo Rd., Kapaa* ☎ *808/823–0559* ⊕ *www. villagekauai.com* 🖃 *$5.*

Keahua Forestry Arboretum. Tree-lined and grassy, this is a perfect spot for a picnic—and there are lots of picnic tables scattered throughout the parklike setting. A shallow, cascading stream makes for a fun spot for kids to splash, although the water's a bit chilly. After crossing the stream on the brand-new bridge, the 1-mile walking trail meanders through mango, monkeypod, and exquisite rainbow eucalyptus trees. This is an exceptionally peaceful place—good for yoga and meditation—that is, unless the resident roosters decide to crow. ⊠ *Kuamoo Rd., Wailua (Kauai County).*

Kealia Scenic Viewpoint. This ocean overlook is perfect for spotting whales during their winter migration. In fact, on three Saturdays in winter, the Hawaiian Islands Humpback Whale National Marine Sanctuary conducts its annual whale count from this spot, one of several around the island. The lookout was rebuilt and doubled in size a few years ago, and it's now easy to hop on the cement bike and walking path just below for a coastal stroll or ride. Most days you can see clear to Lihue and beyond. If you packed them, bring your binoculars. ⊠ *Rte. 56, Kapaa* ✛ *Between mile markers 9 and 10.*

Sleeping Giant. Although its true name is Nounou, this landmark mountain ridge is better known as the Sleeping Giant because of its resemblance to a very large man sleeping on his back. Legends differ on whether the giant is Puni, who was accidentally killed by rocks launched at invading canoes by the Menehune, or Nunui, a gentle creature who

One of the best places for a luau is here at Smith's Tropical Paradise.

has not yet awakened from the nap he took centuries ago after building a massive temple and enjoying a big feast. ✉ *Rte. 56, Kapaa ✛ About 1 mile north of Wailua River.*

FAMILY **Smith's Tropical Paradise.** Nestled next to Wailua Marina along the mighty Wailua River, this 30-acre botanical and cultural garden offers a glimpse of exotic foliage, including fruit orchards, a bamboo rain forest, and tropical lagoons. Take the tram and enjoy a narrated tour or stroll along the mile-long pathways during the luau. It's a popular spot for wedding receptions and other large events, and its nightly luau is one of the island's oldest and best. ✉ *3-5971 Kuhio Hwy., just south of Wailua River, Kapaa* ☎ *808/821–6895* ⊕ *smithskauai.com.*

Spalding Monument. The Colonel Zephaniah Spalding monument commemorates the Civil War veteran who purchased this splendid property overlooking an area from Anahola to Kapaa in 1876 and soon established what became the Kealia Sugar Plantation. Turn onto Kealia Road just after mile marker 10 for an off-the-beaten-track scenic detour. Immediately on your right are a small post office and a food truck and, on your left, rodeo grounds often in use on summer weekends. The road ascends, and 2½ miles later you'll reach a grassy area with the concrete remains of a onetime monument. It's a nice spot to picnic or to simply gaze at the nearby grazing horses. If you're an early riser, this is a great spot to watch the sun rise; if not, check the local newspaper for the next full moon and bring a bottle of wine. It's possible to continue on for another very bumpy 2 miles, where you'll reconnect with Highway 56 near the town of Anahola, but your bike or car will not thank you for it. You're better off doubling back. ✉ *Kealia Rd., Kapaa.*

Steelgrass Chocolate Farm. Hawaii is the only state in the country where *theobroma cacao* grows. As every chocolate connoisseur knows, the tree that grows the precious seed that becomes chocolate is the cacao tree. The Lydgates are on a mission to grow enough cacao on their family farm with the hope that one day they will produce an identifiable Kauai homegrown chocolate. For now, you can tour this organic farm (in addition to cacao, they grow vanilla, timber, bamboo, and many tropical fruits) and learn how chocolate is made, "from branch to bar," as they put it. The three-hour tour includes, of course, plenty of chocolate tastings. Reservations are required for the morning tour, which runs weekdays at 9 am. Children 12 and under are free. ✉ *5730 Olohena Rd., Kapaa* ☎ *808/821–1857* ⊕ *www.steelgrass.org* 🏷 *$75.*

LIHUE

7 miles southwest of Wailua.

The commercial and political center of Kauai County, which includes the islands of Kauai and Niihau, Lihue is home to the island's major airport, harbor, and hospital. This is where you can find the state and county offices that issue camping and hiking permits and the same fast-food eateries and big-box stores that blight the mainland. The county is seeking help in reviving the downtown; for now, once your business is done, there's little reason to linger in lackluster Lihue.

GETTING HERE AND AROUND

Route 56 leads into Lihue from the north and Route 50 comes here from the south and west. The road from the airport (where Kauai's car rental agencies are) leads to the middle of Lihue. Many of the area's stores and restaurants are on and around Rice Street, which also leads to Kalapaki Bay and Nawiliwili Harbor.

TOP ATTRACTIONS

Fodor's Choice ★
Alekoko (Menehune) Fishpond. No one knows just who built this intricate aquaculture structure in the Huleia River. Legend attributes it to the Menehune, a mythical—or real, depending on who you ask—ancient race of people known for their small stature, industrious nature, and superb stoneworking skills. Volcanic rock was cut and fit together into massive walls 4 feet thick and 5 feet high, forming an enclosure for raising mullet and other freshwater fish that has endured for centuries. ✉ *Hulemalu Rd., Niumalu.*

Fodor's Choice ★
Kauai Museum. Maintaining a stately presence on Rice Street, the historic museum building is easy to find. It features a permanent display, "The Story of Kauai," which provides a competent overview of the Garden Island and Niihau, tracing the Islands' geology, mythology, and cultural history. Local artists are represented in changing exhibits in the second-floor Mezzanine Gallery. The expanded gift shop alone is worth a visit, with a fine collection of authentic Niihau shell lei, feather hatband lei, hand-turned wooden bowls, reference books, and other quality arts, crafts, and gifts—many of them locally made. ✉ *4428 Rice St., Lihue* ☎ *808/245–6931* ⊕ *www.kauaimuseum.org* 🏷 *$15.*

WORTH NOTING

Grove Farm Homestead. Guided tours of this carefully restored 80-acre country estate offer a fascinating and authentic look at how upper-class Caucasians experienced plantation life in the mid-19th century. The tour focuses on the original home, built by the Wilcox family in 1860 and filled with a quirky collection of classic Hawaiiana. You can also see the workers' quarters, farm animals, orchards, and gardens that reflect the practical, self-sufficient lifestyle of the island's earliest Western inhabitants. Tours of the homestead are conducted twice a day, three days a week. To protect the historic building and its furnishings, tours may be canceled on very wet days. ■TIP➔ With a six-person limit per tour, reservations are essential. ⊠ *4050 Nawiliwili Rd., Lihue* ☎ *808/245–3202* ⊕ *www.grovefarm.org* ✉ *$20 requested donation.*

FAMILY **Kilohana Plantation.** This estate dates back to 1850, shortly after the "Great Mahele"—the division of land by the Hawaiian people. Plantation manager Albert Spencer Wilcox developed it as a working cattle ranch, and his nephew, Gaylord Parke Wilcox, took over in 1936, building Kauai's first mansion. Today the 16,000-square-foot, Tudor-style home houses specialty shops, art galleries, the Koloa Rum Co. and Gaylord's, a pretty restaurant with courtyard seating. Nearly half the original furnishings remain, and the gardens and orchards were replanted according to the original plans. You can tour the grounds for free, or take a 40-minute train ride and learn the agricultural story of Kauai while viewing a working farm. ⊠ *3-2087 Kaumualii Hwy., Lihue* ☎ *808/245–5608* ⊕ *www.kilohanakauai.com* ✆ *Train tours $19.*

THE SOUTH SHORE

As you follow the main road south from Lihue, the landscape becomes lush and densely vegetated before giving way to drier conditions that characterize Poipu, the South Side's major resort area. Poipu owes much of its popularity to a steady supply of sunshine and a string of sandy beaches, although the beaches are smaller and more covelike than those on the West Side. With its extensive selection of accommodations, services, and activities, the South Shore attracts more visitors than any other area of Kauai. It also attracted developers with big plans for the onetime sugarcane fields that are nestled in this region and enveloped by mountains. There are few roads in and out, and local residents are concerned about increased traffic as well as noise and dust pollution as a result of chronic construction. If you're planning to stay on the South Side, be sure to ask if your hotel, condo, or vacation rental will be impacted by the development during your visit.

Both Poipu and nearby Koloa (site of Kauai's first sugar mill) can be reached via Route 520 (Maluhia Road) from the Lihue area. Route 520 is known locally as Tree Tunnel Road, due to the stand of eucalyptus trees lining the road that were planted at the turn of the 20th century by Walter Duncan McBryde, a Scotsman who began cattle ranching on Kauai's South Shore. The canopy of trees was ripped to literal shreds twice—in 1982 during Hurricane Iwa and again in 1992

2

SUNSHINE MARKETS

If you want to rub elbows with the locals and purchase fresh produce and flowers at (somewhat) reasonable prices, head for Sunshine Markets, also known as Kauai's farmers' markets. These busy markets are held throughout the week, usually in the afternoon, at locations all around the island—just ask any local person. They're good fun, and they support neighborhood farmers. Arrive a little early, bring dollar bills to speed up transactions and your own shopping bags to carry your produce, and be prepared for some pushy shoppers. Farmers are usually happy to educate visitors about unfamiliar fruits and veggies, especially when the crowd thins. For schedules and information on all of the Sunshine Markets, call ☎ *808/241–6303*; and check out Kauai's government website at ⊕ *www.kauai.gov*.

East Side Sunshine Markets
⊠ *Vidinha Stadium, Lihue, ½ mile south of airport on Rte. 51*, Friday 3 pm. ⊠ *Kapaa, turn mauka on Rte. 581/Olohena Rd. for 1 block*, Wednesday 3 pm.

North Shore Sunshine Markets
⊠ *Waipa, mauka of Rte. 560 north of Hanalei after mile marker 3, Hanalei*, Tuesday 2 pm. ⊠ *Kilauea Neighborhood Center, on Keneke St., Kilauea*, Thursday 4:30 pm. ⊠ *Hanalei Community Center, 5299 Kuhio Hwy, Hanalei*, Saturday 9:30 am.

South Shore Sunshine Markets
⊠ *Ballpark, Koloa, north of intersection of Koloa Rd. and Rte. 520*, Monday noon.

West Side Sunshine Markets
⊠ *Kalaheo Community Center, on Papalina Rd. just off Kaumualii Hwy., Kalaheo*, Tuesday 3 pm. ⊠ *Hanapepe Park, Hanapepe*, Thursday 3 pm. ⊠ *Kekaha Neighborhood Center, Elepaio Rd., Kekaha*, Saturday 9 am.

during Hurricane Iniki. And, true to Kauai, both times the trees grew back into an impressive tunnel. It's a distinctive way to announce, "You are now on vacation," for there's a definite feel of leisure in the air here. There's still plenty to do—snorkel, bike, walk, horseback ride, take an ATV tour, surf, scuba dive, shop, and dine—everything you'd want on a tropical vacation. From the west, Route 530 (Koloa Road) slips into downtown Koloa, a string of fun shops and restaurants, at an intersection with the only gas station on the South Shore.

KOLOA

11 miles southwest of Lihue.

Hawaii's lucrative foray into sugar was born in this sleepy town, where the first sugar was milled back in 1830. You can still see the mill's old stone smokestack. Little else remains, save for the charming plantation-style buildings that have kept Koloa from becoming a tacky tourist trap for Poipu-bound visitors. The original small-town character has been preserved by converting historic structures along the main street into boutiques, restaurants, and shops. Placards describe the original tenants and life in the old mill town. Look for Koloa Fish Market,

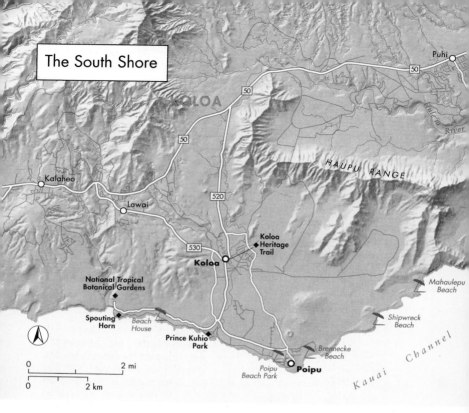

which offers poke and sashimi takeout, and Progressive Expressions, a popular local surf shop.

TOP ATTRACTION

Fodor's Choice ★

Old Koloa Town. Koloa's first sugar mill opened in 1835, ushering in an era of sugar production throughout the Islands, with more than 100 plantations established by 1885. Many of the workers came from the Philippines, Japan, China, Korea and Portugal, creating Hawaii's multiethnic mélange. Today, many of Koloa's historic buildings beneath the shade of ancient monkeypod trees have been converted into fun shops and restaurants. You'll just want to stroll and take it all in; favorites include Island Soap and Candleworks, Crazyshirts, and Lappert's, Hawaiian-inspired ice cream made daily in nearby Hanapepe. Try the Kauai Pie and Luau Delight flavors. ■ TIP→ Be sure to approach Old Koloa Town via the Tree Tunnel, a romantic canopy of eucalyptus trees planted more than a century ago along a stretch of Maluhia Road. ⊠ Koloa Rd., Koloa ⊕ www.oldkoloa.com.

WORTH NOTING

Koloa Heritage Trail. Throughout the South Shore, you'll find brass plaques with details of 14 historical stops along the 10-mile Koloa Heritage Trail—bike it, hike it, or drive it, your choice. You'll learn about Koloa's whaling history, sugar industry, ancient Hawaiian cultural sites, the island's volcanic formation, and more. Pick up a free self-guided trail map at most any shop in Koloa town. ⊠ *Koloa.*

POIPU

2 miles southeast of Koloa.

Thanks to its generally sunny weather and a string of golden-sand beaches dotted with oceanfront lodgings, Poipu is a top choice for many visitors. Beaches are user-friendly, with protected waters for *keiki* (children) and novice snorkelers, lifeguards, restrooms, covered pavilions, and a sweet coastal promenade ideal for leisurely strolls. Some experts have even ranked Poipu Beach Park number one in the nation. It depends on your preferences, of course, though it certainly does warrant high accolades.

GETTING HERE AND AROUND

Poipu is the one area on Kauai where you could get by without a car, though that could mean an expensive taxi ride from the airport and limited access to other parts of the island. To reach Poipu by car, follow Poipu Road south from Koloa. After the traffic circle, the road curves to follow the coast, leading to some of the popular South Shore beaches.

TOP ATTRACTIONS

National Tropical Botanical Gardens (*NTBG*). Tucked away in Lawai Valley, these gardens include lands and a cottage once used by Hawaii's Queen Emma for a summer retreat. Trams depart on the half hour to transport people from the visitor center to the gardens. The rambling 252-acre McBryde Gardens has a number of exhibits to help visitors learn about biodiversity and plants collected throughout the tropics, including the Life Canoe Garden that features plants originally brought to Hawaii by early voyagers from distant Polynesian islands. It is known as a garden of "research and conservation." The 100-acre Allerton Gardens, which can be visited only on a guided tour, artfully displays statues and water features that were originally developed as part of a private estate. Reservations are required to visit both gardens. The visitor center has a high-quality gift shop with botany-theme merchandise. Besides harboring and propagating rare and endangered plants from Hawaii and elsewhere, NTBG functions as a scientific research and education center. The organization also operates gardens in Limahuli, on Kauai's North Shore, and in Hana, on Maui's east shore, as well as one in Florida. ⊠ *4425 Lawai Rd., Poipu* ☎ *808/742–2623* ⊕ *www.ntbg.org* ✉ *McBryde self-guided tour $30, Allerton guided tour $50.*

Prince Kuhio Park. A triangle of grass behind the Prince Kuhio condominiums honors the birthplace of Kauai's beloved Prince Jonah Kuhio Kalanianaole. Known for his kind nature and good deeds, he lost his chance at the throne when Americans staged an illegal overthrow of Queen Liliuokalani in 1893 and toppled Hawaii's constitutional monarchy. This is a great place to view wave riders surfing a popular break known as PKs and to watch the sun sink into the Pacific. ⊠ *Lawai Rd., Poipu.*

Fodor'sChoice
★
Spouting Horn. If the conditions are right, you can see a natural blowhole in the reef behaving like Old Faithful, shooting salt water high

into the air and making a cool, echoing sound. It's most dramatic during big summer swells, which jam large quantities of water through an ancient lava tube with great force. Vendors hawk inexpensive souvenirs and collectibles in the parking lot. You may find good deals on shell jewelry, but some vendors also carry exotic Niihau-shell creations with prices up to $12,000. ⊠ *End of Lawai Rd., Poipu* ⊕ *www.kauai. com/spouting-horn.*

THE WEST SIDE

Exploring the West Side is akin to visiting an entirely different world. The landscape is dramatic and colorful: a patchwork of green, blue, black, and orange. The weather is hot and dry, the beaches are long, the sand is dark. Niihau, a private island and the last remaining place in Hawaii where Hawaiian is spoken exclusively, can be glimpsed offshore. This is rural Kauai, where sugar is making its last stand and taro is still cultivated in the fertile river valleys. The lifestyle is slow, easy, and traditional, with many folks fishing and hunting to supplement their diets. Here and there modern industry has intruded into this pastoral scene: huge generators turn oil into electricity at Port Allen; seed companies cultivate experimental crops of genetically engineered plants in Kekaha and Waimea; the navy launches rockets at Mana to test the "Star Wars" missile defense system; and NASA mans a tracking station in the wilds of Kokee. It's a region of contrasts that simply shouldn't be missed.

Heading west from Lihue or Poipu, you pass through a string of tiny towns, plantation camps, and historic sites, each with a story to tell of centuries past. There's Hanapepe, whose coastal salt ponds have been harvested since ancient times; Kaumakani, where the sugar industry still clings to life; Fort Elisabeth, from which an enterprising Russian tried to take over the island in the early 1800s; and Waimea, where Captain Cook made his first landing in the Islands, forever changing the face of Hawaii.

From Waimea town you can head up into the mountains, skirting the rim of magnificent Waimea Canyon and climbing higher still until you reach the cool, often-misty forests of Kokee State Park. From the vantage point at the top of this gemlike island, 3,200 to 4,200 feet above sea level, you can gaze into the deep, verdant valleys of the North Shore and Napali Coast. This is where the "real" Kauai can still be found: the native plants, insects, and birds that are found nowhere else on Earth.

HANAPEPE

15 miles west of Poipu.

In the 1980s Hanapepe was fast becoming a ghost town, its farm-based economy mirroring the decline of agriculture. Today it's a burgeoning art colony with galleries, crafts studios, and a lively art-theme street fair on Friday nights. The main street has a new vibrancy enhanced by the restoration of several historic buildings. The emergence of Kauai coffee as a major West Side crop, and expanded activities at Port Allen,

Continued on page 76

BIRTH OF THE ISLANDS

How did the volcanoes of the Hawaiian Islands evolve here, in the middle of the Pacific Ocean? The ancient Hawaiians believed that the volcano goddess Pele's hot temper was the key to the mystery; modern scientists contend that it's all about plate tectonics and one very hot spot.

Plate Tectonics & the Hawaiian Question: The theory of plate tectonics says that the Earth's surface is comprised of plates that float around slowly over the planet's molten interior. The vast majority of earthquakes and volcanic eruptions occur near plate boundaries—the San Francisco earthquakes in 1906 and 1989, for example, were the result of activity along the nearby San Andreas Fault, where the Pacific and North American plates meet. Hawaii, more than 1,988 miles from the nearest plate boundary, is a giant exception. For years scientists struggled to explain the island chain's existence—if not a fault line, what caused the earthquakes and volcanic eruptions that formed these islands?

What's a hotspot? In 1963, J. Tuzo Wilson, a Canadian geophysicist, argued that the Hawaiian volcanoes must have been created by small concentrated areas of extreme heat beneath the plates. Wilson hypothesized that there is a hotspot beneath the present-day position of the Big Island. Its heat produced a persistent source of magma by partly melting the Pacific Plate above it. The magma, lighter than the surrounding solid rock, rose through the mantle and crust to erupt onto the sea floor, forming an active seamount. Each flow caused the seamount to grow until it finally emerged above sea level as an island volcano. Plausible so far, but why then, is there not one giant Hawaiian island?

Holo Mai Pele, often played out in hula, is the Hawaiian creation myth. Pele sends her sister Hiiaka on an epic quest to fetch her lover Lohiau. Overcoming many obstacles, Hiiaka reaches full goddess status and falls in love with Lohiau herself. When Pele finds out, she destroys everything dear to her sister, killing Lohiau and burning Hiiaka's ohia groves. Each time lava flows from a volcano, ohia trees sprout shortly after, in a constant cycle of destruction and renewal.

AGE OF VOLCANIC ROCK	
Kauai	5.1 million yrs
Oahu	3 million yrs
Molokai	1.8 million yrs
Lanai	1.5 million yrs
Maui	1.3 million yrs
Hawaii	400,000 yrs
Loihi	-100,000 yrs

PACIFIC OCEAN

PACIFIC PLATE

SOLID DENSE ROCK

FIXED HOTSPOT

KEY
▲ Volcano
← Direction of plate movement

Volcanoes on the Move: Wilson further suggested that the movement of the Pacific Plate itself eventually carries the island volcano beyond the hotspot. Cut off from its magma source, the island volcano becomes dormant. As the plate slowly moved, one island volcano would become extinct just as another would develop over the hotspot. After several million years, there is a long volcanic trail of islands and seamounts across the ocean floor. The oldest islands are those farthest from the hotspot. The exposed rocks of Kauai, for example, are about 5.1 million years old, but those on the Big Island are less than .5 million years old, with new volcanic rock still being formed.

An Island on the Way: Off the coast of the Big Island, the volcano known as Loihi is still submerged but erupting. Scientists long believed it to be a retired seamount volcano, but in the 1970s they discovered both old and new lava on its flanks, and in 1996 it erupted with a vengeance. It is believed that several thousand years from now, Loihi will be the newest addition to the Hawaiian Islands.

The West Side

OCEAN

PACIFIC

Kee Beach
State Park

Haena
560

Hanale
Bay

Hanalei

Hanakapiai
Beach

NAPALI COAST

Kalalau Trail

Puu ○ Kila
Lookout

Kalalau
Lookout

Kokee State Park

Kokee

Polihale
State Park

550

Waimea
Canyon

Napali-Kona
Forest Reserve

WAIMEA

Kokee Rd

Waimea Canyon Rd

55

552

550

Kekaha Beach
Park

Kekaha

West Kauai
Technology &
Visitor Center

Waimea

Fort
Elizabeth

50

Kaulakahi Channel

TO
NIIHAU

Hanapepe Valley
and Canyon Lookout
Kalaheo

530

Hanapepe
Swinging
Bridge

50

540

Kukuiolono
Park

Lapperts Ice Cream
Hanapepe

Eleele

Salt Pond Beach Park

Port Allen

Hanapepe
Bay

Kauai Coffee
Visitor Center
and Museum

0   5 miles
0   5 km

now the main departure point for tour boats, also gave the town's economy a boost.

GETTING HERE AND AROUND

Hanapepe, locally known as Kauai's "biggest little town," is just past the Eleele Shopping Center on the main highway (Route 50). A sign leads you to the town center, where street parking is easy and there's an enjoyable walking tour.

TOP ATTRACTIONS

Hanapepe Swinging Bridge. This bridge may not be the biggest adventure on Kauai, but it's enough to make your heart hop. It's considered a historic suspension bridge even though it was rebuilt in 1996 after the original was destroyed—like so much of the island—by Hurricane Iniki. What is interesting about this bridge is that it's not just for show; it actually provides the only access to taro fields across the Waimea River. If you're in the neighborhood, it's worth a stroll. ⊠ *Off Hanapepe Rd., next to Banana Patch Studios parking lot, Hanapepe.*

Hanapepe Valley and Canyon Lookout. This dramatic divide and fertile river valley once housed a thriving Hawaiian community of taro farmers, with some of the ancient fields still in cultivation today. From the lookout, you can take in the farms on the valley floor with the majestic mountains as a backdrop. ⊠ *Rte. 50, Hanapepe.*

WORTH NOTING

Hanapepe Walking Tour. This 1½-mile self-guided walking tour takes you to 14 different plaques with historic photos and stories mounted on buildings throughout Hanapepe town. Businesses and shops in town sell a map of the tour for $2; however, you can often pick one up free with a coupon found in many guidebooks on promotional-brochure rack stands. ⊠ *Hanapepe town.*

Kauai Coffee Visitor Center and Museum. Two restored camp houses, dating from the days when sugar was the main agricultural crop on the Islands, have been converted into a museum, visitor center, and gift shop. About 3,100 acres of McBryde sugar land have become Hawaii's largest coffee plantation, producing more than 50% of the state's beans. You can walk among the trees, view old grinders and roasters, watch a video to learn how coffee is processed, sample various estate roasts, and check out the gift store. The center offers a free 15-minute self-guided tour with well-marked signs through a small coffee grove as well as $20 guided tours. From Kalaheo, take Highway 50 in the direction of Waimea Canyon (west) and veer left onto Highway 540. It's 2½ miles from the Highway 50 turnoff. ⊠ *870 Halawili Rd., Kalaheo* ☎ *808/335–0813* ⊕ *www.kauaicoffee.com* ☕ *Free.*

Kukuiolono Park. Translated as "Light of the God Lono," Kukuiolono has serene Japanese gardens, a display of significant Hawaiian stones, and spectacular panoramic views. This quiet hilltop park is one of Kauai's most scenic areas and an ideal picnic spot. There's also a small golf course. ⊠ *Papalina Rd., Kalaheo* ☎ *808/332–9151* ☕ *Free.*

WAIMEA AND WAIMEA CANYON

Waimea is 7 miles northwest of Hanapepe; Waimea Canyon is approximately 10 miles northeast of Waimea.

Waimea is a serene, pretty town that has the look of the Old West and the feel of Old Hawaii, with a lifestyle that's decidedly laid-back. It's an ideal place for a refreshment break while sightseeing on the West Side. The town has played a major role in Hawaiian history since 1778, when Captain James Cook became the first European to set foot on the Hawaiian Islands. Waimea was also the place where Kauai's King Kaumualii acquiesced to King Kamehameha's unification drive in 1810, averting a bloody war. The town hosted the first Christian missionaries, who hauled in massive timbers and limestone blocks to build the sturdy Waimea Christian Hawaiian and Foreign Church in 1846. It's one of many lovely historic buildings preserved by residents who take great pride in their heritage and history.

North of Waimea town, via Route 550, you'll find the vast and gorgeous Waimea Canyon, also known as the Grand Canyon of the Pacific. The spectacular vistas from the lookouts along the road culminate with an overview of Kalalau Valley. There are various hiking trails leading to the inner heart of Kauai. A camera is a necessity in this region.

GETTING HERE AND AROUND

Route 50 continues northwest to Waimea and Kekaha from Hanapepe. You can reach Waimea Canyon and Kokee State Park from either town—the way is clearly marked. Some pull-off areas on Route 550 are fine for a quick view of the canyon, but the designated lookouts have bathrooms and parking.

TOP ATTRACTIONS

Fort Elizabeth. The ruins of this stone fort, built in 1816 by an agent of the imperial Russian government named Anton Scheffer, are reminders of the days when Scheffer tried to conquer the island for his homeland, or so one story goes. Another claims that Scheffer's allegiance lay with King Kaumualii, who was attempting to regain leadership of his island nation from the grasp of Kamehameha the Great. The crumbling walls of the fort are not particularly interesting, but the signs loaded with historical information are. ⊠ *Rte. 50, Waimea (Kauai County).*

Kalalau Lookout. At the end of the road, high above Waimea Canyon, Kalalau Lookout marks the start of a 1-mile (one-way) hike to **Puu o Kila Lookout.** On a clear day at either spot, you can see a dreamy landscape of gaping valleys, sawtooth ridges, waterfalls, and turquoise seas, where whales can be seen spouting and breaching during the winter months. If clouds block the view, don't despair—they tend to blow through fast, giving you time to snap that photo of a lifetime. You may spot wild goats clambering on the sheer, rocky cliffs, and white tropic birds. If it's very clear to the northwest, drink in the shining sands of Kalalau Beach, gleaming like golden threads against the deep blue of the Pacific. ⊠ *Waimea Canyon Dr.* ✛ *4 miles north of Kokee State Park.*

Kokee State Park. This 4,345-acre wilderness park is 3,600 feet above sea level, an elevation that affords you breathtaking views in all directions

and a cooler, wetter climate. You can gain a deeper appreciation of the island's rugged terrain and dramatic beauty from this vantage point. Large tracts of native ohia and koa forest cover much of the land, along with many varieties of exotic plants. Hikers can follow a 45-mile network of trails through diverse landscapes that feel wonderfully remote—until the tour helicopters pass overhead. ⊠ *Hwy. 50, Kekaha* ✛ *15 miles north of Kekaha* ⊕ *kokee.org.*

Kokee Natural History Museum. When you arrive at Kokee State Park, Kokee Natural History Museum is a great place to start your visit. The friendly staff is knowledgeable about trail conditions and weather, while informative displays and a good selection of reference books can teach you more about the unique attributes of the native flora and fauna. You may also find that special memento or gift you've been looking for. ⊠ *Rte. 550, Kokee* ☎ *808/335–3353* ⊕ *kokee.org* ▨ *Donations accepted.*

QUICK BITES

Kokee Lodge. There's only one place to buy food and hot drinks in Kokee State Park, and that's the dining room of rustic Kokee Lodge. It's known for its Portugese bean soup and corn bread, of all things. ⊠ *Kokee State Park, 3600 Kokee Rd., mile marker 15, Kokee* ☎ *808/335–6061* ⊕ *kokeelodge. com* ☽ *No dinner.*

Fodor's Choice ★

Waimea Canyon. Carved over countless centuries by the Waimea River and the forces of wind and rain, Waimea Canyon is a dramatic gorge nicknamed the "Grand Canyon of the Pacific"—but not by Mark Twain, as many people mistakenly think. Hiking and hunting trails wind through the canyon, which is 3,600 feet deep, 2 miles wide, and 10 miles long. The cliff sides have been sharply eroded, exposing swatches of colorful soil. The deep red, brown, and green hues are constantly changing in the sun, and frequent rainbows and waterfalls enhance the natural beauty. This is one of Kauai's prettiest spots, and it's worth stopping at both the **Puu ka Pele** and **Puu Hinahina** lookouts. Clean public restrooms and parking are at both lookouts. ⊠ *Hwy. 550 (Kokee Rd.), Waimea (Kauai County)* ☎ *808/274–3444* ⊕ *dlnr.hawaii.gov/dsp/ parks/kauai/.*

WORTH NOTING

West Kauai Technology & Visitor Center. Cultural information and local exhibits highlight this museum-style resource center in the middle of Waimea town. Weekly events include historic walks and lei making with reservations required. This small center has a gift shop with island-made items, Niihau shell jewelry, books, and more. ⊠ *9565 Kaumualii Hwy., (Rte. 50), Waimea (Kauai County)* ☎ *808/338–1332* ⊕ *www. westkauaivisitorcenter.org/* ▨ *Free.*

3

BEACHES

Updated by
Joan Conrow

Kauai may be nicknamed the Garden Island, but with more sandy beaches per mile of coastline than any other Hawaiian Island, it could easily be called the Sandy Island as well. Totaling more than 50 miles, Kauai's beaches make up 44% of the island's shoreline—almost twice that of Oahu, second on this list.

It is, of course, because of Kauai's age as the eldest sibling of the inhabited Hawaiian Islands, allowing more time for water and wind erosion to break down rock and coral into sand.

But not all of Kauai's beaches are the same. Each beach is unique unto itself. Conditions and scenery can change throughout the day and certainly throughout the year, transforming, say, a tranquil, lakelike ocean setting in summer into monstrous waves drawing internationally ranked surfers from around the world in winter.

There are sandy beaches, rocky beaches, wide beaches, narrow beaches, skinny beaches, and alcoves. Generally speaking, surf kicks up on the North Shore in winter and the South Shore in summer, although summer's southern swells aren't nearly as frequent or as big as the northern winter swells that attract those surfers. Kauai's longest and widest beaches are found on the North Shore and West Side and are popular with beachgoers, although during winter's rains, everyone heads to the drier South Shore and West Side. The East Side beaches tend to be narrower and have onshore winds less popular with sunbathers, yet fishers abound. Smaller coves are characteristic of the South Shore and attract all kinds of water lovers year-round, including monk seals.

In Hawaii, all beaches are public, but their accessibility varies greatly. Some require an easy ½-mile stroll, some require a four-wheel-drive vehicle, others require boulder-hopping, and one takes an entire day of serious hiking. And then there are those "drive-in" beaches adjacent to parking areas. Kauai is not Disneyland, so don't expect much signage to help you along the way. One of the top-ranked beaches in the whole world—Hanalei—doesn't have a single sign in town directing you to the beach. Furthermore, the majority of Kauai's beaches on Kauai's vast coastline are remote, offering no facilities. It's important to note that drownings are common on Kauai, in part because many beaches have no lifeguards and tricky ocean conditions. When in doubt, stay out. ■TIP➔ **If you want the convenience of restrooms, picnic tables, lifeguards, and the like, stick to county beach parks.**

THE NORTH SHORE

If you've ever dreamed of Hawaii—and who hasn't—you've dreamed of Kauai's North Shore. *Lush, tropical,* and *abundant* are just a few words to describe this rugged and dramatic area. And the views to the sea aren't the only attraction—the inland views of velvety-green valley folds and carved mountain peaks will take your breath away. Rain is the reason for all the greenery on the North Shore, and winter is the rainy season. Not to worry, though; it rarely rains *everywhere* on the island at one time. ■TIP➔ **The rule of thumb is to head south or west when it rains in the north.**

The waves on the North Shore can be big—and we mean huge—in winter, drawing crowds to witness nature's spectacle. By contrast, in summer the waters can be completely serene. ⚠ **Following extensive flooding in early 2018, areas of Haena, including Haena Beach Park and Kee Beach, are undergoing repairs. Please check before visiting to make sure places are open.**

HANALEI, HAENA, AND WEST

Fodor's Choice ★ **Haena Beach Park.** This is a drive-up beach park popular with campers year-round. The wide bay here—named Makua—is bordered by two large reef systems creating favorable waves for skilled surfers during peak winter conditions. In July and August, waters at this same beach usually are as calm as a lake. Entering the water can be dangerous in winter when the big swells roll in. ■TIP➔ **During the summer months only, this is a premier snorkeling site on Kauai.** It's not unusual to find a food vendor parked here selling sandwiches and drinks out of a converted bread van. **Amenities:** food and drink; lifeguards; parking; showers; toilets. **Best for:** snorkeling; surfing; walking. ⊠ *Near end of Rte. 560, across from "Dry Cave", Haena.*

Hanakapiai Beach. If you're not up for the full 11-mile haul to Kalalau Beach, you can explore Napali Coast via a 2-mile hike to Hanakapiai Beach, which fronts a tropical valley. It'll take about two hours, and you'll have plenty of company on the trail. This is no longer a secluded beach, although it is still wilderness, and you'll find no amenities except pit toilets. The ocean here is what locals like to call "confused," and Hanakapiai Bay has been the site of numerous drownings. In the winter, surf often eats up the beach, exposing lava-rock boulders backing the sand. Be cautious when crossing the stream that runs through the valley, as it can quickly flood, stranding hikers on the wrong side. This has resulted in helicopter rescues and even deaths, as people are swept out to sea while attempting to cross. ■TIP➔ **A new bridge makes the passage easier, but don't attempt to cross during heavy rain. Amenities:**

Kauai
Beaches

Puu Poa Beach
Pali Ke Kua Beach
Haena Beach Park
Hanalei Bay
Lumahai Beach
Anini Beach Park
Kalihiwai Beach
Kee Beach
Hanalei Bay
Kauapea Beach
Hanakapiai Beach
Princeville
Kahili Beach
Kalalau
Haena
Hanalei
Kilauea
Larsen's Beach
NAPALI COAST
North Shore
56
Aliomanu Beach
Kalalau Trail
Anahola Beach Park
Kalalau Lookout
Kokee State Park
Anahola
Donkey Beach
Polihale State Park
Waialeale 5,148 ft.
East Side
Kealia Beach
550
581
Kealia
Kapaa
Baby Beach
580
Wailua Beach
WAIMEA CANYON
Wailua
Wailua Bay
Lydgate State Park
552
550
Kilohana Crater 1,138 ft.
583
56
Hanamaulu
Lihue
Lihue Airport
Kekaha
Kekaha Beach Park
50
58
Kalapaki Beach
Waimea
Nawiliwili Bay
Lucy Wright Beach Park
Kalaheo
Mahaulepu Beach
Kaulakahi Channel
50
Hanapepe
Eleele
Beach House Beach
Koloa
Keoniloa Beach
Kauai Channel
Salt Pond Beach Park
Hanapepe Bay
Lawai Kai
Waiohai Beach
Brennecke Beach
Kukuiula Small Boat Harbor
Poipu Beach Park
Poipu
South Shore

0   10 mi
0   10 km

toilets. **Best for:** sunset. ⊠ *Kalalau Trail, End of Rte. 560, 7 miles west of Hanalei, Hanalei* ⊕ *www.hawaiistateparks.org.*

FAMILY
Fodor'sChoice
★ **Hanalei Bay.** This 2-mile crescent beach cradles a wide bay in a setting that is quintessential Hawaii. The sea is on one side, and behind you are the mountains, often ribboned with waterfalls and changing color in the shifting light. In winter, Hanalei Bay boasts some of the biggest onshore surf breaks in the state, attracting world-class surfers, and the beach is plenty wide enough for sunbathing and strolling. In summer, the bay is transformed—calm waters lap the beach, sailboats moor in the bay, and outrigger-canoe paddlers ply the sea. Pack the cooler, haul out the beach umbrellas, and don't forget the beach toys, because Hanalei Bay is worth scheduling for an entire day, maybe two. Several county beach parks, some with pavilions, can be found along the bay. **Amenities:** lifeguards; parking; showers; toilets. **Best for:** sunset; surfing; swimming; walking. ⊠ *Weke Rd., Hanalei.*

Fodor'sChoice
★ **Kalalau.** Located at the end of the trail with the same name, Kalalau is a remote beach in spectacular Napali Coast State Wilderness Park. Reaching it requires an arduous 11-mile hike along sea cliff faces, through steaming tropical valleys, and across sometimes-raging streams. Another option is to paddle a kayak to the beach—summer only, though; otherwise the surf is way too big. The beach is anchored

by a *heiau* (a stone platform used as a place of worship) on one end and a waterfall on the other. The safest time to come is summer, when the trail is dry and the beach is wide, cupped by low, vegetated sand dunes and a large walk-in cave on the western edge. Day hikes into the valley offer waterfalls, freshwater swimming pools, and wild, tropical fruits. Though state camping permits are required, the valley often has a significant illegal crowd, which has strained park facilities and degraded much of its former peaceful solitude. Helicopter overflights are near-constant in good weather. **Amenities:** none. **Best for:** sunset; walking. ⊠ *Trailhead starts at end of Rte. 560, 7 miles west of Hanalei* ⊕ *www.hawaiistateparks.org.*

Fodor'sChoice
★
Kee Beach. Highway 560 on the North Shore literally dead-ends at this beach, pronounced kay-eh. This is also the start of the famous Kalalau Trail, and a culturally significant area to Native Hawaiians, who still use an ancient *heiau* dedicated to hula. (It's not appropriate to hang out on the grass platform or leave offerings there.) The setting is gorgeous, with Makana (a prominent peak that Hollywood dubbed "Bali Hai" in the blockbuster musical *South Pacific*) dramatically imposing itself on the lovely coastline and lots of lush tropical vegetation. The small beach is protected by a reef—except during high surf—creating a small sandy-bottom lagoon that's a popular snorkeling spot. There can be a strong current in winter. Unfortunately, it's so heavily visited that parking is difficult, if not impossible. Expect to park quite a distance from the beach. It's a great place to watch the sunset lighting up Napali Coast. **Amenities:** lifeguards; parking; showers, toilets. **Best for:** snorkeling; sunset; swimming; walking. ⊠ *End of Rte. 560, 7 miles west of Hanalei.*

Lumahai Beach. Famous as the beach where Nurse Nellie washed that man right out of her hair in *South Pacific,* Lumahai's setting is picturesque, with a river and ironwood grove on the western end, and stands of hala (pandanus) trees and black lava rock on the eastern side. In between is a long stretch of thick olivine-flecked sand that can be wide or narrow, depending on surf. It can be accessed in two places from the highway; one involves a steep hike from the road. The ocean can be very dangerous here, with a snapping shore break year-round and monster swells in the winter. The current can be strong near the river. Parking is very limited along the road, or in a rough dirt lot near the river. **Amenities:** none. **Best for:** solitude; sunset; walking. ⊠ *On winding section of Rte. 560, near mile marker 5, Hanalei.*

PRINCEVILLE AND KILAUEA

FAMILY **Anini Beach Park.** A great family park, Anini features one of the longest and widest fringing reefs in all Hawaii, creating a shallow lagoon that is good for snorkeling and kids splashing about. It is safe in all but the highest of winter surf. The reef follows the shoreline for some 2 miles and extends 1,600 feet offshore at its widest point. There's a narrow ribbon of sandy beach and lots of grass and shade, as well as a county campground at the western end and a small boat ramp. **Amenities:** lifeguard; parking; showers; toilets. **Best for:** sunrise; swimming; walking. ⊠ *Anini Rd., off Rte. 56, Princeville.*

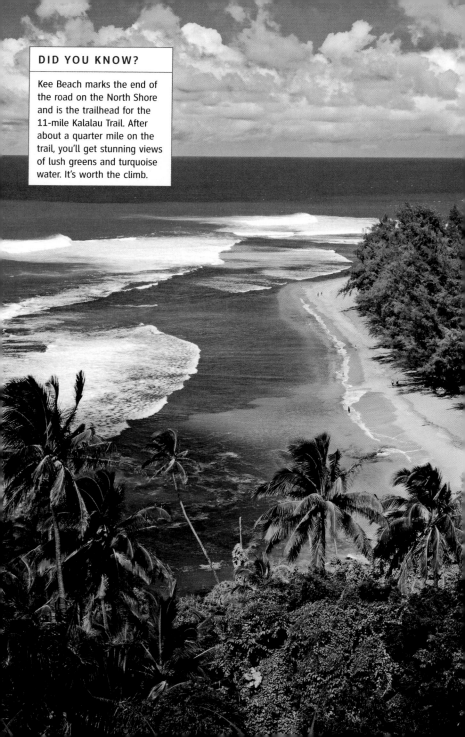

DID YOU KNOW?

Kee Beach marks the end of the road on the North Shore and is the trailhead for the 11-mile Kalalau Trail. After about a quarter mile on the trail, you'll get stunning views of lush greens and turquoise water. It's worth the climb.

Kahili Beach (*Rock Quarry*). You wouldn't know it today, but this beach on Kilauea Bay was once an interisland steamer landing and a rock quarry. Today, it's a fairly quiet beach, although when the surf closes out many other North Shore surf spots, the break directly offshore from Kilauea Stream near the abandoned quarry is still rideable. For the regular ocean goer, summer's your best bet, although the quickly sloping ocean bottom makes for generally treacherous swimming. The stream estuary is quite beautiful, and the ironwood trees and false kamani growing in the generous sand dunes at the rear of the beach provide protection from the sun. It's a wonderful place to observe seabirds. **Amenities:** none. **Best for:** solitude; surfing; walking. ⊠ *Off Wailapa Rd., turn left on dirt road and follow to the end, Kilauea.*

Kalihiwai Beach. A winding road leads down a cliff face to picture-perfect Kalihiwai Beach, which fronts a bay of the same name. It's another one of those drive-up beaches, so it's very accessible. Most people park under the grove of ironwood trees, near the stream, where young kids like to splash and older kids like to body board. Though do beware: the stream carries leptospirosis, a potentially lethal bacteria that can enter through open cuts. In winter months, beware of a treacherous shore break. Summer is the only truly safe time to swim. There's a local-favorite winter surf spot off the eastern edge of the beach, for advanced surfers only. The toilets here are the portable kind, and there are no showers. **Amenities:** parking; toilets. **Best for:** surfing; swimming; walking. ⊠ *Kalihiwai Rd., on Kilauea side of Kalihiwai Bridge, Kilauea.*

Kauapea Beach (*Secret Beach*). This beach went relatively unknown— except by local fishermen, of course—for a long time, hence the common reference to it as "Secret Beach." You'll understand why once you stand on the coarse white sands of Kauapea and see the solid wall of rock that runs the length of the beach, making it fairly inaccessible. For the hardy, there is a steep hike down the western end. From there, you can walk for a long way in either direction in summer. During winter, big swells cut off access to sections of the beach. You may witness dolphins just offshore, and it's a great place to see seabirds, as the Kilauea Point National Wildlife Refuge and its historic lighthouse lie at the eastern end. Nudity is not uncommon, though it is illegal in Hawaii. A consistent onshore break makes swimming here typically very dangerous. **Amenities:** parking. **Best for:** solitude; sunrise; walking. ⊠ *Kalihiwai Rd., just past turnoff for Kilauea, Kilauea.*

Larsen's Beach. The long, wide fringing reef here is this beach's trademark. The waters near shore are generally too shallow for swimming; if you go in, wear a rash guard to protect against prickly sea urchins and sharp coral on the bottom. This area is known for its tricky currents, especially during periods of high surf, and has been the site of numerous drownings. It can be dangerous to snorkel here. There's some nudity at the western end. Accessing this long strand of coarse, white sand requires hiking down a steep, rocky trail. Slippery when wet. **Amenities:** parking. **Best for:** solitude; sunrise; walking. ⊠ *Off Koolau Rd., look for dirt road and "beach access" sign, Kilauea.*

Pali Ke Kua Beach (*Hideaways Beach*). This is actually two very small pocket beaches separated by a narrow rocky point. The beach area itself is narrow and can all but disappear in wintertime. However, in summer, the steep, rocky trail (don't trust the rusty handrails and rotting ropes) that provides access reduces the number of beachgoers, at times creating a deserted beach feel. Winter's high surf creates dangerous conditions. ■TIP→ Don't attempt the trail after a heavy rain—it turns into a mudslide. Amenities: parking. Best for: sunset; surfing. ⊠ *End of Ka Haku Rd., on dirt trail between parking lot and condominium complex, Princeville.*

Puu Poa Beach. The coastline along the community of Princeville is primarily made up of sea cliffs with a couple of pockets of beaches. The sea cliffs end with a long, narrow stretch of beach just east of the Hanalei River and at the foot of the St. Regis Princeville Resort. Public access is via 100-plus steps around the back of the hotel; hotel guests can simply take the elevator down to sea level. The beach itself is subject to the hazards of winter's surf, narrowing and widening with the surf height. On calm days, snorkeling is good thanks to a shallow reef system pocked with sand. Sometimes a shallow sandbar extends across the river to Black Pot Beach Park, part of the Hanalei Beach system, making it easy to cross the river. On high-surf days, the outer edge of the reef near the river draws internationally ranked surfers. The resort's pool is off-limits to nonguests, but the restaurants and bars are not. **Amenities:** food and drink; parking. **Best for:** snorkeling; sunset; surfing. ⊠ *End of Ka Haku Rd., off Rte. 560, Princeville.*

> ## COUNTY AND STATE BEACH PARKS
>
> If restrooms, covered picnic areas, showers, and easy accessibility are important to you, stick to these county and state beach parks:
>
> - Anahola Beach Park
> - Anini Beach Park
> - Haena State Park
> - Hanalei Beach Park
> - Kekaha Beach Park
> - Kukuiula Landing
> - Lydgate State Park
> - Salt Pond Beach Park

THE EAST SIDE

The East Side of the island is considered the "windward" side, a term you'll often hear in weather forecasts. It simply means the side of the island receiving onshore winds. The wind helps break down rock into sand, so there are plenty of beaches here. Unfortunately, only a few of those beaches are protected, so many are not ideal for beginning ocean goers, though they are perfect for long sunrise ambles. On superwindy days, kiteboarders sail along the east shore, sometimes jumping waves and performing acrobatic maneuvers in the air.

⚠ Following extensive flooding in early 2018, areas along the Wailua River, including Wailua Beach, are undergoing repairs. Please check before visiting to make sure places are open.

BEACH SAFETY ON KAUAI

Hawaii's world-renowned, beautiful beaches can be extremely dangerous at times due to large waves and strong currents—so much so that the state rates wave hazards using three signs: a yellow square (caution), a red stop sign (high hazard), and a black diamond (extreme hazard). Signs are posted and updated three times daily or as conditions change.

Visiting beaches with lifeguards is strongly recommended, and you should swim only when there's a normal caution rating. Never swim alone or dive into unknown water or shallow breaking waves. If you're unable to swim out of a rip current, tread water and wave your arms in the air to signal for help.

Even in calm conditions, there are other dangerous things in the water to be aware of, including razor-sharp coral, jellyfish, eels, and sharks, to name a few.

Jellyfish cause the most ocean injuries, and signs are sometimes posted along beaches when they're present. Reactions to a sting are usually mild (burning sensation, redness, welts); however, in some cases they can be severe (breathing difficulties). If you're stung, pick off the tentacles, rinse the affected area with water, and apply ice.

The chances of getting bitten by a shark in Hawaiian waters are very low; sharks attack swimmers or surfers three or four times per year. Of the 40 species of sharks found near Hawaii, tiger sharks are considered the most dangerous because of their size and indiscriminate feeding behavior. They're easily recognized by their blunt snouts and vertical bars on their sides.

Here are a few tips to reduce your shark-attack risk:

■ Swim, surf, or dive with others at beaches patrolled by lifeguards.

■ Avoid swimming at dawn, dusk, and night, when some shark species may move inshore to feed.

■ Don't enter the water if you have open wounds or are bleeding.

■ Avoid murky waters, harbor entrances, areas near stream mouths (especially after heavy rains), channels, or steep drop-offs.

■ Don't wear high-contrast swimwear or shiny jewelry.

■ Don't swim near dolphins, which are often prey for large sharks.

■ If you spot a shark, leave the water quickly and calmly; never provoke or harass a shark, no matter how small.

The website ⊕ *oceansafety.ancl. hawaii.edu* provides statewide beach hazard maps as well as weather and surf advisories.

KAPAA AND WAILUA

Aliomanu Beach. This narrow beach is lined with homes, most of them set back a bit and screened with vegetation that blocks access along the sand in a number of places when the surf is up or tide is high. The waters off Aliomanu Beach are protected by the fringing reef 100 yards or so out to sea, and there are pockets for swimming. However, currents can be tricky, especially near the stream tucked in the beach's elbow toward the northern end, and at the river mouth on the southern end

No matter what time of year you visit Kauai, there's a good chance you'll have a beach all to yourself.

that demarcates neighboring Anahola Beach. This beach is in Hawaiian Homelands, an area held in trust for Native Hawaiians by the State of Hawaii, and is frequently used by fishermen and local families for camping. **Amenities:** parking. **Best for:** solitude; sunrise. ⊠ *Aliomanu Rd., north of mile marker 14, Anahola.*

Anahola Beach Park. Anahola is part of the Hawaiian Homelands on Kauai, so Anahola Beach Park is definitely a locals' hangout, especially for families with small children. The shallow and calm water at the beach road's end is tucked behind a curving finger of land and perfect for young ones. As the beach winds closer to the river mouth, there's less protection and a shore break favorable for body boarders if the trades are light or *kona* (south) winds are present. The long, sandy beach is nice for a morning or evening stroll, but the campground often makes this beach busier in summer. **Amenities:** lifeguards; parking;showers; toilets. **Best for:** surfing; swimming; walking. ⊠ *Anahola Rd., south of mile marker 14, Anahola.*

FAMILY **Baby Beach.** There aren't many safe swimming beaches on Kauai's East Side; however, this one usually ranks highly with parents because there's a narrow, lagoonlike area between the beach and the near-shore reef perfect for small children. In winter, watch for east and northeast swells that would make this not such a safe option. There are no beach facilities—no lifeguards—so watch your babies. There is an old-time shower spigot (cold water only) along the roadside available to rinse the salt water. **Amenities:** parking; showers. **Best for:** sunrise; swimming. ⊠ *Moanakai Rd., Kapaa.*

Donkey Beach (*Paliku Beach*). This beach gets its unusual name from the former Lihue Plantation Company, which once kept a herd of mules and donkeys in the pasture adjacent to the beach. If the waves are right, body boarders and surfers might be spotted offshore. However, the waters here are rough and not recommended for swimming and snorkeling. Instead, we suggest a morning walk along the easy trail that overlooks the beach, starting at the northern end of Kealia Beach. **Amenities:** none. **Best for:** solitude; sunrise; surfing. ⊠ *Rte. 56, north of Kealia Kai subdivision, Kealia.*

Kealia Beach. A half mile long and adjacent to the highway heading north out of Kapaa, Kealia Beach attracts body boarders and surfers year-round. It's a favorite with locals and visitors alike. Kealia is not generally a great beach for swimming, but it's a place to sunbathe and enjoy the beach scene. The waters are usually rough and the waves crumbly due to an onshore break (no protecting reef) and northeasterly trade winds. A scenic lookout on the southern end, accessed off the highway, is a superb location for saluting the morning sunrise or spotting whales during winter. A level, paved trail with small, covered pavilions runs along the coastline here, and is very popular for walking and biking. **Amenities:** lifeguard; parking; showers; toilets. **Best for:** sunrise; surfing; swimming; walking. ⊠ *Rte. 56, at mile marker 10, Kealia.*

FAMILY **Lydgate State Park.** This is by far the best family beach park on Kauai. The waters off the beach are protected by a hand-built breakwater, creating two boulder-enclosed saltwater pools for safe swimming and snorkeling most of the year. The smaller of the two pools is perfect for *keiki* (children). Behind the beach is Kamalani Playground; children of all ages—that includes you—enjoy the swings, lava-tube slides, tree house, and more. Picnic tables abound in the park, and pavilions for day use and overnight camping are available by permit. The Kamalani Kai Bridge is a second playground, south of the original. (The two are united by a bike and pedestrian path that is part of the coastal multiuse path.) ■TIP→ **This park system is perennially popular; the quietest times to visit are early mornings and weekdays. Amenities:** lifeguards; parking; showers; toilets. **Best for:** partiers; sunrise; swimming; walking. ⊠ *Leho Dr., just south of Wailua River, Wailua (Kauai County).*

Wailua Beach. At the mouth of Hawaii's only navigable river, Wailua Beach has considerable cultural significance. At the river's mouth, petroglyphs carved on boulders are sometimes visible during low surf and tide conditions. Surfers and stand-up paddlers enjoy this beach, and many families spend the weekend days under the Wailua Bridge at the river mouth, even hauling out their portable grills and tables to go with their beach chairs. The great news about Wailua Beach is that it's almost impossible to miss; however, parking can be a challenge. The best parking for the north end of the beach is on Papaloa Road behind the Shell station. For the southern end of the beach, park at Wailua River State Park. **Amenities:** parking; showers; toilets. **Best for:** surfing; swimming; walking; windsurfing. ⊠ *Kuhio Hwy., Wailua (Kauai County).*

LIHUE

FAMILY **Kalapaki Beach.** Five minutes south of the airport in Lihue, you'll find this wide, sandy-bottom beach fronting the Kauai Marriott. This beach is almost always safe from rip currents and undertows because it's around the back side of a peninsula, in its own cove. There are tons of activities here, including all the usual water sports—beginning and intermediate surfing, body boarding, bodysurfing, and swimming—plus, there are two outrigger canoe clubs paddling in the bay and the Nawiliwili Yacht Club's boats sailing around the harbor. **Kalapaki** is the only place on Kauai where double-hulled canoes are available for rent (at Kauai Beach Boys, which fronts the beach next to Duke's Canoe Club restaurant). Visitors can also rent snorkel gear, surfboards, body boards, and kayaks from Kauai Beach Boys. A volleyball court on the beach is often used by a loosely organized group of local players; visitors are always welcome. ■TIP→ **Beware the stream on the south side of the beach, though, as it often has high bacteria counts.** Duke's Canoe Club restaurant is one of only a couple of restaurants on the island actually on a beach; the restaurant's lower level is casual, even welcoming beach attire and sandy feet, perfect for lunch or an afternoon cocktail. **Amenities:** food and drink; lifeguard; parking; showers; toilets; water sports. **Best for:** partiers; surfing; swimming; walking. ⊠ *Off Rice St., Lihue* ⊕ *www.kauai.com/kalapaki-beach.*

THE SOUTH SHORE

The South Shore's primary access road is Highway 520, a tree-lined, two-lane, windy road. As you drive along it, there's a sense of tunneling down a rabbit hole into another world, à la Alice. And the South Shore is certainly a wonderland. On average, it rains only 30 inches per year, so if you're looking for fun in the sun, this is a good place to start. The beaches, with their powdery-fine sand, are consistently good year-round, except during high surf, which, if it hits at all, will be in summer. If you want solitude, this isn't it; if you want excitement—well, as much excitement as quiet Kauai offers—this is the place for you.

POIPU

Beach House Beach. Don't pack the beach umbrella, beach mats, and cooler for this one. Just your snorkel gear, when the seas are calm. The beach, named after the neighboring Beach House restaurant and on the road to Spouting Horn, is a small slip of sand during low tide and a rocky shoreline when it's high; however, it is conveniently located by the road's edge, and its rocky coastline and somewhat rocky bottom make it great for snorkeling. (As a rule, sandy-bottom beaches are not great for snorkeling. The rocks create safe hiding places and grow the food that fish and other marine life like to eat.) A sidewalk along the coastline on the restaurant side of the beach makes a great vantage point from which to peer into the water and look for *honu,* the Hawaiian green sea turtle. It's also a very popular gathering spot to watch the sun set. ■TIP→ **Make reservations for dinner at the Beach House in advance**

A lush mountain backdrop, a long stretch of sand, and beautiful surf. It all comes together at Hanalei Bay, a quintessential Hawaii beach.

and time it around sunset. You can park in the public lot across from the beach. **Amenities:** parking; showers; toilets. **Best for:** snorkeling; sunset; surfing. ✉ *Lawai Rd., off Poipu Rd., Poipu.*

Brennecke Beach. This beach is synonymous on Kauai with board surfing and bodysurfing, thanks to its shallow sandbar and reliable shore break. Because the beach is small and often congested, surfboards are prohibited near shore. The water on the rocky eastern edge of the beach is a good place to see the endangered green sea turtles noshing on plants growing on the rocks. **Amenities:** food and drink; parking. **Best for:** sunset; surfing. ✉ *Hoone Rd., off Poipu Rd., Poipu.*

Keoniloa Beach (*Shipwreck Beach*). Few—except the public relations specialists at the Grand Hyatt Kauai Resort and Spa, which backs the beach, but is separated by water features and vegetation—refer to this beach by anything other than its common name: Shipwreck Beach. Its Hawaiian name means "long beach." Both make sense. It is a long stretch of crescent-shape beach punctuated by stunning sea cliffs on both ends, and, yes, a ship once wrecked here. With its onshore break, the waters off Shipwreck are best for body boarding and bodysurfing; however, the beach itself is plenty big for sunbathing, sand-castle building, Frisbee, and other beach-related fun. The eastern edge of the beach is the start of an interpretive dune walk (complimentary) held by the hotel staff; check with the concierge for dates and times. **Amenities:** food and drink; parking; showers; toilets. **Best for:** sunrise; surfing; walking. ✉ *Ainako Rd., continue on Poipu Rd. past Hyatt, turn makai on Ainako Rd., Poipu.*

BEST BEACHES

He says "to-mah-toe," and she says "to-may-toe." When it comes to beaches on Kauai, the meaning behind that axiom holds true: people are different. What rocks one person's world wreaks havoc for another's. Here are some additional tips on how to choose a beach that's right for you.

BEST FOR FAMILIES

Lydgate State Park, East Side. The kid-designed playground, the protected swimming pools, and Kamalani Bridge guarantee you will not hear these words from your child: "Mom, I'm bored."

Poipu Beach Park, Poipu, South Shore. The *keiki* (children's) pool and lifeguards make this a safe spot for kids. The near-perpetual sun isn't so bad, either.

BEST STAND-UP PADDLING

Anini Beach Park, North Shore. The reef and long stretch of beach give beginners to stand-up paddling a calm place to give this new sport a try. You won't get pummeled by waves here.

Wailua Beach, East Side. On the East Side, the Wailua River bisects the beach and heads inland 2 miles, providing stand-up paddlers with a long and scenic stretch of water before they have to figure out how to turn around.

BEST SURFING

Hanalei Bay Beach Park, North Shore. In winter, Hanalei Bay offers a range of breaks, from beginner to advanced. Surfing legends Laird Hamilton and the Irons Brothers grew up surfing the waters of Hanalei.

Waiohai Beach, South Shore. Surf instructors flock to this spot with their students for its gentle, near-shore break. Then, as students advance, they can paddle out a little farther to an intermediate break—if they dare.

BEST SUNSETS

Kee Beach, North Shore. Even in winter, when the sun sets in the south and out of view, you won't be disappointed here, because the "magic hour," as photographers call the time around sunset, paints Napali Coast with a warm gold light. But it can be tough to find parking here.

Polihale State Park, West Side. This due-west-facing beach may be tricky to get to, but it does offer the most unobstructed sunset views on the island. The fact that it's so remote means you won't have strangers in your photos, but you will want to depart right after sunset or risk getting lost in the dark.

BEST FOR CELEB SPOTTING

Haena Beach Park, North Shore. Behind those gated driveways and heavily foliaged yards that line this beach live—at least, part-time—some of the world's most celebrated music and movie moguls.

Hanalei Bay Beach Park, North Shore. We know we tout this beach often, but it deserves the praise. It's a mecca for everyone—regular joes, surfers, fishers, young, old, locals, visitors, and, especially, the famous. You may also recognize Hanalei Bay from the movie *The Descendants*.

FAMILY **Kukuiula Small Boat Harbor.** This is a great beach to sit and people-watch as diving and fishing boats, kayakers, and canoe paddlers head out to sea. Shore and throw-net fishermen frequent this harbor as well. It's not a particularly large harbor, so it retains a quaint sense of charm, unlike Nawiliwili Harbor or Port Allen. The bay is a nice, protected area for limited swimming, but with all the boat traffic kicking up sand and clouding the water, it's typically not good for snorkeling. Outside the breakwater, there is a decent surf spot. **Amenities:** parking; showers; toilets. **Best for:** solitude; sunset; swimming. ⊠ *Lawai Rd., off Poipu Rd., Poipu.*

Fodor'sChoice   **Lawai Kai.** One of the most spectacular beaches on the South Shore is
★   inaccessible by land unless you tour the National Tropical Botanical Garden's Allerton Garden, which we highly recommend. On the tour, you'll see the beach, but you won't visit it. One way to legally access the beach on your own is by paddling a kayak 1 mile from Kukuiula Harbor. However, you have to rent the kayaks elsewhere and haul them on top of your car to the harbor. Also, the wind and waves usually run westward, making the in-trip a breeze but the return trip a workout against Mother Nature. ■ TIP→ **Do not attempt this beach in any manner during a south swell. Amenities:** none. **Best for:** solitude; sunset. ⊠ *4425 Lawai Rd., off Poipu Rd.* ☎ *808/742–2433 for tour information at the National Tropical Botanical Garden's Allerton Garden* ⊕ *http://ntbg.org.*

Fodor'sChoice   **Mahaulepu Beach.** This 2-mile stretch of coast, with its sand dunes, lime-
★   stone hills, sinkholes, and caves, is unlike any other on Kauai. Remains of a large, ancient settlement, evidence of great battles, and the discovery of a now-underwater petroglyph field indicate that Hawaiians lived in this area as early as AD 700. Mahaulepu's coastline is unprotected and rocky, which makes venturing into the ocean hazardous. There are three beach areas with bits of sandy-bottom swimming; however, the best way to experience Mahaulepu is simply to roam, especially in the morning. ■ TIP→ **Access to this beach is via private property. The owner allows access during daylight hours, but be sure to depart before sunset or risk getting locked in for the night. Amenities:** parking. **Best for:** solitude; sunrise; walking. ⊠ *Poipu Rd., past Hyatt Hotel, Poipu.*

FAMILY   **Poipu Beach Park.** The most popular beach on the South Shore is Poipu
Fodor'sChoice   Beach Park. During calm seas, the snorkeling and swimming are good,
★   and when the surf's up, the body boarding and surfing are good, too. Frequent sunshine, grassy lawns, and easy access add to the appeal, especially with families. The beach is frequently crowded and great for people-watching. Even the endangered Hawaiian monk seal often makes an appearance. **Amenities:** food and drink; lifeguards; parking; showers; toilets. **Best for:** partiers; snorkeling; sunbathing; swimming. ⊠ *Hoone Rd., off Poipu Rd., Poipu* ☎ *808/742–7444.*

Waiohai Beach. The first hotel built in Poipu in 1962 overlooked this beach, adjacent to Poipu Beach Park. Actually, there's little to distinguish where one starts and the other begins other than a crescent reef at the eastern end of Waiohai Beach. That crescent, however, is important. It creates a small, protected bay—good for snorkeling and beginning

CLOSE UP

Seal-Spotting on the South Shore

When strolling on one of Kauai's lovely beaches, don't be surprised if you find yourself in the rare company of Hawaiian monk seals. These are among the most endangered of all marine mammals, with perhaps fewer than 1,200 remaining. They primarily inhabit the northwestern Hawaiian Islands, although more are showing their sweet faces on the main Hawaiian Islands, especially on Kauai. They're fond of hauling out on the beach for a long snooze in the sun, particularly after a night of gorging on fish. They need this time to rest and digest, safe from predators.

Female seals regularly birth their young on the beaches around Kauai, where they stay to nurse their pups for upward of six weeks. It seems the seals enjoy particular beaches for the same reasons we do: the shallow, protected waters.

If you're lucky enough to see a monk seal, keep your distance and let it be. Although they may haul out near people, they still want and need their space. Stay several hundred feet away, and forget photos unless you've got a zoom lens. It's illegal to do anything that causes a monk seal to change its behavior, with penalties that include big fines and even jail time. In the water, seals may appear to want to play. It's their curious nature. Don't try to play with them. They are wild animals—mammals, in fact, with teeth.

If you have concerns about the health or safety of a seal, or just want more information, contact the **Hawaiian Monk Seal Conservation Hui** (☎ 808/651–7668 ⊕ www.kauaiseals. com).

surfers. If you're a beginner, this is the spot. However, when a summer swell kicks up, the near-shore conditions become dangerous; offshore, there's a splendid surf break for experienced surfers. The beach itself is narrow and, like its neighbor, gets very crowded in summer. **Amenities:** parking. **Best for:** snorkeling; sunset; surfing; swimming. ⊠ *Hoone Rd., off Poipu Rd., Poipu.*

THE WEST SIDE

The West Side of the island receives hardly enough rainfall year-round to water a cactus, and because it's also the leeward side, there are few tropical breezes. That translates to sunny and hot with long, languorous, and practically deserted beaches. You'd think the leeward waters—untouched by wind—would be calm, but there's no reef system, so the beach drops off quickly and currents are common. Rivers often turn the ocean water murky. ■ TIP→ **The best place to gear up for the beaches on the West Side is on the South Shore or East Side.** Although there's some catering to visitors here, it's not much.

South Shore beaches have good surf breaks. Head to Poipu Beach for board rentals or lessons.

HANAPEPE

FAMILY **Salt Pond Beach Park.** A great family spot, Salt Pond Beach Park features a naturally made, shallow swimming pond behind a curling finger of rock where *keiki* (children) splash and snorkel. This pool is generally safe except during a large south swell, which usually occurs in summer, if at all. The center and western edge of the beach is popular with body boarders and bodysurfers. Pavilions with picnic tables offer shade, and there's a campground that tends to attract a rowdy bunch at the eastern end. On a cultural note, the flat stretch of land to the east of the beach is the last spot in Hawaii where ponds are used to harvest salt in the dry heat of summer. The beach park is popular with locals and it can get crowded on weekends and holidays. **Amenities:** lifeguard; parking; showers; toilets. **Best for:** sunset; swimming; walking. ✉ *Lolokai Rd., off Rte. 50, Hanapepe.*

WAIMEA AND WAIMEA CANYON

Kekaha Beach Park. This is one of the premier spots on Kauai for sunset walks and the start of the state's longest beach. We don't recommend much water activity here without first talking to a lifeguard. The beach is exposed to open ocean and has an onshore break that can be hazardous any time of year. However, there are some excellent surf breaks—for experienced surfers only. Or, if you would like to run or stroll on a beach, this is the one—the hard-packed sand goes on for miles, all the way to Napali Coast, but you won't get past the Pacific Missile Range Facility and its post-9/11 access restrictions. Another bonus for this beach is its relatively dry weather year-round. If it's raining where you are, try Kekaha Beach Park. Toilets here are the portable kind. **Amenities:** lifeguards; parking; showers; toilets. **Best for:** sunset; surfing; walking. ⊠ *Rte. 50, near mile marker 27, Kekaha.*

Lucy Wright Beach Park. Named in honor of the first Native Hawaiian schoolteacher, this beach is on the western banks of the Waimea River. It is also where Captain James Cook first came ashore in the Hawaiian Islands in 1778. If that's not interesting enough, the sand here is not the white, powdery kind you see along the South Shore. It's a combination of pulverized, black lava rock and lighter-color reef. In a way, it looks a bit like a mix of salt and pepper. Unfortunately, the intrigue of the beach doesn't extend to the waters, which are reddish and murky (thanks to river runoff) and choppy (thanks to an onshore break). Instead, check out the Waimea Landing State Recreation Pier, from which fishers drop their lines. It's located about 100 yards west of the river mouth. **Amenities:** parking; showers; toilets. **Best for:** sunset; surfing; walking. ⊠ *Pokile Rd., off Rte. 50, Waimea (Kauai County).*

Fodor's Choice ★ **Polihale State Park.** The longest stretch of beach in Hawaii starts in Kekaha and ends about 15 miles away at the start of Napali Coast. At Napali end of the beach is the 5-mile-long, 140-acre Polihale State Park. In addition to being long, this beach is 300 feet wide in places and backed by sand dunes 50 to 100 feet tall. It is frequently very hot, with minimal shade and scorching sand in summer. Polihale is a remote beach accessed via a rough, 5-mile haul-cane road (four-wheel drive needed in wet weather) at the end of Route 50 in Kekaha. ■ TIP→ **Be sure to start the day with a full tank of gas and a cooler filled with food and drink.** Though it's a popular camping and day-use beach location, the water here is typically rough and not recommended for recreation. No driving is allowed on the beach. The Pacific Missile Range Facility (PMRF), operated by the U.S. Navy, is adjacent to the beach and access to the coastline in front of the base is restricted. **Amenities:** parking; showers; toilets. **Best for:** solitude; sunset; walking. ⊠ *Dirt road at end of Rte. 50, Kekaha* ☎ *808/587–0300.*

WHERE TO EAT

Updated by
Joan Conrow

On Kauai, if you're lucky enough to win an invitation to a potluck, baby luau, or beach party, don't think twice—just accept. The best grinds (food) are homemade, and so you'll eat until you're full, then rest, eat some more, and make a plate to take home, too.

But even if you can't score a spot at one of these parties, don't despair. Great local-style food is easy to come by at countless low-key places around the island. As an extra bonus, these eats are often inexpensive, and portions are generous. Expect plenty of meat—usually deep-fried or marinated in a teriyaki sauce and grilled *pulehu*-style (over an open fire)—and starches. Rice is standard, even for breakfast, and often served alongside potato–macaroni salad, another island specialty. Another local favorite is *poke,* made from chunks of raw tuna or octopus seasoned with sesame oil, soy sauce, onions, and pickled seaweed. It's a great *pupu* (appetizer) when paired with a cold beer.

Kauai's cultural diversity is apparent in its restaurants, which offer authentic Chinese, Korean, Japanese, Thai, Mexican, Italian, Vietnamese, and Hawaiian specialties. Less specialized restaurants cater to the tourist crowd, serving standard American fare—burgers, pizza, sandwiches, surf-and-turf combos, and so on. Poipu and Kapaa offers the best selection of restaurants, with options for a variety of tastes and budgets; most fast-food joints are in Lihue.

KAUAI DINING PLANNER

EATING-OUT STRATEGY

Where should we eat? With dozens of island eateries competing for your attention, it may seem like a daunting question. But our expert writers and editors have done most of the legwork—the dozens of selections here represent the best eating experience this island has to offer. Find a restaurant quickly—reviews are ordered alphabetically within their geographic area. *Restaurant reviews have been shortened. For full information, visit Fodors.com.*

WITH KIDS

Hawaii is a kid-friendly destination in many regards, and that includes taking the little ones out to eat with you. Because of the overall relaxed vibe and casual dress here, you won't have to worry too much about your tot's table manners or togs—within reason, of course. Take advantage of treats and eating experiences unique to Hawaii, such as shave ice, sunshine markets (perfect for picnic lunches or beach provisions), and luau.

SMOKING

Smoking is prohibited in all Hawaii restaurants and bars.

RESERVATIONS

It's always a good idea to make reservations when you can, and if you plan to dine at one of Kauai's top eateries, reservations are essential. However, you'll find that many places on the island don't take reservations at all, and service is first come, first served.

WHAT TO WEAR

Just about anything goes on Kauai. At lunch you can dine in a sarong, or T-shirt and shorts, and flip-flops at most places. Dinner is only a slight step up. That said, if you're out for a special occasion and want to don your fanciest duds, no one will look twice.

HOURS AND PRICES

Restaurants on Kauai significantly quiet down by 9 pm; the limited bar scene continues past midnight—but not much past. It seems as if the entire island is in bed before 10 pm to get up early the next day and play. In general, peak dining hours here tend to be on the earlier side, during sunset hours from 6 to 8 pm. A tip of 18% to 20% is standard for good service.

WHAT IT COSTS			
$	$$	$$$	$$$$
Restaurants	under $18	$18–$26	$27–$35	over $35

Prices in the restaurant reviews are the average cost of a main course at dinner or, if dinner is not served, at lunch; taxes and service charges are generally included.

THE NORTH SHORE

Because of the North Shore's isolation, restaurants have enjoyed a captive audience of visitors who don't want to make the long, dark trek into Kapaa town for dinner. As a result, dining in this region has been characterized by expensive fare that isn't especially tasty, either. Fortunately, the situation is slowly improving as new restaurants open and others change hands or menus.

Still, dining on the North Shore can be pricier than other parts of the island, and not especially family-friendly. Most of the restaurants are found either in Hanalei town or the Princeville resorts. Consequently, you'll encounter delightful mountain and ocean views, but just one restaurant with oceanfront dining. ⚠ Following extensive flooding in early 2018, areas of Haena and the Napali Coast are undergoing repairs. Please check before visiting to make sure places are open.

$$
AMERICAN

✕**Hanalei Gourmet.** This spot in Hanalei's restored old schoolhouse offers dolphin-safe tuna, low-sodium meats, fresh-baked breads, and homemade desserts as well as a casual atmosphere where both families and the sports-watching crowd can feel equally comfortable. Lunch and dinner menus feature sandwiches, burgers, hearty salads, a variety of pupus, and nightly specials of fresh local fish. **Known for:** friendly bar; consistently good food; fresh bread. ⑤ *Average main: $25* ✉ *Hanalei Center, 5-5161 Kuhio Hwy., Hanalei* ☎ *808/826–2524* ⊕ *www. hanaleigourmet.com.*

$$$$
ECLECTIC
Fodor's Choice
★

✕**Kauai Grill.** Savor an artful meal created by world-renowned chef Jean-Gorges Vongerichten, surrounded by a dramatic Hanalei Bay scene that's positively stunning at sunset. Located at the luxurious St. Regis Princeville Resort, Kauai Grill has dark-wood decor and an ornate chandelier, the centerpiece of the room. **Known for:** skill on the grill; Hawaii-grown ingredients; attentive service. ⑤ *Average main: $50* ✉ *St. Regis Princeville, 5520 Ka Haku Rd., Princeville* ☎ *808/826–9644* ⊕ *www.kauaigrill.com* ☉ *Closed Sun. and Mon. No lunch.*

$$
AMERICAN
FAMILY

✕**Kilauea Bakery and Pau Hana Pizza.** Open from 6:30 am, the bakery serves coffee drinks, delicious fresh pastries, bagels, and breads in the morning. Late risers beware: breads and pastries sell out quickly. **Known for:** its starter of Hawaiian sourdough made with guava; specialty pizzas topped with eclectic ingredients; fresh chocolate chip cookies made in-house daily. ⑤ *Average main: $20* ✉ *Kong Lung Center, 2484 Keneke St., Kilauea* ☎ *808/828–2020* ⊕ *www.kilaueabakery.com.*

$$$$
HAWAIIAN
FAMILY

✕**Makana Terrace.** There's no doubt this spot is pricey, but you're paying for the view—sit on the terrace if you can—and for an attentive staff. The menu is simple and the focus is on local dishes like taro waffles and Molokai sweet potato pancakes or island-caught fish and grilled beef tenderloin. **Known for:** breathtaking panoramic view of Hanalei Bay; lavish daily breakfast/brunch buffet. ⑤ *Average main: $42* ✉ *St. Regis Princeville Resort, 5520 Ka Haku Rd., Princeville* ☎ *808/826–9644* ⊕ *www.stregisprinceville.com* ☉ *Closed Tues. and Wed. No lunch.*

$$$
HAWAIIAN
FAMILY

✕**Nanea Restaurant and Bar.** This is the signature restaurant of the Westin Princeville Ocean Resort Villas, and its casual, open-air seating is the perfect compliment to an island-style menu that is sure to please a wide range of diners. The grilled rib eye is served with bacon and sour cream mashed potatoes, while the half-chicken—smoked kalua style—is accompanied by Molokai sweet potatoes. **Known for:** kids eat free; inventive cocktails; local ingredients. ⑤ *Average main: $35* ✉ *Westin Princeville Ocean Resort Villas, 3838 Wyllie Rd., Princeville* ☎ *808/827–8808* ⊕ *www.westinprinceville.com.*

$$
BRAZILIAN

✕**Neide's Salsa and Samba.** The only restaurant serving authentic Brazilian food on Kauai, Neide's Salsa and Samba is also one of the most affordable establishments on the North Shore. The first half of the menu focuses on Mexican food, but it's the Brazilian dishes here that deserve your attention. **Known for:** authentic Brazilian food; great view of the

Where to Eat on the North Shore

Restaurant	No.
Hanalei Gourmet	**2**
Kauai Grill	**6**
Kilauea Bakery and Pau Hana Pizza	**9**
Makana Terrace	**7**
Nanea Restaurant and Bar	**8**
Neide's Salsa & Samba	**4**
Opakapaka Grill and Bar	**1**
Postcards Café	**5**
Restaurant Bar Acuda	**3**

BUDGET-FRIENDLY EATS: NORTH SHORE

It's not easy to find cheap food on the North Shore, but these little eateries serve up dinner for two for under $20.

Foodland. In a pinch, you can pick up pretty good sushi, ready-to-eat hot entrées, deli items, bakery goods, and panini sandwiches at the Foodland grocery store. ⊠ *Princeville Shopping Center, 5–4280 Kuhio Hwy., Princeville* ☎ *808/826–9880.*

Harvest Market. Health foods, such as rice dishes, soups, and salads, are served in the back of this natural-foods store at the Hanalei Center; takeout only. ⊠ *5-5161 Kuhio Hwy., Hanalei* ☎ *808/826-0089.*

Neide's Salsa & Samba. This is one of the better low-cost eateries on the North Shore, with tasty Brazilian and Mexican food, which is not commonly found on the island, to take out or eat in an informal garden setting at the Hanalei Center. ⊠ *5-5161 Kuhio Hwy., Hanalei* ☎ *808/826–1851.*

Tropical Taco. This place is a safe choice for very basic Mexican food, though the prices are high for the cuisine. Takeout or limited outdoor seating. ⊠ *5-5088 Kuhio Hwy., Hanalei* ☎ *808/827–8226* ⊕ *www. tropicaltaco.com.*

Hanalei mountains; relaxed service. ⑤ *Average main: $22* ⊠ *5-5161 Kuhio Hwy., Hanalei* ☎ *808/826–1851.*

$$
FUSION
✕**Opakapaka Grill and Bar.** A trip to this oceanfront oasis requires a narrow, cliff-hugging ride along the exquisite North Shore coastline or a short walk from the condos at Hanalei Colony Resort. The menu features the regular choices of burgers, sandwiches, and salads for lunch, while dinner options include fresh island fish, pasta, and meats and chicken dishes, as well as a good selection of small plates. **Known for:** oceanfront setting and view; Hawaiian fusion menu; good selection of pupu (appetizers). ⑤ *Average main: $26* ⊠ *Hanalei Colony Resort, 5-7130 Kuhio Hwy., Haena* ☎ *808/826–9875* ⊕ *www.hcr.com/dining.*

$$$
AMERICAN
✕**Postcards Café.** This plantation-cottage restaurant has a menu full of seafood but also offers additive-free vegetarian and vegan options. Top menu picks include taro fritters, wasabi-crusted ahi, fennel-crusted lobster tail, and baked portobello mushrooms. **Known for:** meat-free menu; cozy dining room; historic setting. ⑤ *Average main: $35* ⊠ *5-5075A Kuhio Hwy., Hanalei* ☎ *808/826–1191* ⊕ *postcardscafe.com* ☽ *No lunch.*

$$$$
TAPAS
Fodor's Choice
★
✕**Restaurant Bar Acuda.** This hip and pricey tapas bar is a top place in Hanalei in terms of tastiness, creativity, and pizzazz. Owner-chef Jim Moffat's brief menu changes regularly: you might find grilled short rib skewers with horseradish chimichurri, or Hawaiian mahimahi with roasted shimeji mushrooms. **Known for:** sophisticated cuisine; innovative specials; eclectic menu. ⑤ *Average main: $40* ⊠ *Hanalei Center, 5-5161 Kuhio Hwy., Hanalei* ☎ *808/826–7081* ⊕ *www.restaurantbaracuda.com.*

THE EAST SIDE

Because the East Side is the island's largest population center, it makes sense that it should boast a wide selection of restaurants. It's also a good place to get both cheaper meals and the local-style cuisine that residents favor.

Most of the eateries are found along Kuhio Highway between Kapaa and Wailua; a few are tucked into shopping centers and resorts. In Lihue, it's easier to find lunch than dinner because many restaurants cater to the business crowd.

You'll find all the usual fast-food joints in both Kapaa and Lihue, as well as virtually every ethnic cuisine available on Kauai. Although fancy gourmet restaurants are less abundant in this part of the island, there's plenty of good, solid food, and a few stellar attractions. But unless you're staying on the East Side, or passing through, it's probably not worth the long drive from the North Shore or Poipu resorts to eat here.

4

KAPAA AND WAILUA

In recent years, the most affordable, hip new eateries on the island have opened in Kapaa. Unlike the resort-dominated South and North shores, Kapaa is local, fun, and eclectic, with food trucks on the side of the road, vegetarian venues, and bars serving up artful appetizers. Diversity is the key to this area; there is something for everyone, especially those on a budget. ⚠ **Following extensive flooding in early 2018, areas along the Wailua River are undergoing repairs. Please check before visiting to make sure places are open.**

$$$
STEAKHOUSE

✕ **Bull Shed.** The A-frame structure makes this popular restaurant look distinctly rustic from the outside, but inside, light-color walls and a full wall of glass highlight an ocean view that is one of the best on Kauai. The food is simple, but they know how to do surf and turf. **Known for:** views of the surf crashing on the rocks; unlimited salad bar; quiet bar. $ *Average main: $35* ☒ *796 Kuhio Hwy.* ☎ *808/822–3791, 808/822–1655* ⊕ *www.bullshedrestaurant.com* ⊗ *No lunch.*

$$
VEGETARIAN

✕ **Eat Healthy Cafe.** A restored plantation cottage surrounded by tropical foliage is the casual setting for this island café. The menu emphasizes local and organic products, with many vegan, vegetarian, and gluten-free options including nori wraps and tofu-based entrées. **Known for:** outdoor seating in the vine-covered garden; delicious food with healthy ingredients; smoothies like Chocolate & Coffee Kiss and I Heart Blueberries. $ *Average main: $24* ☒ *4-369 Kuhio Hwy., Wailua (Kauai County)* ☎ *808/822–7990* ⊕ *eathealthykauai.com* ⊗ *No dinner Sun. and Mon.*

$$
AMERICAN
Fodor'sChoice
★

✕ **Hukilau Lanai.** Relying heavily on superfresh island fish and local meats and produce, this restaurant offers quality food that is competently and creatively prepared. The nightly fish specials—served grilled, steamed, or sautéed with succulent sauces—shine here. **Known for:** nightly fish specials; gluten-free options; delicious desserts. $ *Average main: $25* ☒ *Kauai Coast Resort, Coconut Marketplace, 520 Aleka Loop, Wailua (Kauai County)* ☎ *808/822–0600* ⊕ *www.hukilaukauai.com* ⊗ *Closed Mon.*

$$$
ECLECTIC
Fodor's Choice
★

✕ **JO2 Restaurant.** This is the newest creation of Jean-marie Josselin, the renowned chef who brought Hawaii regional cuisine to Kauai in 1990, and it reflects his growth as a chef. The food is very imaginative, with its French, Japanese, and Islands influences, and served with flair in a chic, yet casual, dining room that's tucked away in a nondescript strip mall. **Known for:** the $35 prix fix 5–6 pm; inventive cuisine; excellent service. ⑤ *Average main: $35* ⊠ *4-971 Kuhio Hwy., Kapaa* ☎ *808/212–1627* ⊕ *www.jotwo.com.*

$$
ITALIAN

✕ **Kauai Pasta.** This simple yet elegant establishment offers some of the best Italian food on the island at moderate prices. Their specials are delicious, and their 10-inch pizzettas make a fine meal for one. **Known for:** chocolate crème brûlée; good value; gluten-free options. ⑤ *Average main: $26* ⊠ *4-939B Kuhio Hwy.* ⊕ *www.kauaipasta.com.*

$
AMERICAN
FAMILY

✕ **Kountry Kitchen.** If you like a hearty breakfast, try this family-friendly restaurant with its cozy, greasy-spoon atmosphere, and friendly service; it's a great spot for omelets, banana pancakes, waffles, and eggs Benedict in two sizes. Lunch selections include sandwiches, burgers, and *loco mocos* (a popular local rice, beef, gravy, and eggs concoction). **Known for:** all day breakfast; take-out options; hearty portions. ⑤ *Average main: $14* ⊠ *1485 Kuhio Hwy., Kapaa* ☎ *808/822–3511* ⊕ *www.kountrystylekitchen.com* ☾ *No dinner.*

$$
ASIAN FUSION

✕ **Lemongrass Grill.** The inside of Kapaa's Lemongrass Grill may remind you of a Pacific Rim–theme rustic tavern, with its stained wood interior, numerous paintings and carvings, and eclectic Asian-influenced menu. There's something for everybody here: salads, poultry, steaks and ribs, vegetarian fare, and, of course, a wide selection of seafood, all with an island flair. **Known for:** curries and satays; live, acoustic music; fresh fish. ⑤ *Average main: $25* ⊠ *4-871 Kuhio Hwy., Kapaa* ☎ *808/821–2888* ⊕ *www.lemongrasskauai.com* ☾ *No lunch.*

$
AMERICAN

✕ **Papaya's.** Kauai's largest natural-foods market contains a limited, buffet-style café with decent vegan and vegetarian food at low prices. Food items change daily, but there's always a salad bar, and favorites like wraps, taro burgers, and fish tacos for lunch and dinner, as well as smoothies, a juice bar, coffee, and muffins. **Known for:** vegan and vegetarian food at good prices; fresh, organic produce; tasty tempeh dishes. ⑤ *Average main: $9* ⊠ *4-901 Kuhio Hwy., Kapaa* ☎ *808/823–0190* ⊕ *www.papayasnaturalfoods.com.*

$$
JAPANESE
Fodor's Choice
★

✕ **Restaurant Kintaro.** If you want to eat at a lively restaurant that's a favorite with locals, visit Kintaro, but be prepared to wait—or better yet, make reservations— because the dining room and sushi bar are always busy. Try the soft-shell crab roll or the unbeatable Bali Hai bomb, a roll of crab and smoked salmon, baked and topped with wasabi mayonnaise. **Known for:** local favorite; lively bar; friendly service. ⑤ *Average main: $22* ⊠ *4-370 Kuhio Hwy., Wailua (Kauai County)* ☎ *808/822–3341* ☾ *Closed Sun. No lunch.*

$
INDIAN

✕ **Shivalik Indian Cuisine.** This eatery provides a refreshing alternative to the typical surf and turf offerings at most of Kauai's restaurants. Boasting no particular Indian regional style, this small-plaza hideaway turns out delectable biryani and tandoori, light and flavorful naan, many vegetarian items, as well as curries and chicken and lamb dishes.

Known for: Wednesday and Friday night all-you-can eat buffet; tandoor oven; extensive menu. $ *Average main: $17* ✉ *4-771 Kuhio Hwy., Wailua (Kauai County)* ☎ *808/821–2333* ⊕ *www.shivalikindianfood. com* ⊗ *Closed Tues.*

$ ✗ **Tiki Tacos.** Tiki Tacos is a notch above most Kauai taco joints, with
MEXICAN excellent authentic Mexican food at reasonable prices. The meals are made from quality ingredients, many of them organic and locally sourced. **Known for:** large potions; good value; friendly service. $ *Average main: $8* ✉ *4-971 Kuhio Hwy., Kapaa* ☎ *808/823–8226.*

$ ✗ **Verde.** Combining classic Mexican food with chili-based sauces and
MEXICAN creations from the chef's home state of New Mexico, Verde's menu includes tostadas, enchiladas, and tacos served with fresh fish or slow-cooked chicken or local grass-fed beef. The seared tuna tacos with red chili aioli and the stacked enchilada, with chicken or beef short ribs smothered in red or green chili sauce, are favorites. **Known for:** super hot sauce; quality local ingredients; casual setting. $ *Average main: $13* ✉ *4-1101 Kuhio Hwy., Kapaa* ☎ *808/821–1400* ⊕ *www. verdehawaii.com.*

4

LIHUE

You will probably find yourself in Lihue at least a few times during your stay. When it comes to restaurants, Lihue isn't especially outstanding. There are some decent restaurants and some good low-cost eateries that feed locals and the business-lunch crowd—but nothing really stellar. If you are in town for lunch, don't pass up some of the authentic local spots.

$$$ ✗ **Café Portofino.** The lengthy menu at this mostly authentic northern
ITALIAN Italian restaurant is as impressive as the views of Kalapaki Bay and the Haupu range, and packed with many pasta, veal, chicken, and fresh fish selections, as well as vegetarian entrées. Linger over coffee and ice cream–filled profiteroles or traditional tiramisu while enjoying harp music Thursday through Monday. **Known for:** roasted rack of lamb; romantic ambience; open-air dining. $ *Average main: $30* ✉ *Kauai Marriott Resort & Beach Club, 3481 Hoolaulea Way, Kalapaki Beach, Lihue* ⊕ *www.cafeportofino.com* ⊗ *No lunch.*

$ ✗ **Dani's Restaurant.** Kauai residents frequent this eatery near the Lihue
HAWAIIAN Fire Station for hearty, local-style food at breakfast and lunch; it's a
FAMILY good place to try traditional luau cuisine without commercial luau prices. You can order Hawaiian-style *laulau* (pork and taro leaves wrapped in ti leaves and steamed) or kalua pig, slow roasted in an underground oven. **Known for:** local-style dining; low prices; casual setting. $ *Average main: $8* ✉ *4201 Rice St., Lihue* ☎ *808/245–4991* ⊗ *Closed Sun. No dinner.*

$$$ ✗ **Duke's Canoe Club.** Surfing legend Duke Kahanamoku is immortalized
SEAFOOD at this casual bi-level restaurant and bar on Kalapaki Beach where surfboards, photos, and other memorabilia marking Duke's long tenure as a waterman adorn the walls. Downstairs, you'll find simple fare ranging from fish tacos and stir-fried cashew chicken to hamburgers, served 11 am to 11 pm, while upstairs, at dinner, fresh fish prepared in a variety

Where to Eat on the East Side

of styles is the best choice, though the prime rib is a favorite among locals. **Known for:** live music; lively bar; hula pie ice-cream dessert. $ *Average main: $30 ⊠ Kauai Marriott Resort & Beach Club, 3610 Rice St., Kalapaki Beach, Lihue ☎ 808/246–9599 ⊕ www. dukeskauai.com.*

$$$
ECLECTIC
✕**Gaylord's.** Located in what was once Kauai's most expensive plantation estate, Gaylord's pays tribute to the elegant dining rooms of 1930s high society—candlelit tables sit on a cobblestone patio that surrounds a fountain and overlooks a wide lawn. The menu is eclectic, ranging from tender seared scallops served in a fennel cream to grilled filet mignon. **Known for:** lavish Sunday brunch buffet; quiet dining; delightful outdoor seating. $ *Average main: $30 ⊠ Kilohana Plantation, 3-2087 Kaumualii Hwy., Puhi ☎ 808/245–9593 ⊕ www. gaylordskauai.com.*

$
ASIAN
Fodor'sChoice
★
✕**Hamura Saimin.** Folks just love this funky old plantation-style diner—locals and tourists stream in and out all day long, and neighbor islanders stop in on their way to the airport to pick up take-out orders to bring home. Their famous *saimin* soup is the big draw, and each day the Hiraoka family dishes up about 1,000 bowls of steaming broth and homemade noodles, topped with a variety of garnishes. **Known for:** classic Kauai experience; grilled chicken and beef sticks; counter-style dining. $ *Average main: $7 ⊠ 2956 Kress St., Lihue ☎ 808/245–3271* 🞐 *No credit cards.*

$$$
AMERICAN
✕**JJ's Broiler.** This spacious, low-key restaurant serves hearty fare, with dinner specials such as lobster and Slavonic steak, a broiled sliced tenderloin dipped in buttery wine sauce, and local-style kalua pig and cabbage; you can save money by ordering from the lunch menu at dinner time. On sunny afternoons, ask for a table on the lanai overlooking Kalapaki Bay and try one of the generous salads or appetizers and a drink. **Known for:** one of the best ocean views in Lihue; great place for a drink; friendly service. $ *Average main: $30 ⊠ Anchor Cove, 3416 Rice St., Nawiliwili ☎ 808/246–4422 ⊕ www.jjsbroiler.com.*

$$
AMERICAN
✕**Kalapaki Joe's.** Both locations—in Lihue's Kukui Grove and in Poipu—appeal to sports fans who like a rip-roaring happy hour as the appetizer menu is extensive. You can also choose from burgers, salads, sandwiches, fish tacos, steaks, ribs, and fresh fish specials. **Known for:** wide-ranging menu; boisterous bar; affordable, casual dining. $ *Average main: $20 ⊠ 3-2600 Kaumualii Hwy., Lihue ☎ 808/245–6366 ⊕ www.kalapakijoes.com.*

BUDGET-FRIENDLY EATS: EAST SIDE

At these small, local-style eateries, two people can generally eat dinner for less than $20.

Garden Island BBQ and Chinese Restaurant ⊠ 4252-A Rice St., Lihue ☎ 808/245–8868.

Hamura Saimin ⊠ 2956 Kress St., Lihue ☎ 808/245–3271.

Papaya's ⊠ 4-831 Kuhio Hwy., Kapaa ⊕ www.papayasnaturalfoods.com ☎ 808/823–0190.

Waipouli Restaurant ⊠ Waipouli Town Center, 4-771 Kuhio Hwy., Kapaa ☎ 808/822–9311.

4

SHAVE ICE

Nothing goes down quite as nicely as shave ice on a hot day. This favorite island treat has been likened to a sno-cone, but that description doesn't do a good shave ice justice. Yes, it is ice served up in a cone-shaped cup and drenched with sweet syrup, but the similarities end there. As its name implies, the ice should be feathery light—the texture of snowflakes, not frozen slush. And alongside the standard cherry and grape, you'll find all sorts of exotic island flavorings, such as passion fruit, pineapple, coconut, mango, and, of course, a rainbow mix or snow topping of condensed milk.

Not all shave ice meets these high standards, and when you're hot, even the average ones taste great. But a few places are worth seeking out. On the East Side, the best is **Hawaiian Blizzard** (⊠ *Kapaa Shopping Center, 4-1105 Kuhio Hwy.*), a true shave-ice stand that opens up weekday afternoons next to the Big Save grocery store in Kapaa. In Lihue, try **Halo Halo Shave Ice** in the Harbor Mall Shopping Center (⊠ *3501 Rice St.*). And on the hot, dry West Side, make a beeline for **Jo-Jo's Clubhouse** (⊠ *Mile marker 23, Kaumualii, Hwy. 50*), on the main drag in Waimea. All three places have benches where you can sit and slurp.

$$
ECLECTIC
FAMILY
✗ **Kukui's Restaurant and Bar.** The meals at Kukui's feature Hawaiian, Asian, and contemporary American influences, and the open-air setting makes it a pleasant place to dine. It's very spacious, and not as busy and noisy as the other eateries at the Marriott, making it well suited to families and those who want a relaxed setting. **Known for:** garden setting; lavish buffets; evening entertainment. ⑤ *Average main: $25* ⊠ *Kauai Marriott Resort & Beach Club, 3610 Rice St., Kalapaki Beach, Lihue* ☎ *808/245–5050* ⊕ *www.marriott.com.*

$$
ECLECTIC
✗ **Lihue Barbecue Inn.** Few Kauai restaurants are more beloved than this family-owned eatery, a mainstay of island dining since 1940, with a menu that runs from traditional American to Asian. You can dine in comfy booths, and meals include a good miso soup or fresh fruit cup and dessert. **Known for:** homemade cream pie in any flavor; hearty specials like liver and onions; locals hangout. ⑤ *Average main: $18* ⊠ *2982 Kress St., Lihue* ☎ *808/245–2921* ⊙ *Closed Sun.*

THE SOUTH SHORE

Most South Shore restaurants are more upscale and located within the Poipu resorts. If you're looking for a gourmet meal in a classy setting, the South Shore is where you'll find it. Poipu has a number of excellent restaurants in dreamy settings and decidedly fewer family-style, lower-price eateries.

$$$$
ASIAN FUSION
✗ **Beach House.** This restaurant has a dreamy ocean view, making it a good setting for a romantic dinner or a cocktail and appetizer while the sun sinks into the glassy blue Pacific and surfers slice the waves. The prices have gone up, but you can still find satisfaction in the crispy

Nothing beats shave ice (no, not "shaved" ice) on a hot Hawaiian day.

crab-stuffed ahi roll, roasted duck breast, or fresh catch of the day served with lilikoi lemon grass beurre blanc. **Known for:** gluten-free and vegan options; small bar with a big view; outdoor dining. $ *Average main: $38* ✉ *5022 Lawai Rd., Poipu* ☎ *808/742–1424* ⊕ *www.the-beach-house.com.*

$$$
AMERICAN
FAMILY

✕ **Brennecke's Beach Broiler.** Casual and fun, with a busy bar and windows overlooking the beach, Brennecke's specializes in big portions in a wide range of offerings including rib-eye steak, burgers, fish tacos, pasta, shrimp, and the fresh catch of the day; create your own combination meal if you can't pick just one. This place is especially good for happy hour (3 to 5 pm and 8:30 pm to closing), as the drink and pupu menus bring the prices closer to reality. **Known for:** family-friendly setting; wide-ranging menu; take-out deli with shave ice. $ *Average main: $27* ✉ *2100 Hoone Rd., Poipu* ☎ *808/742–7588* ⊕ *www.brenneckes.com.*

$$$$
ITALIAN
Fodor's Choice
★

✕ **Dondero's.** With a beautiful setting, good food, stunning ocean view, and impeccable service, Dondero's is one of Kauai's better restaurants. The elegant tasting menu features Italian dishes or opt for classic dishes like grilled seafood cioppino or the tender veal osso buco. **Known for:** Italianate murals and elegant interior; wonderful outdoor dining experience; emphasis on local ingredients. $ *Average main: $38* ✉ *Grand Hyatt Kauai Resort and Spa, 1571 Poipu Rd., Poipu* ☎ *808/240–6456* ⊕ *kauai.grand.hyatt.com/en/hotel/dining/Donderos.html* ⊗ *Closed Sun. and Mon. No lunch.*

$$$
ASIAN FUSION
Fodor's Choice
★

✕ **Eating House 1849.** Hawaii's culinary superstar, Roy Yamaguchi, has moved his signature Hawaiian-fusion-cuisine restaurant on Kauai's South Shore to an updated shopping-center locale that suits the new name and creative fare. Though billed as "plantation cuisine," the hot

Where to Eat on the South Shore and West Side

Beach House **6**
Brennecke's
  Beach Broiler **13**
Dondero's **16**
Eating House 1849 .... **9**
Joe's on the Green **12**

Kalaheo Café &
  Coffee Co. **5**
Keoki's Paradise **10**
Lappert's Ice Cream **3**
Little Fish Coffee **4**
Makai Sushi **7**
Merriman's Fish House .. **11**

Pizzetta **8**
Plantation Gardens **15**
Plantations BBQ & Bar ... **1**
Red Salt **14**
Tidepools **17**
Wrangler's Steakhouse **2**

pot rice bowl or spicy ramen bowl are about the only items that might have their roots in the days when sugar was king, otherwise, the menu is classic Asian fusion. **Known for:** innovative cuisine; use of local ingredients; lively atmosphere. $ *Average main: $35* ⊠ *Shops at Kukuiula, 2829 Ala Kalanikaumaka Rd., No. A-201, Poipu* ☎ 808/742–5000 ⊕ *www.eatinghouse1849.com.*

$

AMERICAN

✕ **Joe's on the Green.** Located at the Kiahuna Golf Course, the casual atmosphere and generous portions at Joe's makes it a refreshing alternative to the pricier hotel brunch venues in this area. Open-air breakfasts and lunches—think tofu scramble and banana-macadamia-nut pancakes or the quarter-pound hot dog and the build-your-own-salad options—comes with an expansive vista of Poipu, and happy hour, which often features live music, offers local favorites like *manapua* dumplings and ahi poke. **Known for:** upbeat happy hour; outdoor dining; friendly service. $ *Average main: $14* ⊠ *2545 Kiahuna Plantation Dr., Poipu* ☎ 808/742–9696 ⊕ *www.joesonthegreen.com.*

$$

AMERICAN

FAMILY

✕ **Kalaheo Café & Coffee Co.** Folks love this busy roadside café—especially for breakfast, though it's good for lunch and a simple dinner, too—for it's casual atmosphere, and it's frequently busy, especially on weekend mornings. Lots of local products are used here, including Anahola Granola, local fish, and Kauai coffee, which you can buy by the pound; it's a solid choice in an area with limited restaurants. **Known for:** fresh-baked bread; great local coffee; hearty portions like the Kahili Breakfast or the Longboard sandwich. $ *Average main: $22* ⊠ *2-2560 Kaumualii Hwy. (Rte. 50), Kalaheo* ☎ 808/332–5858 ⊕ *www.kalaheo. com* ☉ *No dinner Sun. and Mon.*

$$$

ASIAN

FAMILY

✕ **Keoki's Paradise.** Built to resemble a dockside boathouse, this active, boisterous place fills up quickly at night thanks to a busy bar and frequent live music. The day's fresh catch is available in various styles and sauces that span the tide from appetizers (Thai shrimp sticks) to mains (seafood risotto), and meat-lover options like the *imu*-roasted pork ribs; the bar serves lighter fare. **Known for:** bustling bar with live music; keiki (kids) menu; fresh fish. $ *Average main: $30* ⊠ *Poipu Shopping Village, 2360 Kiahuna Plantation Dr., Poipu* ☎ 808/742–7534 ⊕ *www. keokisparadise.com.*

$

SUSHI

Fodor'sChoice

★

✕ **Makai Sushi.** The menu is simple—poke bowls, sashimi, and four types of sushi rolls—but the freshness of the fish and attention to quality preparation set this tiny sushi bar apart from the crowd and make it a welcome addition to the Poipu Beach food scene. Tucked into a corner of Kukuiula Market, it attracts a steady stream of customers who watch owner Matthew Oliver and an assistant transform spicy ahi, blue crab, avocado, cucumber, tobiko into the Hapa Roll or mix raw ahi, ono, salmon, cucumber, avocado, and sweet Maui onion into the Gorilla Bowl. **Known for:** superfresh fish; friendly sushi chefs; take-out options. $ *Average main: $13* ⊠ *Kukuiula Market, 2728 Poipu Rd., Koloa* ☎ 808/639–7218 ⊕ *makaisushi.com.*

$$$$

MODERN

HAWAIIAN

✕ **Merriman's Fish House.** The regional food served up at chef Peter Merriman's namesake restaurant is enhanced by a sophisticated setting and lovely views from a pretty second-floor dining room. Start at the bar, where fine wines are offered by the glass, and then continue to the

4

dinner menu, which states the origin of the fish, lamb, beef, chicken, and veggies; lunch and simple dinners of pizza and burgers are served downstairs, which has a nice outdoor eating area. **Known for:** upscale, romantic atmosphere; casual menu downstairs; locally caught fish. $ *Average main: $45* ⊠ *2829 Ala Kalanikaumaka St., G-149, Poipu* ☎ *808/742–8385* ⊕ *www.merrimanshawaii.com.*

BUDGET-FRIENDLY: SOUTH SHORE AND WEST SIDE

Grind's Cafe and Espresso ⊠ *Rte. 50, 4469 Waialo Rd.* ☎ *808/335-6027* ⊕ *www.grindscafe.net.*

Puka Dog ⊠ *2650 Kiahuna Plantation Dr., Koloa* ☎ *808/742-6044* ⊕ *www. pukadog.com.*

Wong's ⊠ *Kaumuali Hwy.* ☎ *808/335-5066* ⊕ *www.wongso-moide.com.*

$ ✕ **Pizzetta.** This family-style Italian restaurant has an open-air
ITALIAN
FAMILY deck where hearty portions of pasta, calzones, and thin-crust pizza are served, along with kalua pork and cabbage, grilled fish, and barbecue ribs, all of which can find their way into pizza toppings. Gluten-free crust and pasta are available. **Known for:** neighborhood delivery service; attentive wait staff; fresh, house-made bread. $ *Average main: $17* ⊠ *5408 Koloa Rd., Koloa* ☎ *808/742–8881.*

$$$ ✕ **Plantation Gardens.** A historic plantation manager's home has been
HAWAIIAN converted to a restaurant that serves seafood and meats with a Pacific Rim and Italian influence. Arrive early to enjoy a stroll through the torch-lit orchid gardens and lotus-studded koi ponds before settling in to the cozy European-style dining room. **Known for:** veranda for outdoor dining; unique setting; inspired cocktails and bar menu. $ *Average main: $28* ⊠ *Kiahuna Plantation, 2253 Poipu Rd., Koloa* ☎ *808/742–2121* ⊕ *www.pgrestaurant.com* ⊙ *No lunch.*

$$$$ ✕ **Red Salt.** Smart, sophisticated decor, attentive and skilled service, and
ECLECTIC an exceptional menu that highlights Hawaiian seafood make Red Salt a
Fodor's Choice great choice for leisurely fine dining. A breakfast buffet is also served,
★ and the sushi bar and pool bar offer more of the kitchen's great food, at lower prices. **Known for:** dramatic presentation; $79 tasting menu; perfectly grilled meats. $ *Average main: $48* ⊠ *Koa Kea Resort, 2251 Poipu Rd., Poipu* ☎ *808/742–4288* ⊕ *meritagecollection.com/koakea/dining-at-red-salt/.*

$$$$ ✕ **Tidepools.** Of the Grand Hyatt's many notable restaurants, Tidepools
SEAFOOD is definitely the most tropical and campy, with private grass-thatch huts that seem to float on a koi-filled pond beneath starry skies while torches flicker in the lushly landscaped grounds nearby. The equally distinctive food has an island flavor that comes from the chef's advocacy of Hawaii regional cuisine and extensive use of island-grown products including fresh herbs from the resort's organic garden. **Known for:** Hawaii regional cuisine; extensive use of island-grown products; excellent service. $ *Average main: $45* ⊠ *Grand Hyatt Kauai Resort and Spa, 1571 Poipu Rd., Poipu* ☎ *808/240–6456* ⊕ *kauai.grand.hyatt.com/en/hotel/dining/Tidepools.html* ⊙ *No lunch.*

The Plate-Lunch Tradition

To experience island history firsthand, step up to the counter at one of Hawaii's ubiquitous "plate lunch" eateries, and order a segmented Styrofoam plate piled with beef, chicken, two scoops of rice, macaroni salad, and maybe a pickled vegetable condiment. On the sugar plantations, Native Hawaiians and immigrant workers from many different countries ate together in the fields, sharing food from their "kaukau kits," the utilitarian version of the Japanese *bento* lunch-box. From this "melting pot" came the vibrant language of pidgin and its equivalent in food: the plate lunch.

Along roadsides, and at beaches and events, you will see food trucks, another excellent venue for sampling plate lunches. These portable restaurants are descendants of "lunch wagons" that began selling food to plantation workers in the 1930s. Try the deep-fried chicken *katsu* (rolled in Japanese panko bread crumbs and spices). The marinated beef teriyaki is another good choice, as is miso butterfish. The noodle soup, *saimin*, with its Japanese fish stock and Chinese red-tinted barbecue pork, is a distinctly local medley. Koreans have contributed spicy barbecue *kalbi* ribs, often served with chili-laden *kimchi* (pickled cabbage). Portuguese bean soup and tangy Filipino *adobo* stew are also favorites. The most popular Hawaiian contribution to the plate lunch is the *laulau*, a mix of meat and fish and young taro leaves, wrapped in more taro leaves and steamed.

4

THE WEST SIDE

When it comes to dining on the West Side, pickings are mighty slim. Fortunately, the few eateries that are here are generally worth patronizing.

$
CAFÉ
✕ **Lappert's Ice Cream.** It's not ice cream on Kauai if it's not Lappert's Ice Cream. Guava, mac nut, pineapple, mango, coconut, banana—Lappert's is the ice-cream capital of Kauai. **Known for:** Kauai Pie (coffee ice cream with chocolate fudge, coconut flakes, and macadamia nuts); super-premium ice cream made daily; homemade pastries and local coffee. ⑤ *Average main: $9* ✉ *1-3555 Kaumualii Hwy., Hanapepe* ☎ *808/335–6121* ⊕ *www.lappertshawaii.com.*

$
CAFÉ
FAMILY
✕ **Little Fish Coffee.** For a wholesome breakfast or lunch on the West Side, this friendly, funky, and fun—right down to the marking pens that allow you to leave your own graffiti on the bathroom wall—café is the spot. The coffee is good, with each cup individually dripped, and the fresh bagels come with house-made cream cheese. **Known for:** casual setting; emphasis on wholesome ingredients; smoothies and fresh juices. ⑤ *Average main: $9* ✉ *3900 Hanapepe Rd., Eleele* ☎ *808/335–5000* ⊕ *littlefishcoffee.com* ⊗ *No dinner.*

$
BARBECUE
FAMILY
✕ **Plantations BBQ & Bar.** This casual eatery is located in the equally laid-back Waimea Plantation Cottages; it's a great place to sit with a cocktail and watch the sun set. The fare is simple and hearty: chili fries, burgers, sandwiches, salads, and barrel-smoked BBQ chicken and beef for lunch and dinner, and the usual eggs and pancakes for breakfast. **Known for:** large portions; kid-friendly dining; great selection of sides.

ROMANTIC DINING

For divine sunsets, the **Beach House** (☎ 808/742–1424), in Koloa, is best, as it puts you right on the water. **Café Portofino** (☎ 808/245–2121), at the Kauai Marriott in Lihue, with its second-story view of Kalapaki Bay and harp music, practically caters to couples. Tops overall, though, is **Dondero's** (☎ 808/240–6456), in Koloa, where the food, service, and elegant setting come together to create a special evening. If it's a nice evening, by all means opt for the veranda.

Be sure to make reservations, and don't plan on pinching pennies. If you're on a budget, pick up some take-out food and spread a blanket on the beach for a memorable sunset picnic and dessert beneath brilliant stars.

⑤ *Average main: $15* ✉ *9400 Kaumualii Hwy., Waimea (Kauai County)* ☎ *808/338–1625.*

$$$
STEAKHOUSE
FAMILY
✕ **Wrangler's Steakhouse.** Denim-covered seating, decorative saddles, and a stagecoach in a loft helped to transform the historic Ako General Store in Waimea into a West Side steak house where you can eat under the stars on the deck out back or inside the old-fashioned, wood-panel dining room. Open weekend evenings, the Saddle Room features a bar menu that includes seven styles of burgers and there's live music on Saturday night. **Known for:** special lunch (rice, beef teriyaki, and shrimp tempura with kimchi) served in a three-tier kaukau tin; campy setting; local, grass-fed beef. ⑤ *Average main: $28* ✉ *9852 Kaumualii Hwy., Waimea (Kauai County)* ☎ *808/338–1218* ⊕ *wranglerssteakhouse.com* ⊘ *Closed Sun. No lunch Sat.*

5

WHERE TO STAY

Updated by
Joan Conrow

The Garden Isle has lodgings for every taste, from swanky resorts to rustic cabins, and from family-friendly condos to romantic bed-and-breakfasts. The savvy traveler can also find inexpensive places that are convenient, safe, and accessible to Kauai's special places and activities.

Kauai may seem small on a map, but because it's circular with no through roads, it can take more time than you think to get from place to place. If at all possible, stay close to your desired activities. This way, you'll save time to squeeze in all the things you'll want to do.

Time of year is also a factor. If you're here in winter or spring, consider staying on the South Shore, as the surf on the North Shore and East Side tends to be rough, making many ocean beaches dangerous for swimming or water sports.

Before booking accommodations, think hard about what kind of experience you want to have for your island vacation. There are several top-notch resorts to choose from, and Kauai also has a wide variety of condos, vacation rentals, and bed-and-breakfasts. The Kauai Visitors Bureau provides a comprehensive listing of accommodation choices to help you decide.

KAUAI LODGING PLANNER

HOTELS AND RESORTS

If you want to golf, play tennis, or hang at a spa, stay at a resort. You'll also be more likely to find activities for children at resorts, including camps that allow parents a little time off. The island's hotels tend to be smaller and older, with fewer on-site amenities. The swankiest places to stay on the island are the St. Regis Princeville Resort on the North Shore, where rooms run more than $1,000 per night in high season, and the Grand Hyatt Kauai on the South Shore for a bit less; of course, those with views of the ocean book faster than those without. Many resorts have begun charging a daily "amenities fee" that can add $15 to $30 to the price of the lodging, so be sure to inquire when you make reservations to avoid unpleasant surprises upon checkout. *Hotel reviews have been shortened. For full information, visit Fodors.com.*

B&BS AND INNS

The island's bed-and-breakfasts allow you to meet local residents and more directly experience the aloha spirit. Many have oceanfront settings and breakfasts with everything from tropical fruits and juices, Kauai coffee, and macadamia waffles to breads made with local bananas and mangoes. Some have pools, hot tubs, services such as *lomilomi* massage, and breakfasts delivered to your lanai. Some properties have stand-alone units on-site.

CONDOS AND VACATION RENTALS

Condos and vacation rentals on Kauai tend to run the gamut from fabulous luxury estates to scruffy little dives. It's buyer-beware in this largely unregulated sector of the visitor industry, where there's no inspection of properties and many operate without county permits. If you're planning to stay at one of these, ask for their county permit number and be sure to contact the Kauai Visitors Bureau (☎ *800/262–1400*) to see whether any complaints have been made against it. Also be aware that most do not have air-conditioning.

Properties managed by individual owners can be found on online vacation-rental directories such as HomeAway (⊕ *www.homeaway. com*) and Vacation Rentals By Owner (⊕ *www.vrbo.com*), as well as on the Kauai Visitors Bureau's website (⊕ *www.gohawaii.com/islands/ kauai*). There are also several Kauai-based management companies with vacation rentals.

RESERVATIONS

The rule on Kauai—and for Hawaii in general—is to book as far in advance as possible. Rooms go most quickly during holidays, but there really isn't any low season to speak of. Some places allow 24 hours' notice to cancel; others require a week or will penalize you the cost of one night. Most hotels allow children under a certain age to stay in their parents' room at no extra charge, but others charge for them as extra adults; find out the cutoff age for discounts.

PRICES

Prices listed in our hotel reviews are the lowest cost of a standard double room in high season, which generally includes taxes and service charges but not any optional meal plans. Prices for rentals are the lowest per-night cost for a one-bedroom unit in high season.

WHAT IT COSTS			
$	$$	$$$	$$$$
Hotels	under $180	$180–$260	$261–$340	over $340

Hotel prices are for two people in a standard double room in high season. Condo price categories reflect studio and one-bedroom rates.

WHERE TO STAY IN KAUAI

	Local Vibe	Pros	Cons
The North Shore	Properties here have the "wow" factor with ocean and mountain beauty; laid-back Hanalei and Princeville set the high-end pace.	When the weather is good (summer) this side has it all. Epic winter surf, gorgeous waterfalls, and verdant vistas create some of the best scenery in Hawaii.	Frequent winter rain (being green has a cost) means you may have to travel south to find the sun; expensive restaurants and shopping offer few deals.
The East Side	The most reasonably priced area to stay for the practical traveler; lacks the pizzazz of expensive resorts on North and South shores; more traditional beach hotels.	The best travel deals show up here; more direct access to the local population; plenty of decent restaurants with good variety, along with delis in food stores.	Beaches aren't the greatest (rocky, reefy) at many of the lodging spots; congested traffic at times; some crime issues in parks.
The South Shore	Resort central; plenty of choices where the consistent sunshine is perfect for those who want to do nothing but play golf or tennis and read a book by the pool.	Beautiful in its own right; many enchanted evenings with stellar sunsets; summer surf a bit easier for beginners to handle.	Though resorts are lush, surrounding landscape is desertlike with scrub brush; construction can be brutal on peace of mind.
The West Side	There are few options for lodging in this mostly untouristed setting, with contrasts such as the extreme heat of a July day in Waimea to a frozen winter night up in Kokee.	A gateway area for exploration into the wilds of Kokee or for boating trips on Napali Coast; main hub for boat and helicopter trips; outstanding sunsets.	Least convenient side for most visitors; daytime is languid and dry; river runoff can ruin ocean's clarity.

THE NORTH SHORE

The North Shore is mountainous and wet, which accounts for its rugged, lush landscape. Posh resorts and condominiums await you at Princeville, a community with dreamy views, excellent golf courses, and lovely sunsets. It maintains the lion's share of North Shore accommodations—primarily luxury hotel rooms and condos built on a plateau overlooking the sea. Hanalei, a bay-side town in a broad valley, has a smattering of hotel rooms and numerous vacation rentals, many within walking distance of the beach. Prices tend to be high in this resort area. If you want to do extensive sightseeing on other parts of the island, be prepared for a long drive—one that's very dark at night. ⚠ **Following extensive flooding in early 2018, areas of Haena and the Napali Coast are undergoing repairs. Please check before visiting to make sure places are open.**

$$ 🖼 **Hanalei Bay Resort.** The nicest feature of this condominium resort
RESORT   overlooking Hanalei Bay and Napali Coast is its upper-level pool,
FAMILY   with authentic lava-rock waterfalls, an open-air hot tub, and a kid-friendly sand "beach." Three-story buildings angle down the cliffs, making for some steep walking paths. **Pros:** beautiful views; tennis

courts on property with a children's program; 24-hour fitness center; tropical pool. **Cons:** steep walkways; long walk to beach; no restaurant or lounge. $ *Rooms from: $215* ✉ *5380 Honoiki Rd., Princeville* ☎ *808/826–6522, 877/507–1428* ⊕ *www.hanaleibayresort.com* ⌯ *134 units* ❍| *No meals.*

$$$$
RESORT

🏨 **Hanalei Colony Resort.** The only true beachfront resort on Kauai's North Shore, Hanalei Colony is a laid-back, go-barefoot kind of resort sandwiched between towering mountains and the sea. **Pros:** oceanfront setting; private, quiet property; well-maintained units with Hawaiian-style furnishings. **Cons:** poor cell-phone reception; damp in winter; isolated location. $ *Rooms from: $375* ✉ *5-7130 Kuhio Hwy., Haena* ☎ *808/826–6235, 800/628–3004* ⊕ *www.hcr.com* ⌯ *48 units* ❍| *No meals.*

$
RENTAL

🏨 **Hanalei Inn.** If you're looking for lodgings that won't break the bank a block from gorgeous Hanalei Bay, look no further, as this is literally the only choice among the town's pricey vacation rentals. **Pros:** quick walk to beach, bus stop, and shops; full kitchen; coin-operated laundry on-site. **Cons:** strict cancellation policy; daytime traffic noise; older property. $ *Rooms from: $159* ✉ *5-5468 Kuhio Hwy., Hanalei* ☎ *808/826–9333, 888/773–4730* ⊕ *www.hanaleiinn. net* ⌯ *4 studios* ❍| *No meals.*

$$$$
RESORT
FAMILY
Fodor'sChoice
★

🏨 **St. Regis Princeville Resort.** Built into the cliffs above Hanalei Bay, this swanky Starwood resort offers expansive views of the sea and mountains, including Makana, the landmark peak immortalized as mysterious Bali Hai island in the film *South Pacific.* **Pros:** great views; excellent restaurants; attractive lobby. **Cons:** minimal grounds; beach not ideal for swimming; extremely expensive. $ *Rooms from: $815* ✉ *5520 Ka Haku Rd., Princeville* ☎ *877/787–3447, 808/826–9644* ⊕ *www.stregisprinceville.com* ⌯ *252 rooms* ❍| *No meals.*

$$$$
RESORT
FAMILY
Fodor'sChoice
★

🏨 **Westin Princeville Ocean Resort Villas.** Spread out over 18½ acres on a bluff above Anini Beach, this Westin property marries the comforts of spacious condominium living with the top-notch service and amenities of a luxurious hotel resort. **Pros:** on-site minimarket; ocean views; kids' program. **Cons:** path to the nearby beach is a steep six- to seven-minute walk; whirlpool tub is small; units can be far from parking. $ *Rooms from: $370* ✉ *3838 Wyllie Rd., Princeville* ☎ *808/827–8700, 800/827–8801* ⊕ *www.westinprinceville.com* ⌯ *366 units* ❍| *No meals.*

THE EAST SIDE

Location, location, location. The East Side, or Coconut Coast, is a good centralized home base if you want to see and do it all. This is one of the few resort areas on Kauai where you can actually walk to the beach, restaurants, and stores from your condo, hotel, or vacation-rental unit. It's not only convenient, but comparatively cheap. You pay less for lodging, meals, services, merchandise, and gas here—mainly because much of the coral-reef coastline isn't as ideal as the sandy-bottom bays that front the fancy resorts. We think the shoreline is just fine. There are pockets in the reef to swim in, and the coast is uncrowded and boasts spectacular views. ■ TIP➔ **Traffic on the main highway can be bumper-to-bumper**

Where to Stay on the North Shore

Hanalei Bay Resort **3**

Hanalei Colony Resort **1**

Hanalei Inn **2**

St. Regis
Princeville Resort **4**

Westin Princeville Ocean
Resort Villas **5**

in the afternoon. All in all, it's a good choice for families because the prices are right and there's plenty to keep everyone happy and occupied.

KAPAA AND WAILUA

Since Kapaa is the island's major population center, this area, including Waipouli and Wailua, has a lived-in, real-world feel. This is where you'll find some of the best deals on accommodations and a wider choice of inexpensive restaurants and shops than in the resort areas. The beaches here are so-so for swimming but nice for sunbathing, walking, and watching the sun- and moonrise.

The Wailua area is rather compact and much of it can be accessed from a coastal walking and biking path. The resorts here are attractive to middle-class travelers seeking a good bang for their buck. Wailua had a rich cultural significance for the ancient Hawaiians. Their royalty lived here, and ancient sacred grounds, called *heiau,* are clearly marked. ⚠ **Following extensive flooding in early 2018, areas along the Wailua River are undergoing repairs. Please check before visiting to make sure places are open.**

$$$$ ⛩ **Aloha Cottages.** Owners Charlie and Susan Hoerner restored a three-
RENTAL bedroom plantation home on Kapaa's Baby Beach to reflect the charm
FAMILY of yesteryear with the conveniences of today. **Pros:** comfortable, home-like ambience; good for large groups; safe children's beach. **Cons:** can be windy at times; not great for swimming; facilities shared between the two houses. $ *Rooms from: $447* ✉ *1041 Moana Kai Rd., Kapaa* ☎ *808/823–0543, 877/915–1015* ⊕ *www.alohacottages.com* ↻ *2 cottages* ⊙ *No meals.*

$$ ⛩ **Aston Islander on the Beach.** A low-rise, Hawaii-plantation-style design
HOTEL gives this 6-acre beachfront property a pleasant, relaxed feeling. **Pros:** convenient location; free airport shuttle; online rate deals. **Cons:** small-ish pool; no restaurant on the property; no resort amenities. $ *Rooms from: $239* ✉ *440 Aleka Pl., Wailua (Kauai County)* ☎ *808/822–7417, 866/774–2924* ⊕ *www.astonhotels.com* ↻ *200 rooms* ⊙ *No meals.*

$$ ⛩ **Courtyard Kauai at Coconut Beach.** This popular hotel, one of the few
RESORT true oceanfront properties on Kauai, sits on a ribbon of sand in Kapaa with bright, spacious rooms that face the ocean or pool. **Pros:** convenient location; close to ocean; pleasant grounds. **Cons:** coastline not conducive to swimming; small pool; high daily parking fee. $ *Rooms from: $249* ✉ *650 Aleka Loop, Wailua (Kauai County)* ☎ *808/822–3455, 800/760–8555* ⊕ *www.marriott.com* ↻ *311 rooms* ⊙ *No meals.*

$$$ ⛩ **Hotel Coral Reef.** This small hotel has been in business since 1956 and
HOTEL is something of a Kauai beachfront landmark, with clean, comfortable
FAMILY rooms, some with great ocean views, and a large pool that overlooks the water; expect great sunrises. **Pros:** free parking; oceanfront setting; convenient location. **Cons:** located in a busy section of Kapaa; ocean swimming is marginal; traffic noise. $ *Rooms from: $289* ✉ *4-1516 Kuhio Hwy., Kapaa* ☎ *808/822–4481, 800/843–4659* ⊕ *www.hotel-coralreefresort.com* ↻ *20 rooms* ⊙ *Free Breakfast.*

$ ⛩ **Kapaa Sands.** An old rock etched with *kanji* (Japanese characters)
RENTAL reminds you that the site of this condominium gem was once occupied

by a Shinto temple. **Pros:** discounts for extended stays; walking distance to shops, restaurants, and beach; turtle and monk seal sightings common. **Cons:** no-frills lodging; small bathrooms; traffic noise in rear units. [S] *Rooms from: $179* ⊠ *380 Papaloa Rd., Wailua (Kauai County)* ☎ *808/822–4901, 800/222–4901* ⊕ *www.kapaasands.com* ⤢ *24 units* ⦿ *No meals.*

$$
RENTAL
FAMILY
Fodor's Choice
★

⊡ **Kauai Coast Resort at the Beachboy.** Fronting an uncrowded stretch of beach, this three-story primarily time-share resort is convenient and a bit more upscale than nearby properties. **Pros:** central location; nice sunrises; free parking. **Cons:** beach is narrow; ocean not ideal for swimming; daily housekeeping fee. [S] *Rooms from: $215* ⊠ *520 Aleka Loop, Wailua (Kauai County)* ☎ *808/822–3441, 866/678–3289* ⊕ *www.shell-hospitality.com* ⤢ *108 units* ⦿ *No meals.*

$
HOTEL

⊡ **Kauai Shores.** This oceanfront inn has been transformed into an affordable boutique hotel, thanks to a much-needed renovation of its guest rooms and public spaces. **Pros:** convenient location; free Wi-Fi; great sunrises; discount for LGBT travelers. **Cons:** coral reef makes ocean swimming marginal; modest property; minimal amenities; daily hospitality fee. [S] *Rooms from: $158* ⊠ *420 Papaloa Rd., Wailua (Kauai County)* ☎ *808/822–4951, 800/560–5553* ⊕ *www.kauaishoreshotel. com* ⤢ *202 rooms* ⦿ *No meals.*

$$$
RENTAL

⊡ **Outrigger at Lae Nani.** Ruling Hawaiian chiefs once returned from ocean voyages to this spot, now host to comfortable condominiums. **Pros:** nice beach; walking distance to playground; attractively furnished. **Cons:** third floor is walk-up; no Wi-Fi; cleaning fee. [S] *Rooms from: $339* ⊠ *410 Papaloa Rd., Wailua (Kauai County)* ☎ *808/823–1401, 866/956–4262* ⊕ *www.outrigger.com* ⤢ *84 units* ⦿ *No meals.*

$$
RENTAL

⊡ **Plantation Hale Suites.** These older, plantation-style one-bedroom units have well-equipped kitchenettes and garden lanai and clean, comfortable rooms, some of which have been recently renovated. **Pros:** friendly staff; three pools; walking distance to shops, restaurant, beach. **Cons:** traffic noise in mountain-view units; coral reef makes ocean swimming challenging; property needs a general update. [S] *Rooms from: $199* ⊠ *525 Aleka Loop, Wailua (Kauai County)* ☎ *808/822–4941, 800/775–4253* ⊕ *www.plantation-hale.com* ⤢ *104 units* ⦿ *No meals.*

LIHUE

Lihue is not the most desirable place to stay on Kauai, in terms of scenic beauty, although it does have its advantages, including easy access to the airport. Restaurants and shops are plentiful, and there's lovely Kalapaki Bay for beachgoers. Aside from the Marriott and the Kauai Beach Resort, most of the limited lodging possibilities are smaller and aimed at the cost-conscious traveler.

$$
HOTEL

⊡ **Garden Island Inn.** Budget travelers love this three-story inn near Kalapaki Bay and Anchor Cove shopping center as it's clean, offers free Wi-Fi, and the innkeepers are friendly, sharing fruit, flowers, and beach gear. **Pros:** walk to beach, restaurants, and shops; good for extended stays and budget travel; air-conditioning. **Cons:** some traffic noise; near a busy harbor; limited grounds; no pool. [S] *Rooms from: $185* ⊠ *3445*

Where to Stay on the East Side

Wilcox Rd., Kalapaki Beach, Lihue ☎ *808/245–7227, 800/648–0154* ⊕ *www.gardenislandinn.com* ➔ *21 rooms* ¶⊙¶ *No meals.*

$$$
RESORT

📷 **Kauai Beach Resort.** This plantation-style hotel recently came under the management of Aqua Hotels and Resorts and in 2017 completed a $14 million renovation that upgraded the amenities to provide a relaxing, upscale experience close to the airport, but without the noise. **Pros:** unique sand-bottom pool with 12-foot waterfall; shuttle service to airport; resort amenities. **Cons:** not a good swimming beach; windy at times; no nearby restaurants or resorts. $ *Rooms from: $329* ⊠ *4331 Kauai Beach Dr., Hanamaulu* ☎ *888/805–3843* ⊕ *www.kauaibeachresorthawaii.com* ➔ *357 rooms* ¶⊙¶ *No meals.*

$$$
RESORT
FAMILY

📷 **Kauai Marriott Resort on Kalapaki Beach.** An elaborate tropical garden, waterfalls right off the lobby, Greek statues and columns, and an enormous 26,000-square-foot swimming pool characterize the grand—and grandiose—scale of this resort on Kalapaki Beach, which looks out at the dramatic Haupu Ridge. **Pros:** oceanfront setting; numerous restaurants; convenient location; airport shuttle. **Cons:** airport noise; ocean water quality can be poor at times; located near an industrial area. $ *Rooms from: $339* ⊠ *3610 Rice St., Kalapaki Beach, Lihue* ☎ *808/245–5050, 800/220–2925* ⊕ *www.kauaimarriott.com* ➔ *367 rooms* ¶⊙¶ *Free Breakfast.*

$
HOTEL

📷 **Kauai Palms Hotel.** Not only is this low-cost alternative close to the airport, but it's also a great base for day trips to all sides of the island. **Pros:** friendly staff; inexpensive; centrally located. **Cons:** bare-bones amenities; smallish rooms; traffic noise. $ *Rooms from: $95* ⊠ *2931 Kalena St., Lihue* ☎ *808/246–0908* ⊕ *www.kauaipalmshotel.com* ➔ *33 rooms* ¶⊙¶ *No meals.*

THE SOUTH SHORE

Sunseekers usually head south to the condo-studded shores of Poipu, where three- and four-story complexes line the coast and the surf is generally ideal for swimming. As the island's primary resort community, Poipu has the bulk of the island's accommodations, and more condos than hotels, with prices in the moderate to expensive range. Although it accommodates many visitors, its extensive, colorful landscaping and low-rise buildings save it from feeling dense and overcrowded, and it has a delightful coastal promenade perfect for sunset strolls. Surprisingly, the South Shore doesn't have as many shops and restaurants as one might expect for such a popular resort region, but the new Kukuiula shopping plaza is doing its best to fill the gaps. ■ TIP➔ **The area's beaches are among the best on the island for families, with sandy shores, shallow waters, and grassy lawns adjacent to the sand.**

$$$$
RESORT
FAMILY
Fodor'sChoice
★

📷 **Grand Hyatt Kauai Resort and Spa.** Dramatically handsome, this classic Hawaiian low-rise is built into the cliffs overlooking an unspoiled coastline; it's taken great strides to reduce its carbon footprint and boasts mouthwatering restaurants, which helps to make it Kauai's best megaresort. **Pros:** fabulous pool; excellent restaurants; Hawaiian ambience. **Cons:** poor and somewhat dangerous swimming beach during summer swells; small balconies; $35 daily resort fee. $ *Rooms from: $424*

✉ *1571 Poipu Rd., Poipu* ☎ *808/742–1234, 800/633–7313* ⊕ *www. grandhyattkauai.com* ⇖ *639 rooms* ⦿ *No meals.*

$$
RENTAL
⊞ Hideaway Cove. Just one block from the ocean's edge in the heart of Poipu, Hideway Cove was once two homes that have been converted to seven complete vacation homes, ranging from a studio to a five-bedroom unit; each unit is appointed with resort-quality furniture and original artwork. **Pros:** high-quality furnishings; private lanai; rates drop with a seven-night stay, effectively making the seventh night free. **Cons:** not on the ocean; cleaning fee; neighborhood can be noisy. ⑤ *Rooms from: $225* ✉ *2307 Nalo Rd., Poipu* ☎ *808/635–8785, 866/849–2426* ⊕ *www.hideawaycove.com* ⇖ *7 units* ⦿ *No meals.*

$
RENTAL
⊞ Kauai Cove Cottages. Located in a residential neighborhood, this property includes a modern studio cottage at the mouth of Waikomo Stream, about two blocks from a nice snorkeling cove, as well as a full bedroom suite and a guest room with shared bath in a larger house a few miles away in the resort community at Poipu Kai. The airy tropical-theme studio has a cathedral ceiling, a complete kitchen, and a private patio with a gas grill. **Pros:** clean; great snorkeling nearby; quiet neighborhood. **Cons:** not on beach; $60–$75 cleaning fee upon departure; no shops or restaurants nearby. ⑤ *Rooms from: $169* ✉ *2672 Puuholo Rd., Poipu* ☎ *808/742–2562, 800/624–9945* ⊕ *www.kauaicove.com* ⇖ *1 cottage, 2 rooms* ⦿ *No meals.*

$$$
RENTAL
FAMILY
⊞ Kiahuna Plantation Resort Kauai by Outrigger. This longtime Kauai condo project consists of 42 plantation-style, low-rise buildings with individually owned one- and two-bedroom units that arc around a large, grassy field leading to a lovely beach. **Pros:** great sunset and ocean views are bonuses in some units; convenient to restaurants and shops; swimmable beach and lawn for picnics and games. **Cons:** no air-conditioning; be prepared for stairs; somewhat lackluster property. ⑤ *Rooms from: $299* ✉ *2253 Poipu Rd., Poipu* ☎ *808/742–6411, 800/542–4862* ⊕ *www.outrigger.com* ⇖ *333 units* ⦿ *No meals.*

$$$$
RESORT
Fodor's Choice
★
⊞ Koa Kea Hotel and Resort. This boutique property offers a luxurious, high-end experience without the bustle of many larger resorts, making it a great place to forget it all while relaxing at the spa or lounging by the pool. **Pros:** incredibly comfortable beds; friendly service; romantic spa; perfect romantic getaway. **Cons:** not much for children; all parking is valet, but it feels more like a convenience than a burden; the area is very busy. ⑤ *Rooms from: $429* ✉ *2251 Poipu Rd., Poipu* ☎ *808/828–8888, 888/898–8958* ⊕ *www.koakea.com* ⇖ *121 rooms* ⦿ *No meals.*

$$$
RENTAL
⊞ Makahuena at Poipu. Situated close to the center of Poipu, on a rocky point over the ocean, the large, individually owned one-, two-, and three-bedroom condos are near Shipwreck and Poipu beaches; they are a better deal for the price than some of the nearby properties; **Pros:** tennis court; scenic setting; right on the ocean. **Cons:** no swimming beach; no air-conditioning; individually owned condos means the decor and upkeep vary, and some are dated. ⑤ *Rooms from: $309* ✉ *1661 Pee Rd., Poipu* ☎ *808/742–2482, 800/367–5004* ⊕ *www.castleresorts.com/ kauai/makahuena-at-poipu/* ⇖ *78 units* ⦿ *No meals.*

$
RENTAL
⊞ Poipu Crater Resort. Set within a nicely landscaped resort built on an extinct volcanic crater known as *Piha Keakua* , or "place of the gods,"

Where to Stay on the South Shore and West Side

Grand Hyatt Kauai
Resort and Spa **16**
Hideaway Cove **15**
Kalaheo Inn **3**
Kauai Cove Cottages **5**
Kiahuna Plantation Resort **7**
Kauai by Outrigger **7**

Koa Kea
Hotel and Resort **13**
Kokee Lodge **1**
Makahuena at Poipu **14**
Poipu Crater Resort **9**
Poipu Kai Resort **8**
Poipu Kapili Resort **6**

Poipu Plantation
Resort **11**
Poipu Shores **12**
Sheraton Kauai Resort ... **10**
Waimea Plantation
Cottages **2**
Whalers Cove Resort **4**

0   4 miles
0   4 km

these two-bedroom condominium units are fairly spacious, with large windows and high ceilings, and full kitchens. **Pros:** attractive and generally well kept; pretty setting on the South Shore; located just 700 yards from Keoniloa Bay (Shipwreck Beach). **Cons:** beach isn't good for swimming; few resort amenities; individually owned units means upkeep and decor varies. ⑤ *Rooms from: $150* ✉ *2330 Hoohu Rd., Poipu* ☎ *808/742–7400* ⊕ *www.parrishkauai.com* ⤳ *30 units* ⓄⒾ *No meals.*

$$ 🏨 **Poipu Kai Resort.** Condominiums, many with cathedral ceilings and all with large furnished lanai and big windows overlooking the lawns,
RENTAL give the resort the feeling of a spacious, quiet retreat inside and out.
FAMILY **Pros:** close to ocean; full kitchens; good rates for the location. **Cons:** some units don't have air-conditioning; closest beaches not ideal for swimming; two-night minimum stay is required. ⑤ *Rooms from: $225* ✉ *1941 Poipu Rd., Koloa* ☎ *808/742–6464, 800/367–8020* ⊕ *villasat-poipukai.com* ⤳ *150 units* ⓄⒾ *No meals.*

$$$ 🏨 **Poipu Kapili Resort.** White-frame exteriors and double-pitched roofs
RENTAL complement the tropical landscaping at this resort, which offers spa-
FAMILY cious one- and two-bedroom condo units—with full kitchens, entertainment centers, and garden or ocean views—that are minutes from Poipu's restaurants and across the street from a nice beach. **Pros:** units are roomy; parking is close to the unit; units are well spaced. **Cons:** units are ocean-view but not oceanfront; a three-night minimum stay is required; minimal amenities. ⑤ *Rooms from: $300* ✉ *2221 Kapili Rd., Poipu* ☎ *808/742–6449, 800/443–7714* ⊕ *www.poipukapili.com* ⤳ *60 units* ⓄⒾ *No meals.*

$ 🏨 **Poipu Plantation Resort.** Plumeria, ti, and other tropical foliage create
B&B/INN a lush landscape for this resort, which rents four suites in a bed-and-breakfast–style plantation home and nine one- and two-bedroom cottage apartments. **Pros:** attractively furnished; full breakfast at B&B; free Wi-Fi. **Cons:** three-night minimum; not on the ocean; no resort amenities. ⑤ *Rooms from: $155* ✉ *1792 Pee Rd., Poipu* ☎ *808/742–6757, 800/634–0263* ⊕ *www.poipubeach.com* ⤳ *4 rooms, 9 cottages* ⓄⒾ *Free Breakfast.*

$$$ 🏨 **Poipu Shores.** Perched on a rocky point above pounding surf—perfect
RENTAL for whale- or turtle-watching—three low-rise buildings have individually owned condos with full kitchens and a washer-dryer; there's a pool in front of the middle one. **Pros:** every unit faces the water; oceanfront pool; wildlife viewing. **Cons:** units vary widely in style; no resort amenities; swimming beach is 10-minute walk away. ⑤ *Rooms from: $298* ✉ *1775 Pee Rd., Koloa* ☎ *808/742–7700, 800/367–1912* ⊕ *www.castleresorts.com* ⤳ *39 units* ⓄⒾ *No meals.*

$$$ 🏨 **Sheraton Kauai Resort.** The Sheraton is a sprawling resort with rooms
RESORT that offer views of the ocean and its lovely landscaped gardens; it's
Fodor's Choice worth splurging on the newly renovated ocean-wing accommodations,
★ which are so close to the water you can practically feel the spray of the surf as it hits the rocks below. **Pros:** ocean-view pool; quiet; great restaurant with spectacular views. **Cons:** parking can be a ways from the room; some rooms feel dated; $30 daily resort fee. ⑤ *Rooms from: $340* ✉ *2440 Hoonani Rd., Poipu Beach, Koloa* ☎ *808/742–1661, 888/488–3535* ⊕ *www.sheraton-kauai.com* ⤳ *405 rooms* ⓄⒾ *No meals.*

$$$$
RENTAL
FAMILY

⬚ **Whalers Cove Resort.** Perched about as close to the water's edge as they can get, these condos are the most luxurious on the South Shore, available in one-, two-, or three-bedroom units. **Pros:** on-site staff; outstanding setting; spacious, fully equipped units. **Cons:** rocky beach not ideal for swimming; no air-conditioning; resort fee, but no resort amenities. ⑤ *Rooms from: $430* ✉ *2640 Puuholo Rd., Poipu* ☎ *808/742–7571, 800/225–2683* ⊕ *www.whalerscoveresort.com* ↩ *39 units* ⦿ *No meals.*

THE WEST SIDE

To do a lot of hiking or immerse yourself in the island's history, find a room in Waimea. You won't find many resorts, restaurants, or shops, but you will encounter quiet days, miles of largely deserted beach, and a rural environment.

$
B&B/INN

⬚ **Kalaheo Inn.** It isn't easy to find good lodgings on the southwest side of the island, but this old-fashioned budget inn with studios or one-, two-, and three-bedroom suites does the job in Kalaheo town. **Pros:** some units have kitchens; walking distance to restaurants; lots of beach gear to lend out. **Cons:** property is a ways from the beach; no air-conditioning; poor cell-phone service. ⑤ *Rooms from: $87* ✉ *4444 Papalina Rd., Kalaheo* ☎ *808/332–6023, 888/332–6023* ⊕ *www.kalaheoinn.com* ↩ *15 units* ⦿ *No meals.*

$
RENTAL

⬚ **Kokee Lodge.** If you're an outdoors enthusiast, you can appreciate Kauai's mountain wilderness from the 12 rustic cabins that make up this lodge; cabins are austere, to say the least, but more comfortable than a tent, and the mountain setting is grand. **Pros:** outstanding setting; more refined than camping; cooking facilities. **Cons:** austere accommodations in a remote location; no restaurants for dinner; $45 cleaning fee. ⑤ *Rooms from: $79* ✉ *Kokee State Park, 3600 Kokee Rd., at mile marker 15, Kokee* ☎ *808/652–6852* ⊕ *www.kokeelodge.com* ↩ *12 cabins* ⦿ *No meals.*

$
RENTAL
Fodor's Choice
★

⬚ **Waimea Plantation Cottages.** Originally built in the early 1900s, history buffs will adore these relocated and refurbished one- to five-bedroom sugar-plantation cottages, which are tucked among coconut trees along a lovely, walkable stretch of beach on the sunny West Side. **Pros:** unique lodging experience; quiet and low-key; free Wi-Fi. **Cons:** not a good swimming beach; rooms are not luxurious; minimal amenities. ⑤ *Rooms from: $170* ✉ *9400 Kaumualii Hwy., Box 367, Waimea (Kauai County)* ☎ *808/338–1625, 800/716–6199* ⊕ *www.coasthotels.com* ↩ *61 cottages* ⦿ *No meals.*

NIGHTLIFE AND PERFORMING ARTS

Updated by
Joan Conrow

Kauai has never been known for its nightlife. It's a rural island, where folks tend to retire early, and the streets are dark and deserted well before midnight. The island does have its night-spots, though, and the after-dark entertainment scene keeps expanding, especially in areas frequented by tourists.

Most of the island's dinner and luau shows are held at hotels and resorts. Hotel lounges are a good source of live music, often with no cover charge, as are a few bars and restaurants around the island.

Check the local newspaper, the *Garden Island,* for listings of weekly happenings. Free publications such as *Kauai Gold, This Week on Kauai,* and *Essential Kauai* also list entertainment events. You can pick them up at Lihue Airport near the baggage claim area, as well as at numerous retail areas on the island.

NIGHTLIFE

For every new venue that opens on Kauai, another one closes, mainly because most island residents tend to retire early. It is, after all, a rural island. But still, there are a number of places to shake your booty, hear local music, and simply enjoy a drink. Nightclubs that stay open until the wee hours are rare on Kauai, and the bar scene is limited. The major resorts generally host their own live entertainment and happy hours. All bars and clubs that serve alcohol must close at 2 am, except those with a cabaret license, which allows them to close at 4 am.

THE NORTH SHORE

BARS AND CLUBS

Hanalei Gourmet. The sleepy North Shore stays awake—until 10:30, that is—each evening in this small, convivial deli and bar inside Hanalei's restored old school building. There's local live Hawaiian, jazz, rock, and folk music on Sunday and Wednesday evening. ⊠ *Hanalei Center, 5-5161 Kuhio Hwy., Hanalei* ☎ *808/826–2524* ⊕ *www.hanaleigourmet.com.*

Fodor's Choice ★ **Happy Talk Lounge.** Want to sip an umbrella cocktail while you gaze at the original Bali Hai? Open on two sides, Happy Talk Lounge offers breezy views across Hanalei Bay to plush emerald mountains. If you think the scene looks familiar, maybe you've seen the film classic *South Pacific*, filmed here. The film version of Bali Hai is actually Kauai's Mount Makana. Order a tropical cocktail and *pupu* (Hawaiian hors d'oeuvres) and enjoy a truly enchanting evening as the sun sets over the sparkling waters. ■**TIP→** Nearby Tunnels Beach (aka Haena Beach and Makua) is often called Nurses' Beach, where Mitzi Gaynor sang about washing that man right outta her hair; Hanalei Bay is where Bloody Mary sang "Bali Hai." ⊠ *Hanalei Bay Resort, 5380 Honoiki Rd., Princeville* ☎ *808/431–4084* ⊕ *www.happytalk-lounge.com.*

MAI TAIS

Hard to believe, but the cocktail known around the world as the mai tai has been around for more than 50 years. While the recipe has changed slightly over the years, the original formula, created by bar owner Victor J. "Trader Vic" Bergeron, included 2 ounces of 17-year-old J. Wray & Nephew rum over shaved ice, ½ ounce Holland Dekuyper orange curaçao, ¼ ounce Trader Vic's rock candy syrup, ½ ounce French Garier orgeat syrup, and the juice of one fresh lime. Done the right way, this tropical drink still lives up to the name "mai tai!" meaning, "out of this world!"

St. Regis Bar. This spacious and comfortable lounge with a gorgeous view of Hanalei Bay offers drinks daily from 3:30 to 11 and a Champagne toast at sunset. Stop by between 5:30 and 10 for *pupu* (hors d'oeuvres), with a popular Hawaiian music and hula show from 6:30 to 9 on Sunday night. ⊠ *Princeville Resort, 5520 Ka Haku Rd., Princeville* ☎ *808/826–9644* ⊕ *www.stregisprinceville.com.*

Tahiti Nui. This venerable and funky institution in sleepy Hanalei still offers its famous luau at 5 on Wednesday evenings, although the bar is the big attraction. Spirits are always high at this popular hangout for locals and visitors alike, which houses live nightly entertainment and Hawaiian slack key guitar music on Friday evenings. Open until 1 am. ⊠ *5-5134 Kuhio Hwy., Hanalei* ☎ *808/826–6277* ⊕ *www.thenui.com.*

THE EAST SIDE

BARS AND CLUBS

Duke's Barefoot Bar. This is one of the liveliest bars in Nawiliwili. Contemporary Hawaiian music is usually performed at this beachside bar and restaurant every day but Tuesday during "Aloha Hours" from 4 to 6 pm. On Thursday, Friday, and Saturday nights, live music is held from 8:30 to 10:30 pm. ⊠ *Kalapaki Beach, 3610 Rice St., Lihue* ☎ *808/246–9599* ⊕ *www.dukeskauai.com.*

Fodor's Choice ★ **Hukilau Lanai.** This open-air bar and restaurant is on the property of the Kauai Coast Resort but operates independently. Trade winds trickle through the modest little bar, which looks out into a coconut grove. If the mood takes you, go on a short walk to the sea, or recline in big, comfortable chairs in Wally's Bar in the lobby while listening to mellow jazz or Hawaiian slack-key guitar. Live music plays from 6 to 9 every night, though the restaurant and bar are closed on Monday. Poolside happy hour runs from 3 to 5. Freshly infused tropical martinis—perhaps locally grown lychee and pineapple or a Big Island vanilla bean infusion—are house favorites. ⊠ *520 Aleka Loop, Wailua (Kauai County)* ☎ *808/822–0600* ⊕ *www.hukilaukauai.com.*

Rob's Good Times Grill. Let loose at this popular restaurant and sports bar, which has live music Monday through Thursday from 4 to 6 pm. Tuesday offers swing dancing from 7:30 to 10 pm, Friday features live music until midnight, Saturday has late-night club dancing with DJ, while Sunday through Thursday go full-on karaoke until closing. ⊠ *4303 Rice St., Lihue* ☎ *808/246–0311* ⊕ *www.kauaisportsbarandgrill.com.*

Trees Lounge. This funky bar and restaurant is popular with a middle-aged crowd. It hosts live music nightly that gets people out on the tiny dance floor. It's behind the Coconut Marketplace and next to the Kauai Coast Resort in Kapaa. Closed Sunday. ⊠ *440 Aleka Pl., Kapaa* ☎ *808/823–0600* ⊕ *www.treesloungekauai.com.*

COFFEEHOUSES

The island has few coffeehouses, and even fewer that are open at night, aside from Starbucks in the Kukui Grove, Kauai Village, and Poipu Shopping Village malls.

EatHealthy Cafe. Nestled in a bamboo forest draped in bougainvillea and flowering vines and hidden from view off the Kuhio Highway is a charming little venue where local musicians perform most evenings. Previously known as Caffé Coco, it now offers vegan fare, including *pupu* (appetizers), entrées, and desserts. It may not have a liquor license, but don't let that stop you from enjoying the entertainment in a pleasant outdoor setting; just bring your own wine or beer. It's open Tuesday through Saturday until 9. ⊠ *4-369 Kuhio Hwy., Kapaa* ☎ *808/822–7990* ⊕ *eathealthykauai.com.*

THE SOUTH SHORE

BARS AND CLUBS

Keoki's Paradise. A young, energetic crowd makes this a lively spot on Friday and Saturday night. When the dining room clears out, there's a bit of a bar scene for singles. Live music every night and two happy hours—one 3–5 pm and the other from 9:30 until closing at 10:30 pm—keep the Bamboo Bar a happening place. ⊠ *Poipu Shopping Village, 2360 Kiahuna Plantation Dr., Poipu* ☎ *808/742–7534* ⊕ *www.keokisparadise.com.*

Lavas at Poipu Beach. This poolside bar and grill is a great place to be on the South Shore to celebrate sunset with a drink, because the ocean view is unsurpassed. Happy hour is from 3 to 5 pm, and there's live music Friday and Sunday night, as well as a hula show on Wednesday from 6 to 7 pm. ⊠ *Sheraton Kauai Resort, 2440 Hoonani Rd., Poipu* ☎ *808/742–1661* ⊕ *www.sheraton-kauai.com/dining.*

Kauai: Undercover Movie Star

Though Kauai has played itself in the movies, most recently starring in *The Descendants* (2011), most of its screen time has been as a stunt double for a number of tropical paradises. The island's remote valleys portrayed Venezuelan jungle in Kevin Costner's *Dragonfly* (2002) and a Costa Rican dinosaur preserve in Steven Spielberg's *Jurassic Park* (1993). Spielberg was no stranger to Kauai, having filmed Harrison Ford's escape via seaplane from Menehune Fishpond in *Raiders of the Lost Ark* (1981).

The fluted cliffs and gorges of Kauai's rugged Napali Coast play the misunderstood beast's island home in *King Kong* (1976), and a jungle dweller of another sort, in *George of the Jungle* (1997), frolicked on Kauai. Harrison Ford returned to the island for 10 weeks during the filming of *Six Days, Seven Nights* (1998), a romantic adventure set in French Polynesia. Part-time Kauai resident Ben Stiller used the island as a stand-in for the jungles of Vietnam in *Tropic Thunder* (2008) and Johnny Depp came here to film some of *Pirates of the Caribbean: On Stranger Tides* (2011). But these are all relatively contemporary movies. What's truly remarkable is that Hollywood discovered Kauai in 1933 with the making of *White Heat,* which was set on a sugar plantation and—like *South Pacific* (also filmed on Kauai)—dealt with an interracial love story.

Then, it was off to the races, as Kauai saw no fewer than a dozen movies filmed on the island in the 1950s, not all of them Oscar contenders. Rita Hayworth starred in *Miss Sadie Thompson* (1953) and no one you'd recognize starred in the tantalizing *She Gods of Shark Reef* (1956).

The movie that is still immortalized on the island in the names of restaurants, real estate offices, a hotel, and even a sushi item is *South Pacific* (1957). (You guessed it, right?) That mythical place called Bali Hai is never far away on Kauai.

In the 1960s Elvis Presley filmed *Blue Hawaii* (1961) and *Girls! Girls! Girls!* (1962) on the island. A local movie tour likes to point out the stain on a hotel carpet where Elvis's jelly doughnut fell.

Kauai has welcomed a long list of Hollywood's A-List: John Wayne in *Donovan's Reef* (1963); Jack Lemmon in *The Wackiest Ship in the Army* (1961); Richard Chamberlain in *The Thorn Birds* (1983); Gene Hackman in *Uncommon Valor* (1983); Danny DeVito and Billy Crystal in *Throw Momma from the Train* (1987); and Dustin Hoffman, Morgan Freeman, Renee Russo, and Cuba Gooding Jr. in *Outbreak* (1995).

Kauai has also appeared on a long list of TV shows and made-for-TV movies, including *Gilligan's Island, Fantasy Island, Starsky & Hutch, Baywatch Hawaii*—even reality TV shows *The Bachelor* and *The Amazing Race 3.*

For the record, just because a movie did some filming here doesn't mean the entire movie was filmed on Kauai. *Honeymoon in Vegas* filmed just one scene here, while the murder mystery *A Perfect Getaway* (2009) was set on the famous Kalalau Trail and featured beautiful Kauaian backdrops but was shot mostly in Puerto Rico.

6

THE WEST SIDE

Port Allen Sunset Grill & Bar. One of the few places for nightlife on the West Side, this casual eatery overlooks the harbor at Port Allen in Eleele and has a friendly bar, with karaoke, that stays open until 10:30 pm. ✉ *4353 Waialo Rd., Eleele* ☎ *808/335–3188.*

PERFORMING ARTS

Although luau remain a primary source of evening fun for families on vacation, there are a handful of other possibilities. There are no traditional dinner cruises, but some boat tours do offer an evening buffet with music along Napali Coast. A few times a year, Women in Theater (WIT), a local women's theater group, performs dinner shows at the Hukilau Lanai in Wailua and the Kauai Community Players offers regular performances at its Puhi Theatrical Warehouse. Kauai Community College Performing Arts Center also draws well-known artists.

VENUES

Kauai Community College Performing Arts Center. This is a main venue for island entertainment, hosting a concert music series, visiting musicians, dramatic productions, and special events such as educational forums. ✉ *3-1901 Kaumualii Hwy., Lihue* ☎ *808/245–8311* ⊕ *www.kauai.hawaii.edu/pac.*

FESTIVAL

FAMILY **Bon Festival.** Traditional Japanese celebrations in honor of loved ones who have died are held from late June through August at various Buddhist temples all over the island. It sounds somber, but it's really a community festival of dance. To top it off, you're welcome to participate. Dance, eat, play carnival games, and hear Japanese *taiko* drumming at one of the Bon folk dances, which take place on temple lawns every Friday and Saturday night from dusk to midnight. Some dancers wear the traditional kimono; others wear board shorts and a tank top. The moves are easy to follow, the event is lively and wholesome, and it's free. A different temple hosts a dance each weekend. Watch the local paper for that week's locale.

LUAU

Although the commercial luau experience is a far cry from the backyard luau thrown by local residents to celebrate a wedding, graduation, or baby's first birthday, they're nonetheless entertaining and a good introduction to the Hawaiian food that isn't widely sold in restaurants. With many, you can watch a roasted pig being carried out of its *imu*, a hole in the ground used for cooking meat with heated stones. Besides the feast, and free mai tais, there's often an exciting dinner show with Polynesian-style music and dancing. It all makes for a fun evening that's suitable for couples, families, and groups, and the informal setting is

Unlike many luau, Luau Kalamaku is organized like a theatrical performance, telling the story of the settlement of the Hawaiian Islands.

conducive to meeting other people. Every luau is different, reflecting the cuisine and tenor of the host facility, so compare prices, menus, and entertainment before making your reservation. Most luau on Kauai are offered only on a limited number of nights each week, so plan ahead to get the luau you want. We tend to prefer those *not* held on resort properties, because they feel a bit more authentic.

The luau shows listed below are our favorites.

Grand Hyatt Kauai Luau. Excellent food and an exciting dance performance characterize this traditional luau buffet, held in a garden setting near majestic Keoneloa Bay. ⊠ *Grand Hyatt Kauai Resort and Spa, 1571 Poipu Rd., Poipu* ☎ 808/240–6456 ⊕ *kauai.grand.hyatt.com/en/hotel/dining/grand-hyatt-kauai-luau.html* ✉ *From $113.*

Luau Kalamaku. Set on historic sugar-plantation land, this luau bills itself as the only "theatrical" luau on Kauai. The luau feast is served buffet style, there's an open bar, and the performers aim to both entertain and educate about Hawaiian culture. Guests sit at tables around a circular stage; tables farther from the stage are elevated, providing unobstructed views. Additional packages offer visitors the opportunity to watch the show only, tour the 35-acre plantation via train, or special romantic perks like a lei greeting and Champagne. ⊠ *3-2087 Kaumualii St., Lihue* ☎ 877/622–1780 ⊕ *www.luaukalamaku.com* ✉ *From $57.*

Fodor's Choice ★ **Smith's Tropical Paradise Luau.** A 30-acre tropical garden on the Wailua River provides the lovely setting for this popular luau, which begins with the traditional blowing of the conch shell and *imu* (pig roast) ceremony, followed by cocktails, an island feast, great music, and an international show in the amphitheater overlooking a torch-lighted lagoon. It's fairly authentic and a better deal than the pricier resort events. ✉ *174 Wailua Rd., Kapaa* ☎ *808/821–6895* ⊕ *www.smiths-kauai.com* 🍴 *$98.*

MUSIC

Check *The Garden Island,* Kauai's newspaper, for outdoor reggae and Hawaiian-music shows.

Hanalei Slack Key Concerts. Relax to the instrumental music form created by Hawaiian *paniolo* (cowboys) in the early 1800s. Shows are Wednesday in Kapaa at All Saints Church and Tuesday at the Princeville Community Center. If you're looking for a scenic setting, head to Hale Halawai Ohana O Hanalei, on Friday and Sunday; it's *mauka* (toward the mountains) down a dirt access road across from St. William's Catholic Church (Malolo Road) and then left down another dirt road. ✉ *5-5299 Kuhio Hwy., Hanalei* ☎ *808/826–1469* ⊕ *www. hawaiianslackkeyguitar.com* 🍴 *From $10.*

Kauai Concert Association. This group offers a seasonal program at the Kauai Community College Performing Arts Center that features well-known classical musicians, including soloists and small ensembles. ✉ *3-1901 Kaumualii Hwy., Lihue* ☎ *808/245–7464* ⊕ *www.kauai-concert.org* 🍴 *From $30.*

THEATER

Kauai Community Players. This talented local group presents plays throughout the year in its intimate theater. ✉ *4411 Kikowaena St., across from Kauai Community College, Lihue* ☎ *808/245–7700* ⊕ *www.kauaicommunityplayers.org* 🍴 *From $10.*

7

SHOPS AND SPAS

Updated by
Joan Conrow

There aren't a lot of shops and spas on Kauai, but what you will find here are a handful of places very much worth checking out for the quality of their selection of items sold and services rendered. Many shops now make an effort to sell as many locally made products as possible. When buying an item, ask where it was made or even who made it.

Often you will find that a product handcrafted on the island may not be that much more expensive than a similar product made overseas. You can also look for the purple "Kauai Made" sticker many merchants display.

Along with one major shopping mall, a few shopping centers, and a growing number of big-box retailers, Kauai has some delightful mom-and-pop shops and specialty boutiques with lots of character. The Garden Isle also has a large and talented community of artisans and fine artists, with galleries all around the island showcasing their creations. You can find many island-made arts and crafts in the small shops, and it's worthwhile to stop in at crafts fairs and outdoor markets to look for bargains and mingle with island residents.

If you're looking for a special memento of your trip that is unique to Kauai County, check out the distinctive Niihau shell lei. The tiny shells are collected from beaches on Kauai and Niihau, pierced, and strung into beautiful necklaces, chokers, and earrings. It's a time-consuming and exacting craft, and these items are much in demand, so don't be taken aback by the high price tags. Those made by Niihau residents will have certificates of authenticity and are worth collecting. You often can find cheaper versions made by non-Hawaiians at crafts fairs.

Kauai is often touted as the healing island, and local spas try hard to fill that role. With the exception of the Hyatt's ANARA Spa, the facilities aren't as posh as some might want, but it's in the human element that Kauai excels. Many island residents are known for their warmth, kindness, and humility, and you can often find all these attributes in the massage therapists and technicians who work long hours at the resort spas. These professionals take their therapeutic mission seriously;

they genuinely want you to experience the island's relaxing, restorative qualities. Private massage services abound on the island, and your spa therapist may offer the same services at a much lower price outside the resort, but if you're looking for a variety of health-and-beauty treatments, an exercise workout, or a full day of pampering, a spa will prove most convenient.

Though most spas on Kauai are associated with resorts, none is restricted to guests only. And there's much by way of healing and wellness to be found on Kauai beyond the traditional spa—or even the day spa. More and more retreat facilities are offering what some would call alternative healing therapies. Others would say there's nothing alternative about them; you can decide for yourself.

Open Hours. Stores are typically open daily from 9 or 10 am to 5 pm, although some stay open until 9 pm, especially those near resorts. Don't be surprised if the posted hours don't match the actual hours of operation at the smaller shops, where owners may be fairly casual about keeping to a regular schedule.

SHOPS

THE NORTH SHORE

7

The North Shore has three main shopping areas, all in towns off the highway. Hanalei has two shopping centers directly across from each other, which offer more than you would expect in a remote, relaxed town. Princeville Shopping Center is a bustling little mix of businesses, necessities, and some unique, often pricey, shops. Kilauea is a bit more sprawled out and offers a charming, laid-back shopping scene with a neighborhood feel.

AREAS AND SHOPPING CENTERS

Ching Young Village. This popular shopping center has its roots in the Chinese immigrants who came to Hawaii in the early 19th century. Hanalei's only full-service grocery store is here along with a number of other shops useful to locals and visitors, such as a music shop selling ukulele and CDs, jewelry stores, art galleries, a surf shop, variety store, and several restaurants. ⊠ *5-5190 Kuhio Hwy., near mile marker 2, Hanalei.*

Hanalei Center. Once an old Hanalei schoolhouse, the Hanalei Center is now a bevy of boutiques and restaurants. You can dig through '40s and '50s vintage memorabilia, find Polynesian artifacts, or search for that unusual gift. Buy beach gear as well as island wear and women's clothing. Find a range of fine jewelry and paper art jewelry. There are a full-service salon and a yoga studio in the two-story modern addition to the center, which also houses a small natural foods grocery. ⊠ *5-5161 Kuhio Hwy., near mile marker 2, Hanalei* ☎ *808/826–7677.*

Princeville Shopping Center. The big draws at this small center are a full-service grocery store and a hardware store, but there's also a fun toy store, bar, mailing service, a very nice sandal boutique, women's clothing, and an ice-cream shop. This is also the last stop for gas and banking when you're heading to the North Shore. ✉ *5-4280 Kuhio Hwy., near mile marker 28, Princeville* ☎ *808/826–9497* ⊕ *www.princevillecenter.com.*

GIFTS

Kong Lung Co. Sometimes called the Gump's of Kauai, this gift store sells elegant clothing, exotic glassware, ethnic books, gifts, and artwork—all very lovely and expensive. The shop is housed in a beautiful 1892 stone building in the heart of Kilauea. It's the showpiece of the pretty little Kong Lung Center, where everything from handmade soaps to hammocks can be found. A great bakery and pizzeria round out the offerings, along with an exhibit of historical photos. ✉ *2484 Keneke St., Kilauea* ☎ *808/828–1822* ⊕ *www.konglungkauai.com.*

Village Variety Store. How about a fun beach towel for the folks back home? That's just one of the gifts you can find here, along with shell lei, Kauai shirts, macadamia nuts, and other souvenirs at low prices. The store also has many small, useful items such as envelopes, housewares, and toiletries. ✉ *Ching Young Village, 5-5190 Kuhio Hwy., Hanalei* ☎ *808/826–6077.*

JEWELRY

Crystal & Gems Gallery. Sparkling crystals of every shape, size, type, and color, as well as jewelry and paintings, are sold in this small, amply stocked boutique. The knowledgeable staff can help you choose crystals for specific healing purposes. ✉ *4489 Aku Rd., Hanalei* ☎ *808/826–9304* ⊕ *www.crystals-gems.com.*

THE EAST SIDE

KAPAA AND WAILUA

Kapaa is the most heavily populated area on Kauai, so it's not surprising that it has the most diverse shopping opportunities on the island. Unlike the North Shore's retail scene, shops here are not neatly situated in centers; they are spread out along a long stretch of road, with many local retail gems tucked away that you may not find if you're in a rush.

AREAS AND SHOPPING CENTERS

Kauai Village Shopping Center. The buildings of this Kapaa shopping village are in the style of a 19th-century plantation town. **ABC Discount Store** sells sundries; **Safeway** carries groceries and alcoholic beverages; **Papaya's** has health foods and a minimalist café. There's also a **Ross Dress for Less** and a **UPS store**. Other shops sell jewelry, art, and home decor. Restaurants include Chinese, and Vietnamese options, and there's also a **Starbucks** and two bars. ✉ *4-831 Kuhio Hwy., Kapaa* ☎ *808/822–3777.*

Kinipopo Shopping Village. Kinipopo is a tiny little center on Kuhio Highway. **Korean Barbeque** fronts the highway, as does **Goldsmith's Kauai Gallery**, which sells handcrafted Hawaiian-style gold jewelry. **Monico's** has authentic Mexican food, and is the center's biggest draw. There's also a clothing shop, beauty salon, bakery, cake shop, and a healing-arts center. ✉ *4-356 Kuhio Hwy., Kapaa* ⊕ *www.kinipopovillage.com.*

Waipouli Town Center. Foodland is the focus of this small retail plaza, one of three shopping centers anchored by grocery stores in Kapaa. You can also find a **McDonald's, Fun Factory** video arcade, and **The Coffee Bean**, along with a local-style restaurant. ✉ *4-771 Kuhio Hwy., Kapaa.*

CLOTHING

A Ell Atelier. Clothing designer Angelique Ell sells everything from custom wedding gowns to men's aloha shirts to children's clothing, using all-natural fabrics. Home linens are also sold in this distinctive boutique, as are soaps, jewelry, candles, handbags, and artwork by local artists. ✉ *4–1320 Kuhio Hwy., Kapaa* ☎ *808/212–7550* ⊕ *www.aelldesign.com.*

Deja Vu Surf Hawaii: Kapaa. This family operation has a great assortment of surf wear and clothes for outdoors fanatics, including tank tops, visors, swimwear, and Kauai-style T-shirts. They also carry body boards and water-sports accessories. Good deals can be found at sidewalk sales. ✉ *4-1419 Kuhio Hwy., Kapaa* ☎ *808/822–4401* ⊕ *www.dejavusurf.com.*

Divine Planet. This friendly, hip boutique sells unusual merchandise from India and other exotic Asian locales. Dangly earrings, loose, natural clothing, beads, campy home furnishings, and other eclectic offerings make this fun shop worth a stop. If you miss it here, you can check out the Hanalei location at Ching Young Village, 5–1590 Kuhio Highway. ✉ *4-831 Kuhio Hwy., Kapaa* ☎ *808/821–1835* ⊕ *www.divine-planet.com.*

Marta's Boat. This charming boutique sells handmade, one-of-a-kind clothing by husband-and-wife team Ambrose and Marta Curry. He creates silk-screen art with nontoxic paint on fabric in his studio next door; then she cuts and sews the fabric into bags and clothing for men, women, and children. ✉ *4-770 Kuhio Hwy., Kapaa* ☎ *808/822–3926.*

GALLERIES

ALOHA Images. ALOHA stands for "Affordable Location of Original Hawaiian Art." A self-proclaimed "candy store for art lovers," it has a large selection of Hawaiian-theme art, ranging from $75 up to the rare $15,000, and owner Ray offers layaway plans to those who request one. ✉ *4504 Kukui St., Kapaa* ☎ *808/631–8026* ⊕ *www.alohaimages.com.*

Kela's Glass Gallery. The colorful vases, bowls, and other fragile items sold in this distinctive gallery, now expanded into a new, larger space, are definitely worth viewing if you appreciate quality handmade glass art. It's expensive, but if something catches your eye, they'll happily pack it for safe transport home. They also ship worldwide. ✉ *4-1400 Kuhio Hwy., Kapaa* ☎ *808/822–4527* ⊕ *www.glass-art.com.*

GIFTS

Pagoda. Pagoda is a tiny shop big on exceptional antiques, Hawaiiana, and gifts. The owner, Liane, has been collecting rare finds most of her life and now has a place to showcase them. ✉ *4-369 Kuhio Hwy., Kapaa* ☎ *808/821–2172* ⊕ *www.pagodakauai.com* ☉ *Closed Sun. and Mon.*

Vicky's Fabric Shop. This small store is packed full of tropical and Hawaiian prints, silks, slinky rayons, soft cottons, and other fine fabrics. A variety of sewing patterns and notions are featured as well, making it a must-stop for any seamstress, and a great place to buy unique island-made gifts. Check out the one-of-a-kind selection of purses, aloha wear, and other quality hand-sewn items. ⊠ *4-1326 Kuhio Hwy., Kapaa* 🕾 *808/822–1746* ⊕ *www.vickysfabrics.com* ☉ *Closed Sun.*

HOME DECOR

Otsuka's. Family-owned Otsuka's has a large clientele of visitors, who appreciate the wide selection of unique furniture, artwork, candles, tropical-print pillows, accessories, and knickknacks that can be found here. ⊠ *4-1624 Kuhio Hwy., Kapaa* 🕾 *808/822–7766* ⊕ *www.otsukas.com* ☉ *Closed Sun. and Mon.*

JEWELRY

Jim Saylor Jewelers. Jim Saylor and his team of jewelers have been designing beautiful keepsakes for more than 40 years on Kauai. Gems from around the world, including black pearls, diamonds, and more, appear in his unusual settings. ⊠ *4-1318 Kuhio Hwy., Kapaa* 🕾 *808/822–3591* ⊕ *www.jimsaylorjewelers.com* ☉ *Closed Sun.*

MARKET

Kauai Products Fair. Open daily, the Kauai Products Fair outdoor market features an assortment of stalls selling fresh produce, tropical plants and flowers, clothing, aloha wear, jewelry, and gifts. ⊠ *4-1613 Kuhio Hwy., Kapaa* 🕾 *808/246–0988.*

LIHUE

Lihue is the business area on Kauai, as well as home to all the big-box stores (Costco, Home Depot, Walmart, and Big K) and the only real mall. Do not mistake this town as lacking in rare finds, however. Lihue is steeped in history and diversity while simultaneously welcoming new trends and establishments.

AREAS AND SHOPPING CENTERS

Kilohana Plantation. This 16,000-square-foot Tudor mansion contains art galleries, a jewelry store, and the restaurant Gaylord's. Kilohana Plantation is filled with antiques from its original owner, and the restored outbuildings house a craft shop and a Hawaiian-style clothing shop. Train rides on a restored railroad are available, with knowledgeable guides reciting the history of sugar on Kauai. The site is also now the home of Luau Kalamaku and Koloa Rum Company. ⊠ *3-2087 Kaumualii Hwy., Lihue* 🕾 *808/245–5608* ⊕ *www.kilohanakauai.com.*

Kukui Grove Center. This is Kauai's only true mall. Besides Kmart, anchor tenants are Longs Drugs, Macy's, Ross, Pier One Imports, Kukui Grove Cinemas, and Times Supermarket. The mall's stores offer women's clothing, surf wear, art, toys, athletic shoes, jewelry, a hair salon, and locally made crafts. Restaurants range from fast food and sandwiches to sushi and Korean, with a popular Starbucks and Jamba Juice. The center stage often has entertainment, especially on Friday night, and there is a farmers' market on Monday. ⊠ *3-2600 Kaumualii Hwy., Lihue* 🕾 *808/245–7784* ⊕ *www.kukuigrovecenter.com.*

The gift shop at the Kauai Museum is one of the best places on the island to find reasonably priced local crafts and books.

CLOTHING

Hilo Hattie, The Store of Hawaii. This is the big name in aloha wear for tourists throughout the Islands, and Hilo Hattie, the Store of Hawaii has only one store on Kauai. Located a mile from Lihue Airport, come here for cool, comfortable aloha shirts and muumuu in bright floral prints, as well as other souvenirs. Also, be sure to check out the line of Hawaii-inspired home furnishings. ✉ *3252 Kuhio Hwy., Lihue* ☎ *808/245–3404* ⊕ *www.hilohattie.com.*

FOOD SPECIALTIES

Kauai Fruit and Flower Company. At this shop near Lihue and five minutes away from the airport, you can buy fresh Hawaii Gold pineapple, sugarcane, ginger, tropical flowers, coconuts, local jams, jellies, and honey, plus papayas, bananas, and mangoes from Kauai. Some of the fruit at Kauai Fruit and Flower Company cannot be shipped out of state. ✉ *3-4684 Kuhio Hwy., Lihue* ☎ *808/245–1814* ⊕ *www.kauaifruit.com* ⊙ *Closed Sat. afternoon and Sun.*

GIFTS

Fodor's Choice ★ **Kapaia Stitchery.** Hawaiian quilts made by hand and machine, a beautiful selection of fabrics, quilting kits, handmade aloha shirts, and unique fabric arts fill Kapaia Stitchery, a cute little red plantation-style building. There are also many locally made gifts and quilts for sale in this locally owned store. The staff is friendly and helpful, even though a steady stream of customers keeps them busy. ✉ *3-3551 Kuhio Hwy., Lihue* ☎ *808/245–2281* ⊕ *kapaia-stitchery.com* ⊙ *Closed Sun.*

Fodor's Choice ★ **Kauai Museum.** The gift shop at the museum sells some fascinating books, maps, and prints, as well as lovely authentic Niihau shell jewelry, handwoven *lau hala* hats, and koa wood bowls. Also featured at the Kauai Museum are tapa cloth, authentic *tikis* (hand-carved wooden figurines), as well as other good-quality local crafts and books at reasonable prices. ✉ *4428 Rice St., Lihue* ☎ *808/245–6931* ⊕ *www.kauaimuseum.org* ⊙ *Closed Sun.*

HOME DECOR

Two Frogs Hugging. At Two Frogs Hugging, you'll find lots of interesting housewares, accessories, knickknacks, and hand-carved collectibles, as well as baskets and furniture from Indonesia, the Philippines, and China. The shop occupies expansive quarters in the Lihue Industrial Park. ✉ *3094 Aukele St., Lihue* ☎ *808/246–8777* ⊕ *www.twofrogshugging.com* ⊙ *Closed Sun.*

MARKETS

FAMILY

Fodor's Choice

★

Kauai Community Market. This is the biggest and best farmers' market on Kauai, sponsored by the Kauai Farm Bureau at the community college in Lihue, and held on Saturday mornings. You'll find fresh produce and flowers, as well as packaged products like breads, goat cheese, pasta, honey, coffee, soaps, lotions, and more, all made locally. Seating areas are available to grab a snack or lunch from the food booths and lunch wagons set up here. ✉ *3-1901 Kaumualii Hwy., Lihue* ☎ *808/855–5429* ⊕ *www.kauaicommunitymarket.com.*

THE SOUTH SHORE

The South Shore, like the North Shore, has convenient shopping clusters, including Poipu Shopping Village and the upscale The Shops at Kukuiula. There are many high-priced shops, but some unique clothing and gift selections.

AREAS AND SHOPPING CENTERS

FAMILY

Poipu Shopping Village. Convenient to nearby hotels and condos on the South Shore, the two dozen shops at Poipu Shopping Village sell resort wear, gifts, souvenirs, and art. This complex also has a few food choices, from hot-dog stands to casual restaurants. There are a few upscale and appealing jewelry stores and fun clothing stores. Watch a traditional hula show in the open-air courtyard Monday and Thursday at 5 pm. ✉ *2360 Kiahuna Plantation Dr., Poipu* ☎ *808/742–2831* ⊕ *www.poipushoppingvillage.com.*

The Shops at Kukuiula. This is the South Shore's newest shopping center, with chic, high-end shops, exclusive galleries, several great restaurants, and a gourmet grocery store. Check out the Kauai Culinary Market on Wednesday from 3:30 to 6, to see cooking demonstrations, listen to live Hawaiian music, visit the beer and wine garden, and browse wares from local vendors. This attractive open-air, plantation-style center is just beyond the roundabout as you enter Poipu. ✉ *2829 Kalanikaumaka St., Poipu* ☎ *808/742–9545* ⊕ *www.theshopsatkukuiula.com.*

GALLERIES

Fodor's Choice

★

Galerie 103. This gallery sells art, but the owners want you to experience it as well. Sparse and dramatic, the main room at Galerie 103 consists of concrete floors and walls of featured pieces, from internationally acclaimed artists and local Kauai ones. Most of the artwork is contemporary or modern with a focus on nature. ✉ 2829 Kalanikaumaka Rd., Koloa ☎ 808/742–0103 ⊕ www.galerie103.com ⊙ Closed Sun. and Mon.

Halelea Gallery. In addition to offering original works by Kauai artists and others, this stylish gallery doubles as a boutique which sells a unique sampling of clothing, jewelry, and gifts made by local designers. The second branch in Hanalei has a different selection. ✉ 2829 Kalanikaumaka Rd., Suite K, Koloa ☎ 808/742–9525 ⊕ www.haleleagallery.com.

THE WEST SIDE

The West Side is years behind the South Shore in development, offering minimal, simple shops with authentic local flavor.

AREAS AND SHOPPING CENTERS

Eleele Shopping Center. Kauai's West Side has a scattering of stores, including those at this no-frills strip mall. It has several banks, a hardware store, laundromat, and a hair salon and it's a good place to rub elbows with local folk at Longs Drugs or Times Big Save grocery store. There's a McDonald's, Subway, and a few little local eateries. ✉ 4469 Waialo Rd., Eleele ☎ 808/245–7238 ⊕ www.eleeleshoppingcenter.com.

Waimea Canyon Plaza. As the last stop for supplies before heading up to Waimea Canyon, Waimea Canyon Plaza has a Menehune Food Mart with limited groceries, snacks, beverages, fresh and prepared local foods, souvenirs, and island-made gifts for all ages. ✉ 8171 Kekaha Rd., at Rte. 50, Kekaha ☎ 808/337–1335.

BOOKS

Talk Story Bookstore. Located in a historic building in quiet Hanapepe town, this cozy bookstore with its friendly cat is the only bookstore on Kauai. It becomes a gathering place on busy Friday evenings during the weekly art nights when local authors sign their books inside while outside there's live music and food trucks for treats. New, used, and out-of-print books are sold here. ✉ 3785 Hanapepe Rd., Hanapepe ☎ 808/335–6469 ⊕ www.talkstorybookstore.com.

FLOWERS

Kalani Tropicals. Kauai-based Kalani Tropicals will take your order online or by phone and ship heliconia, anthuriums, ginger, and other tropicals as cut flowers or fashioned into distinctive arrangements. ☎ 808/823–6547 ⊕ kalanitropicals.com ⊙ Closed Sun.

FOOD SPECIALTIES

Kauai Coffee Visitor Center and Museum. Kauai produces more coffee than any other island in the state. The local product can be purchased from grocery stores or here at the Kauai Coffee Visitor Center and Museum, where a sampling of the nearly two dozen coffees is available. Be sure to try some of the estate-roasted varieties. ✉ 870 Halawili Rd., off Rte. 50, Kalaheo ☎ 808/335–0813, 800/545–8605 ⊕ www.kauaicoffee.com.

7

SPAS

THE NORTH SHORE

Fodor's Choice ★ **Halelea Spa.** This superb spa at the St. Regis Princeville Resort is indeed a House of Joy, as its Hawaiian name translates, so long as you are prepared to pay handsomely for services. Opened in 2009, the 11,000-square-foot Halelea Spa transports users to a place of tranquility. The spa's 12 luxurious treatment rooms afford a subdued indoor setting outmatched only by the professional service. Take advantage of the dedicated couple's room and enjoy a hot *pohaku* (stone) massage. Follow that with a few hours sipping tea in the relaxation lounge, sweating in the sauna, and rinsing in an overhead rain shower. There is a qualified wellness consultant, and spa programs are inspired by Native Hawaiian healing rituals. ⊠ *The St. Regis Princeville Resort, 5520 Ka Haku Rd., Princeville* ☎ *877/787–3447, 808/826–9644* ⊕ *www.stregisprinceville.com* ✉ *Massage from $185.*

Hanalei Day Spa. As you travel beyond tony Princeville, life slows down. The single-lane bridges may be one reason. Another is the Hanalei Day Spa, an open-air, thatched-roof, Hawaiian-style hut nestled just off the beach on the grounds of Hanalei Colony Resort in Haena. Though this no-frills day spa offers facials, waxing, wraps, scrubs, and the like, its specialty is massage: Ayurveda, Zen Shiatsu, Swedish, four-handed, and even a baby massage (and lesson for Mom, to boot). ⊠ *Hanalei Colony Resort, Rte. 560, Haena* ✛ *6 miles past Hanalei* ☎ *808/826–6621* ⊕ *www.hanaleidayspa.com* ✉ *Massage from $110* ☉ *Closed Sun. and Mon.*

THE EAST SIDE

Alexander Day Spa & Salon at the Kauai Marriott. This sister spa of Alexander Simson's Beverly Hills spa focuses on body care rather than exercise, so don't expect any fitness equipment or exercise classes, just pampering and beauty treatments. The Alexander Day Spa & Salon at the Kauai Marriott is a sunny, pleasant facility. Massages are available in treatment rooms, your room, and on the beach, although the beach locale isn't as private as you might imagine. Wedding-day and custom spa packages can be arranged. ⊠ *Kauai Marriott Resort & Beach Club, 3610 Rice St., Suite 9A, Lihue* ☎ *808/246–4918* ⊕ *www.alexanderspa.com* ✉ *Massage from $130.*

Angeline's Muolaulani Wellness Center. It doesn't get more authentic, or rustic, than this. In the mid-1980s Aunty Angeline Locey opened her Anahola home to offer traditional Hawaiian healing practices. Though she passed on in 2017, her son and granddaughter carry on the tradition. There's a two-hour treatment ($175) that starts with a steam, followed by a sea-salt-and-clay body scrub and a four-handed massage. The real treat, however, is relaxing on Aunty's open-air garden deck. Hot-stone lomi is also available. The Center's mission is to promote a healthy body image; as such, au naturel is an option here, but if you're nudity-shy, you can wear a sarong. Detailed directions are given when you book a treatment. ■TIP→ **This is cash only and you need to bring your own towel.** ✉ *Kamalomaloo Pl., Anahola* ☎ *808/822–3235* ⊕ *www.angelineslomikauai.com.*

Golden Lotus Studio. This small studio, tucked off the main road in Kapaa, offers a variety of yoga and dance classes daily, including heated power vinyasa yoga and aerial yoga. Various types of massage are available by appointment, including lomilomi, Ayurveda, deep tissue, and Thai yoga style, starting at $95 an hour. Check their website for special events and workshops, offered frequently. ✉ *4-941A Kuhio Hwy., Kapaa* ☎ *808/823–9810* ⊕ *www.goldenlotuskauai.org.*

TRY A LOMI MASSAGE

Living in ancient Hawaii wasn't sunbathing and lounging at the beach. Growing taro was hard work, as was building canoes, fishing for dinner, and pounding tapa for clothing, sails, and blankets. Enter *lomilomi*—Hawaiian-style massage. It's often described as being more vigorous, more rhythmic, and faster than Swedish massage, and it incorporates more elbow and forearm work. It might even involve chanting, music, and four hands (in other words, two people).

THE SOUTH SHORE

Fodor's Choice ★ **ANARA Spa.** The luxurious ANARA Spa has all the equipment and services you expect from a top resort spa, along with a pleasant, professional staff. Best of all, it has indoor and outdoor areas that capitalize on the tropical locale and balmy weather, further distinguishing it from the Marriott and St. Regis spas. Its 46,500 square feet of space includes the lovely Garden Treatment Village, an open-air courtyard with private thatched-roof huts, each featuring a relaxation area, misters, and open-air shower in a tropical setting. Ancient Hawaiian remedies and local ingredients are featured in many of the treatments, such as a pineapple-papaya body hydration, and a traditional lomilomi massage. The open-air lava-rock showers are wonderful, introducing many guests to the delightful island practice of showering outdoors. The spa, which includes a full-service salon, adjoins the Hyatt's legendary swimming pool. ✉ *Hyatt Regency Kauai Resort and Spa, 1571 Poipu Rd., Poipu* ☎ *808/240–6440* ⊕ *www.anaraspa.com* 🖎 *Massages from $180.*

THE WEST SIDE

Sweet Lomi Massage. Sweet Lomi Massage offers a variety of services, from Swedish and hot stone massages to an especially good reflexology treatment. The two-hour Sweet Lomi Blend includes a variety of massage techniques and is truly divine. ✉ *4492 Moana Rd., Waimea (Kauai County)* ☎ *808/651–8857* ⊕ *www.sweetlomi.com* 🖎 *Massages from $100* ⊗ *Closed Sun. and Mon.*

8

WATER SPORTS
AND TOURS

Updated by
Joan Conrow

Ancient Hawaiians were water-sports fanatics—they invented surfing, after all—and that propensity hasn't strayed far from today's mind-set. Even if you're not into water sports or sports in general, there's only a slim chance that you'll leave this island without getting out on the ocean, as Kauai's top attraction—Napali Coast—is something not to be missed.

For those who can't pack enough snorkeling, fishing, body boarding, or surfing time into a vacation, Kauai has it all—everything except parasailing, that is, as it's illegal to do it here (though not on Maui, the Big Island, or Oahu). If you need to rent gear for any of these activities, you'll find plenty of places with large selections at reasonable prices. And no matter what part of the island you're staying on, you'll have several options for choice spots to enjoy playing in the water.

One thing to note, and we can't say this enough—the waters off the coast of Kauai have strong currents and can be unpredictable, so always err on the side of caution and know your limits. Follow the tagline repeated by the island's lifeguards—"When in doubt, don't go out."

BOAT TOURS

Deciding to see Napali Coast by boat is an easy decision. Choosing the outfitter to go with is not. There are numerous boat-tour operators to choose from, and, quite frankly, they all do a good job. Before you even start thinking about whom to go out with, answer these three questions: What kind of boat do I prefer? Where am I staying? Do I want to go in the morning or afternoon? Once you settle on these three, you can easily zero in on the tour outfitter.

First, the boat. The most important thing is to match your personality and that of your group with the personality of the boat. If you like thrills and adventure, the rubber, inflatable rafts—often called Zodiacs, which Jacques Cousteau made famous and which the U.S. Coast Guard uses—will entice you. They're fast, likely to leave you drenched and windswept, and quite bouncy. If you prefer a smoother, more leisurely ride, then the large catamarans are the way to go. The next boat choice is size. Both the rafts and catamarans come in small and large. Again—think smaller, more adventurous; larger, more leisurely. ■TIP➜ **Do not choose a smaller boat because you think there will be fewer people. There might be fewer people, but you'll be jammed together sitting atop strangers.** If you prefer privacy over socializing, go with a larger boat, so you'll have more room to spread out. The smaller boats will also take you along the coast at a higher rate of speed, making photo opportunities a bit more challenging. One advantage to smaller boats, however, is that—depending on ocean conditions—some may slip into a sea cave or two. If that sounds interesting to you, call the outfitter and ask their policy on entering sea caves. Some won't, no matter the conditions, because they consider the caves sacred or because they don't want to cause any environmental damage.

Boats leave from three points around the island (Hanalei, Port Allen, and Waimea), and all head to the same spot: Napali Coast. Here's the inside skinny on which is the best: if you're staying on the North Shore, choose to depart out of the North Shore. If you're staying anywhere else, depart out of the West Side. It's that easy. Sure, the North Shore is closer to Napali Coast; however, you'll pay more for less overall time. The West Side boat operators may spend more time getting to Napali Coast; however, they'll spend about the same amount of time along Napali, plus you'll pay less. Finally, you'll also have to decide whether you want to go on a morning tour, which includes a deli lunch and a stop for snorkeling, or an afternoon tour, which does not always stop to snorkel but does include a sunset over the ocean. The morning tours with snorkeling are more popular with families and those who love dolphins, as the animals enjoy the "waves" created by the front of the catamarans and might just escort you down the coast. The winter months will also be a good chance to spot some whales breaching, though surf is much rougher along Napali. You don't have to be an expert snorkeler or even have any prior experience, but if it is your first time, note that although there will be some snorkeling instruction, there might not be much. Hawaiian spinner dolphins are so plentiful in the mornings that some tour companies guarantee you'll see them, though you won't get in the water and swim with them. The afternoon tours are more popular with nonsnorkelers—obviously—and photographers interested in capturing the setting sunlight on the coast. ■TIP➜ **No matter which tour you select, book it online whenever possible.** Most companies offer Web specials, usually around $10 to $20 off per person.

8

CATAMARAN TOURS

Fodor'sChoice
★ **Blue Dolphin Charters.** Blue Dolphin operates 65-foot sailing (rarely raised and always motoring) catamarans designed with three decks of spacious seating with great visibility, as well as motorized rafts. ■TIP➜ **The lower deck is best for shade seekers.** The most popular is a daylong tour of Napali Coast, which includes a detour across

the channel to Niihau for snorkeling and diving. Morning snorkel tours of Napali include a deli lunch. Sunset sightseeing tours include a Hawaiian-style buffet. North Shore and South Shore rafting tours are also available, as are daily sportfishing charters of four to eight hours for no more than six guests. Blue Dolphin promises dolphin sightings and the best mai tais "off the island." Book online for cheaper deals on every tour offered. ⊠ *4353 Waialo Rd., No. 2-6B7B, Eleele* ☎ *808/335–5553, 877/511–1311* ⊕ *www.kauaiboats.com* ⤳ *From $100; 2-hr whale-watching/sunset tours, winter only, $65.*

> ### BOAT TOUR CHECKLIST
>
> ■ Swimsuit
>
> ■ Sunscreen
>
> ■ Hat
>
> ■ Sunglasses
>
> ■ Beach towel
>
> ■ Light jacket
>
> ■ Camera (in waterproof bag, just in case)
>
> ■ Motion sickness meds (take well before departure)
>
> ■ Change of clothes (postcruise)

FAMILY
Fodor's Choice
★

Capt. Andy's Sailing Adventures. Departing from Port Allen and running 55- and 60-foot sailing catamarans, as well as 24-foot inflatables out of Kikiaoloa Harbor in Kekaha, Capt. Andy's offers something for every taste, from raft expeditions to Hawaiian yachting. They have several lunch and snorkeling packages and four-hour sunset tours along Napali Coast. The Zodiac rafts have hydrophones to hear whales and other underwater sounds. The longtime Kauai company also operates a snorkel barbecue sail and dinner sunset sail aboard its *Southern Star* yacht, originally built for private charters. This boat now operates as host for two of Capt. Andy's daily sailing trips for an upgraded feel. For a shorter adventure, they have a two-hour sunset sail, embarking out of Kukuiula Harbor in Poipu along the South Shore—with live Hawaiian music—on Thursday. ■ TIP➔ **If the winds and swells are up on the North Shore, this is usually a good choice—especially if you're prone to seasickness.** This is the only tour-boat operator that allows infants on board—but only on the two-hour trip. Note, if you have reservations for the shorter tour, you'll check in at their Kukuiula Harbor office. ⊠ *4353 Waiola Rd., Suite 1A-2A, Eleele* ☎ *808/335–6833* ⊕ *www.napali.com* ⤳ *From $89, discounts for online booking.*

Captain Sundown. Sundown has one of the few permits to sail from Hanalei Bay and operates the only sailing catamaran there. Captain Bob has been cruising Napali Coast since 1971—six days a week, sometimes twice a day. (And right alongside Captain Bob is his son, Captain Larry.) To say he knows the area is an understatement. Here's the other good thing about this tour: they take a maximum of 17 passengers on the 40-foot boat. The breathtaking views of the waterfall-laced mountains behind Hanalei and Haena start immediately, and then it's around Kee Beach and the magic of Napali Coast unfolds before you. All the while, the captains are trolling for fish, and if they catch any, guests get to reel 'em in. Afternoon sunset sails (summertime only) run three hours and check in around 3 pm—these are BYOB. Cancellations due to rough surf are more frequent in winter. ✉ *5-5134 Kuhio Hwy., Hanalei* ☏ *808/826–5585* ⊕ *www.captain-sundown.com* ✉ *From $165.*

Catamaran Kahanu. Hawaiian-owned and -operated, Catamaran Kahanu has been in business since 1985 and runs a 40-foot power catamaran with 18- to 20-passenger seating. It offers seasonal whale-watching, snorkeling, and sunset cruises, ranging from two to five hours, and departs from Port Allen. The five-hour Na Pali Coast tour includes snorkeling at Nualolo Kai, plus a deli lunch and soft drinks. The four-hour afternoon tour takes in the sunset and includes a hot dinner. The boat is smaller than most

BEST BOAT TOURS
Best for snorkeling: Z-Tourz
Best for romance: Capt. Andy's Poipu Sail
Best for thrill seekers: Napali Explorer (Zodiac 1)
Best for mai tais: Blue Dolphin Charters
Best for pregnant women: Capt. Andy's
Best for charters: Captain Sundown
Best for price: Napali Riders

and may feel a tad crowded, but the tour feels more personal, with a laid-back, *ohana* (family) style. Guests can witness the ancient cultural practice of coconut weaving or other Hawaiian craft demonstrations on board. There's no alcohol allowed. ✉ *4353 Waialo Rd., near Port Allen Marina Center, Eleele* ☏ *808/645–6176, 888/213–7711* ⊕ *www.catamarankahanu.com* ✉ *From $75.*

HoloHolo Charters. Choose between the 50-foot catamaran called *Leila* for a morning snorkel sail to Napali Coast, or the 65-foot *HoloHolo* seven-hour catamaran trip to the "forbidden island" of Niihau. Both boats have large cabins and little outside seating. HoloHolo also offers a four-hour seasonal voyage of Napali from Hanalei Bay on its rigid-hull inflatable rafts, specifically for diving and snorkeling. Originators of the Niihau tour, HoloHolo Charters built their 65-foot powered catamaran with a wide beam to reduce side-to-side motion, and twin 425 HP turbo diesel engines specifically for the 17-mile channel crossing to Niihau. It's the only outfitter running daily Niihau tours. The *HoloHolo* also embarks on a daily sunset and sightseeing tour of Napali Coast. *Leila* can hold 37 passengers, while her big brother can take a maximum of 49. Check-in is at Port Allen Marina Center. ✉ *4353 Waialo Rd., Suite 5A, Eleele* ☏ *808/335–0815, 800/848–6130* ⊕ *www.holoholocharters.com* ✉ *From $70.*

Kauai Sea Tours. This company operates the *Lucky Lady,* a 60-foot sailing catamaran designed almost identically to that of Blue Dolphin Charters—with all the same benefits—including great views and spacious seating. Snorkeling tours anchor near Makole (based on the captain's discretion). If snorkeling isn't your thing, try the four-hour sunset tour, with beer, wine, mai tais, *pupu* (appetizers), and a hot buffet dinner or a two-hour seasonal whale-watching cruise. Tours of Napali, one with a beach landing, are offered on inflatable rafts. Check in at Port Allen Marina Center. ✉ *4353 Waialo Rd., Eleele* ☏ *808/335–5309, 800/733–7997* ⊕ *www.kauaiseatours.com* ✉ *From $79.*

If you choose to sail by yourself in Kauai, be prepared for strong currents and know your limits.

Liko Kauai Cruises. There are many things to like about Liko Kauai Cruises. The 49-foot powered cat will enter sea caves, ocean conditions permitting. Sometimes, even Captain Liko himself—a Native Hawaiian—still takes the captain's helm. We particularly like the layout of his boat—most of the seating is in the bow, so there's good visibility. A maximum of 32 passengers make each trip, which last five hours and include snorkeling, food, and soft drinks. Trips usually depart out of Kikiaola Harbor in Waimea, a bit closer to Napali Coast than those leaving from Port Allen. ⊠ *4516 Alawai Rd., Waimea (Kauai County)* ☎ *808/338–0333, 888/732–5456* ⊕ *www.liko-kauai.com* ✉ *$135.*

Napali Catamaran. One of the few tour groups departing Hanalei, this company, formerly known as Whitey's, has been around since 1973. Once on board, it takes about five minutes before you're witnessing the magnificence of Napali Coast. Taking a maximum of 16 passengers, its new 35-foot powered catamaran is small enough—and with no mast, short enough—to dip into sea caves. Between March and October, they run two four-hour snorkeling tours per day, stopping at the best snorkeling site along Napali—Nualolo Kai. They've also added a two-hour evening cruise along the coast. The rate's are a bit pricey, but the four-hour tour includes a deli-style lunch. ⊠ *Ching Young Village, 5-5190 Kuhio Hwy., Hanalei* ☎ *808/826–6853, 866/255–6853* ⊕ *www.napalicatamaran.com* ✉ *From $179.*

BOAT TOUR WEATHER CANCELLATIONS

If it's raining where you're staying, that doesn't mean it's raining over the water, so don't shy away from a boat tour. Besides, it's not the rain that should concern you—it's the wind and waves. Especially from due north and south, wind creates surface chop and makes for rough riding. Larger craft are designed to handle winter's ocean swells, however, so unless monster waves are out there, your tour should depart without a hitch. If the water is too rough, your boat captain may reroute to calmer waters. It's a tough call to make, but your comfort and safety are always the foremost factor. ■TIP➡ In winter months, North Shore departures are canceled much more often than those departing the West Side. This is because the waves are often too big for the boats to leave Hanalei Bay. If you want the closest thing to a guarantee of seeing Napali Coast in winter, choose a West Side outfitter. Oh, and even if your tour boat says it cruises the "entire Napali," keep in mind that "ocean conditions permitting" is always implied.

RAFT TOURS

Capt. Andy's Raft Expeditions. Departing out of Kikiaola Harbor in Kekaha, Capt. Andy's Raft Expeditions offer both snorkeling and beach-landing excursions. The Zodiac rafts are on the smaller side—24 feet with a maximum of 14 passengers—and all seating is on the rubber hulls, so hang on. They operate three different rafts, so there's a good chance of availability. Trips include snorkeling at Nualolo Kai (ocean conditions permitting), sea caves, sightseeing along Napali Coast, a hiking tour through an ancient Hawaiian fishing village, and a buffet lunch on the beach. A shorter snorkeling tour is also offered. You're closer to the water on the Zodiacs, so you'll have great views of humpbacks, spinner dolphins, sea turtles, and other wildlife. ⊠ *Kikiaola Small Boat Harbor, Kaumualii Hwy., Kekaha* ☎ *808/335–6833, 800/535–0830* ⊕ *www.napali.com* ☎ *From $149.*

Kauai Sea Tours. This company holds a special permit from the state to land at Nualolo Kai along Napali Coast, ocean conditions permitting. Here, you'll enjoy a picnic lunch, as well as an archaeological tour of an ancient Hawaiian fishing village, ocean conditions permitting. Kauai Sea Tours operates four 24-foot inflatable rafts—maximum occupancy 14. These are small enough for checking out the insides of sea caves and the undersides of waterfalls. Four different tours are available, including snorkeling and whale-watching, depending on the season. ⊠ *Port Allen Marina Center, 4353 Waialo Rd., Eleele* ☎ *800/733–7997, 800/733–7997* ⊕ *www.kauaiseatours.com* ☎ *From $110.*

Fodor'sChoice ★ **Napali Explorer.** These tours operate out of Kikialoa Harbor, a tad closer to Napali Coast than most of the other West Side catamaran tours. The company runs two different sizes of inflatable rubber raft: a 48-foot, 36-passenger craft with an onboard toilet, freshwater shower, shade canopy, and seating in the stern (which is surprisingly smooth and comfortable) and bow (which is where the fun is); and a 26-foot,

8

14-passenger craft for the all-out fun and thrills of a white-knuckle ride in the bow. The smaller vessel stops at Nualolo Kai and ties up onshore for a tour of the ancient fishing village. Charters are available. ⊠ *9814 Kaumalii Hwy., Waimea (Kauai County)* ☎ *808/338–9999* ⊕ *www. napaliexplorer.com* ◪ *From $99.*

Napali Riders. This tour-boat outfitter distinguishes itself in two ways. First, it cruises the entire Napali Coast, clear to Kee Beach and back. Second, it has a reasonable price because it's a no-frills tour—no lunch provided, just beverages and snacks. The company runs morning and afternoon four-hour snorkeling, sightseeing, and whale-watching trips out of Kikiaola Harbor in Waimea on a 30-foot inflatable raft with a 28-passenger maximum—that's fewer than they used to take, but can still be a bit cramped. ⊠ *9600 Kaumualii Hwy., Waimea (Kauai County)* ☎ *808/742–6331* ⊕ *www.napaliriders.com* ◪ *$119.*

Z-Tourz. What we like about Z-Tourz is that it's a boat company that makes snorkeling its priority. Its two- and three-hour tours focus solely on the South Shore's abundant offshore reefs. If you want to snorkel with Hawaii's tropical reef fish and turtles (pretty much guaranteed), this is your boat. The craft is a 26-foot rigid-hull inflatable (think Zodiac) with a maximum of 16 passengers. These snorkel tours are guided, so someone actually identifies what you're seeing. Rates include lunch and snorkel gear. ⊠ *3417 Poipu Rd., Poipu* ☎ *808/742–7422, 888/998–6879* ⊕ *www.kauaiztours.com* ◪ *From $99.*

RIVERBOAT TOURS TO FERN GROTTO

Smith's Motor Boat Services. This 2-mile trip up the lush and lovely Wailua River, the only navigable waterway in Hawaii, culminates at the infamous Fern Grotto, a yawning lava tube that is covered with fishtail ferns. During the boat ride, guitar and ukulele players regale you with Hawaiian melodies and tell the history of the river. It's a kitschy, but fun, bit of Hawaiiana and the river scenery is beautiful. Flat-bottom, 150-passenger riverboats (that rarely fill up) depart from Wailua Marina at the mouth of the Wailua River. ■ TIP➡ It's extremely rare, but occasionally after heavy rains the tour doesn't disembark at the grotto; if you're traveling in winter, ask beforehand. Round-trip excursions take 1½ hours, including time to walk around the grotto and environs. Tours run at 9:30, 11, 2, and 3:30 daily. ⊠ *5971 Kuhio Hwy., Kapaa* ☎ *808/821–6895* ⊕ *www.smithskauai.com/fern-grotto/* ◪ *$25.*

BODY BOARDING AND BODYSURFING

The most natural form of wave riding is bodysurfing, a popular sport on Kauai because there are many shore breaks around the island. Wave riders of this style stand waist deep in the water, facing shore, and swim madly as a wave picks them up and breaks. It's great fun and requires no special skills and absolutely no equipment other than a swimsuit. The next step up is body boarding, also called boogie boarding. In this case, wave riders lie with their upper body on a foam board about half the length of a traditional surfboard and kick as the wave propels them toward shore. Again, this is easy to pick up, and there are many places around Kauai to practice. The locals wear short-finned flippers to help them catch waves, which is a good idea to enhance safety in the water. It's worth spending a few minutes watching these experts as they spin, twirl, and flip—that's right—while they slip down the face of the wave. Of course, all beach-safety precautions apply, and just because you see wave riders of any kind in the water doesn't mean the water is safe for everyone. Any snorkeling-gear outfitter also rents body boards.

Some of our favorite bodysurfing and body-boarding beaches are **Brennecke, Wailua, Kealia, Kalihiwai,** and **Hanalei.**

DEEP-SEA FISHING

Simply step aboard and cast your line for mahimahi, ahi, ono, and marlin. That's about how quickly the fishing—mostly trolling with lures—begins on Kauai. The water gets deep quickly here, so there's less cruising time to fishing grounds, which is nice, since Hawaii's seas are notoriously rough. Of course, your captain may elect to cruise to a hot location where he's had good luck lately.

There are oodles of charter fishermen around; most depart from Nawiliwili Harbor in Lihue, and most use lures instead of live bait. Inquire about each boat's "fish policy," that is, what happens to the fish if any are caught. Some boats keep all; others will give you enough for a meal or two, even doing the cleaning themselves. On shared charters, ask about the maximum passenger count and about the fishing rotation; you'll want to make sure everyone gets a fair shot at reeling in the big one. Another option is to book a private charter. Shared and private charters run four, six, and eight hours in length.

BOATS AND CHARTERS

Captain Don's Sport Fishing & Ocean Adventure. Captain Don is very flexible and treats everyone like family—he'll stop to snorkel or whale-watch if that's what the group (four to six) wants. Saltwater fly-fishermen (bring your own gear) are welcome. He'll even fish for bait and let you keep part of whatever you catch. The *June Louise* is a 34-foot twin diesel. ⊠ *Nawiliwili Small Boat Harbor, 2494 Niumalu Rd., Nawiliwili* ☎ *808/639–3012* ⊕ *www.captaindonsfishing.com* ✉ *From $150 (shared); from $650 (private).*

Hana Paa. The advantage with Hana Paa is that it takes fewer people (minimum two, maximum four for a nonprivate excursion), but you pay for it. Charters can accommodate up to six people. The company's fish policy is flexible, and the boat is roomy. The *Maka Hou II* is a 38-foot Bertram. ⊠ *Nawiliwili Small Boat Harbor, 2494 Niumalu Rd., Nawiliwili* ☎ *808/823–6031, 866/776–3474* ⊕ *www.fishkauai.com* ✉ *From $330 (shared); from $600 (private).*

Happy Times Fishing Charters. If you're staying on the West Side, you'll be glad to know that Napali Explorer (of the longtime rafting tour business) runs fishing trips out of Port Allen under the name Happy Times

Niihau: The Forbidden Isle

Seventeen miles from Kauai, across the Kaulakahi Channel, sits the privately owned island of Niihau. It's known as the Forbidden Isle, because access is limited to the Robinson family, which owns it, and the 200 or so Native Hawaiians who were born there.

Niihau was bought from King Kamehameha in 1864 by a Scottish widow, Eliza Sinclair. Sinclair was introduced to the island after an unusually wet winter; she saw nothing but green pastures and thought it would be an ideal place to raise cattle. The cost was $10,000. It was a real deal, or so Sinclair thought.

Unfortunately, Niihau's usual rainfall is about 12 inches a year, and the land soon returned to its normal, desertlike state. Regardless, Sinclair did not abandon her venture, and today the island is owned by Bruce and Keith Robinson, Eliza Sinclair's great-great-grandsons.

Visits to the island are restricted to custom hunting expeditions and tours, with transport by Niihau Helicopter. Tours depart from Kaumakani and avoid the western coastline, especially the village of Puuwai. There's a five-passenger minimum for each flight, and reservations are essential. A picnic lunch on a secluded Niihau beach is included, with time for swimming, beachcombing, and snorkeling. The half-day tour is $440 per person.

For more information, contact **Niihau Tours** (☎ 808/335–3500 or 877/441–3500 ⊕ www.niihau.us).

Fishing Charters. It offers shared and exclusive charters of four, six, and eight hours in a 41-foot Concord called *Happy Times*. The shared tours max out at six fishermen, and a portion of the catch is shared with all. The boat is also used for specialty charters—that is, film crews, surveys, burials, and even Niihau fishing. Rates range from $149 to $600 per person. ⊠ *Port Allen Small Boat Harbor, Waialo Rd., Eleele* ☎ *808/338–9999* ⊕ *www.napaliexplorer.com* 🖃 *From $149 per person.*

Kai Bear. The father of this father-and-son duo has it figured out: he lets the son run the business and do all the work. Or so he says. The prices are reasonable, and they share the catch. Trips run from a four-hour, shared charter (six fishermen max) up to an eight-hour, keep-all-the-fish-you-want exclusive. What's particularly nice about this company are the boats: the 38-foot Bertram, *Kai Bear*, and the 42-foot Bertram, *Grander*, which are well maintained and very roomy. ⊠ *Nawiliwili Small Boat Harbor, 2900 Nawiliwili Rd., Nawiliwili* ☎ *808/652–4556* ⊕ *www.kaibear.com* 🖃 *From $175.*

KAYAKING

Kauai is the only Hawaiian island with navigable rivers. As the oldest inhabited island in the chain, Kauai has had more time for wind and water erosion to deepen and widen cracks into streams and streams into rivers. Because this is a small island, the rivers aren't long, and there are no rapids, which makes them generally safe for kayakers of all levels, even beginners, except when rivers are flowing fast from heavy rains.

For more advanced paddlers, there aren't many places in the world more beautiful for sea kayaking than Napali Coast. If this is your draw to Kauai, plan your vacation for the summer months, when the seas are at their calmest. ■ TIP→ **Tour and kayak-rental reservations are recommended at least two weeks in advance during peak summer and holiday seasons.** In general, tours and rentals are available year-round, Monday through Saturday. Pack a swimsuit, sunscreen, a hat, bug repellent, water shoes (sport sandals, aqua socks, old tennis shoes), and motion sickness medication if you're planning on sea kayaking.

RIVER KAYAKING

Tour outfitters operate on the Huleia, Wailua, and Hanalei rivers with guided tours that combine hiking to waterfalls, as in the case of the first two, and snorkeling, as in the case of the third. Another option is renting kayaks and heading out on your own. Each has its advantages and disadvantages, but it boils down as follows:

If you want to swim at the base of a remote 100-foot waterfall, sign up for a five-hour kayak (4-mile round-trip) and hiking (2-mile round-trip) tour of the **Wailua River.** It includes a dramatic waterfall that is best accessed with the aid of a guide, so you don't get lost. ■ TIP→ **Remember—it's dangerous to swim under waterfalls no matter how good a water massage may sound. Rocks and logs are known to plunge down, especially after heavy rains.** ⚠ **Following extensive flooding in early 2018, areas along the Wailua River are undergoing repairs. Please check before visiting to make sure places are open.**

If you want to kayak on your own, choose the **Hanalei River.** It's most scenic from the kayak itself—there are no trails to hike to hidden waterfalls. And better yet, a rental company is right on the river—no hauling kayaks on top of your car.

If you're not sure of your kayaking abilities, head to the **Huleia River;** 3½-hour tours include easy paddling upriver, a nature walk through a rain forest with a cascading waterfall, a rope swing for playing Tarzan and Jane, and a ride back downriver—into the wind—on a motorized, double-hull canoe.

As for the kayaks themselves, most companies use the two-person sit-on-top style that is quite buoyant—no Eskimo rolls required. The only possible danger comes in the form of communication. The kayaks seat two people, which means you'll share the work (good) with a guide, or your spouse, child, parent, or friend (the potential danger part). On the river, the two-person kayaks are known as "divorce boats." Counseling is not included in the tour price.

SEA KAYAKING

In its second year and second issue, *National Geographic Adventure* ranked kayaking Napali Coast second on its list of America's Best 100 Adventures, right behind rafting the Colorado River through the Grand

Canyon. That pretty much says it all. It's the adventure of a lifetime in one day, involving eight hours of paddling. Although it's good to have some kayaking experience, feel comfortable on the water, and be reasonably fit, it doesn't require the preparation, stamina, or fortitude of, say, climbing Mt. Everest. Tours run May through September, ocean conditions permitting. In the winter months sea-kayaking tours operate on the South Shore—beautiful, but not as dramatic as Napali.

EQUIPMENT AND TOURS

Kayak Kauai. This company pioneered kayaking on Kauai. It offers guided tours on the Wailua River, and sea kayak tours in Hanalei Bay, and along Napali Coast in season. It has consolidated operations, and is now conveniently located in the Wailua Marina. From there, it can launch kayaks right into the Wailua River for its five-hour Secret Falls hike-paddle tour and three-hour paddle to a swimming hole. Kayak Kauai also offers 12-hour escorted summer sea kayak tours and camping trips on Napali Coast. Stand-up paddleboard instruction and sea-kayak whale-watching tours round out its repertoire. The company will shuttle kayakers as needed, and, for rentals, it provides the hauling gear necessary for your rental car. Snorkel gear, body boards, and stand-up paddleboards also can be rented. ⊠ *Wailua Marina, 3-5971 Kuhio Hwy., Wailua (Kauai County)* ☎ *808/826–9844, 888/596–3853* ⊕ *www.kayakkauai.com* ⛵ *From $85 (river tours) and $240 (sea tours); kayak rentals from $95 per day.*

Kayak Wailua. We can't quite figure out how this family-run business offers pretty much the same Wailua River kayaking tour as everyone else—except for lunch and beverages, which are BYO—for the lowest price, but it does. They say it's because they don't discount and don't offer commissions to activities and concierge desks. Their trips, a 4½-hour kayak, hike, and waterfall swim, are offered six times a day, with the last at 1 pm. With the number of boats going out, large groups can be accommodated. No tours are allowed on Wailua River on Sunday. ⊠ *4565 Haleilio Rd., behind old Coco Palms hotel, Kapaa* ☎ *808/822–3388* ⊕ *www.kayakwailua.com* ⛵ *$60.*

Fodor's Choice ★ **Napali Kayak.** A couple of longtime guides ventured out on their own to create this company, which focuses solely on a 17-mile sea-kayaking paddle along Napali Coast from April to October for small groups, or private and honeymoon tours. These guys are highly experienced and still highly enthusiastic about their livelihood—so much so that REI Adventures hires them to run their multiday, multisport tours. If you're an experienced kayaker and want to try camping on your own at Kalalau (you'll need permits), Napali Kayak will provide kayaks outfitted with dry bags, extra paddles, and seat backs, while also offering transportation drop-off and pickup. They also do Napali Coast day tours from Hanalei to Polihale, with a lunch break at Milolii, and rent camping equipment and first-aid kits. ⊠ *5-5075 Kuhio Hwy., next to Postcards Café, Hanalei* ☎ *808/826–6900* ⊕ *www.napalikayak.com* ⛵ *From $225.*

FAMILY **Outfitters Kauai.** This well-established tour outfitter operates year-round river-kayak tours on the Huleia and Wailua rivers, as well as sea-kayaking tours along Napali Coast in summer and the South Shore in winter. Outfitters Kauai's specialty, however, is the Kipu Safari. This all-day adventure starts with kayaking up the Huleia River and includes a rope swing over a swimming hole, a wagon ride through a working cattle ranch, a picnic lunch by a private waterfall, hiking, and two "zips" across the rain-forest canopy (strap on a harness, clip into a cable, and zip over a quarter of a mile). They then offer a one-of-a-kind Waterzip Zipline at their mountain stream–fed blue pool. The day ends with a ride on a motorized double-hull canoe. It's a great tour for the family, because no one ever gets bored. ✉ *2827-A Poipu Rd., Poipu* ☎ *808/742–9667, 888/742–9887* ⊕ *www.outfitterskauai.com* ✉ *Kipu Safari $189.*

Wailua Kayak & Canoe. This purveyor of kayak rentals is right on the Wailua River, which means no hauling your kayak on top of your car (a definite plus). Guided waterfall tours are also offered. This outfitter promotes itself as "Native Hawaiian owned and operated." No Wailua River tours are offered on Sunday. ✉ *162 Wailua Rd., Kapaa* ☎ *808/821–1188* ⊕ *www.wailuariverkayaking.com* ✉ *$50 for a single, $90 for a double; guided tours from $75.*

KITEBOARDING

Several years ago, the latest wave-riding craze to hit the Islands was kiteboarding, and the sport is still going strong. As the name implies, there's a kite and a board involved. The board you strap on your feet; the kite is attached to a harness around your waist. Steering is accomplished with a rod that's attached to the harness and the kite. Depending on conditions and the desires of the kiteboarder, the kite is played out some 30 to 100 feet in the air. The result is a cross between waterskiing—without the boat—and windsurfing. Speeds are fast and aerobatic maneuvers are involved. Though lessons are available, you can also enjoy watching the pros who can put on a pretty spectacular show. The most popular year-round spots for kiteboarding are **Kapaa Beach Park, Anini Beach Park,** and **Mahaulepu Beach.** ■TIP→ Many visitors come to Kauai dreaming of parasailing. If that's you, make a stop at Maui or the Big Island. There's no parasailing or commercial jet skiing on Kauai.

Kiteboard Kauai. Certified instructor Adam Finn is committed to helping students quickly and safely master basic techniques so they can enjoy maximum time on the waves. To that end, he uses waterproof radio helmets to communicate with students in the water. Lessons by appointment only. ✉ *Kapaa* ⊕ *www.kiteboardkauai.com.*

SCUBA DIVING

The majority of scuba diving on Kauai occurs on the South Shore. Boat and shore dives are available, although boat sites surpass the shore sites for a couple of reasons. First, they're deeper and exhibit the complete

SCUBA Q&A

Q: Do I have to be certified to go scuba diving?

A: No. You can try Discover Scuba, which allows you to dive up to 40 feet after an introductory lesson in a pool. Most dive outfitters on Kauai offer this introductory program.

Q: Can I dive if I have asthma?

A: Only if your doctor signs a medical release—the original of which you must present to your dive outfitter.

Q: Can I get certified on Kauai?

A: Yes. Start to finish, it'll take three days. Or, you can complete your classroom and confined-water training at home and just do your check-out dives on Kauai.

Q: How old do you have to be to learn how to dive?

A: Most certifying agencies require that you be at least 12 years old (with PADI it's 10) when you start your scuba-diving course. You will normally receive a junior certification, which can be upgraded to a full certification when you are 15 years old.

Q: Can I wear contact lenses or glasses while diving?

A: You can either wear contact lenses with a regular mask or opt for a prescription mask—just let your dive outfitter know in advance.

Q: What if I forget my certification card?

A: Let your dive outfitter know immediately; with advance notice, they can usually dig up your certification information online.

symbiotic relationship of a reef system, and second, the visibility is better a little farther offshore.

The dive operators on Kauai offer a full range of services, including certification dives, referral dives, boat dives, shore dives, night dives, and drift dives. ■ TIP→ **As for certification, we recommend completing your confined-water training and classroom testing before arriving on the island.** That way, you'll spend less time training and more time diving.

BEST SPOTS

The best and safest scuba-diving sites are accessed by boat on the South Shore of the island, right off the shores of Poipu. The captain selects the actual site based on ocean conditions of the day. Beginners may prefer shore dives, which are best at **Koloa Landing** on the South Shore year-round and **Makua (Tunnels) Beach** on the North Shore in the calm summer months. Keep in mind, though, that you'll have to haul your gear a ways down the beach.

For the advanced diver, the island of Niihau—across an open ocean channel in deep and crystal-clear waters—beckons and rewards, usually with some big fish. Seasport Divers, Fathom Five, and Bubbles Below venture the 17 miles across the channel in summer when the crossing is smoothest. Divers can expect deep dives, walls, and strong currents at

Niihau, where conditions can change rapidly. To make the long journey worthwhile, three dives and Nitrox are included.

EQUIPMENT, LESSONS, AND TOURS

Bubbles Below. Marine ecology is the emphasis here aboard the 36-foot, eight-passenger *Kai Manu*. This longtime Kauai company discovered some pristine dive sites on the West Side of the island where white-tip reef sharks are common—and other divers are not. Thanks to the addition of a 32-foot powered catamaran—the six-passenger *Dive Rocket*—the group also runs Niihau, Napali, and North Shore dives year-round (depending on ocean conditions, of course). They're still known for their South Side trips and lead dives at the East Side walls as well, so they truly do circumnavigate the island. A bonus on these tours is the wide variety of food served between dives. Open-water certification dives, check-out dives, and intro shore dives are available upon request. ✉ *Port Allen Small Boat Harbor, 4353 Waialo Rd., Eleele* ☎ *808/332–7333* ⊕ *www.bubblesbelowkauai.com* 💲 *$140 for 2-tank boat dive; $90 for rider/snorkeler; Niihau charter $350.*

Kauai Down Under Dive Team. This company offers boat dives, but specializes in shore diving, typically at Koloa Landing (year-round) and Tunnels (summers). They're not only geared toward beginning divers—for whom they provide a thorough and gentle certification program as well as the Discover Scuba program—but also offer night dives and scooter (think James Bond) dives. Their main emphasis is a detailed review of marine biology, such as pointing out rare dragon eel and harlequin shrimp tucked away in pockets of coral. ■ TIP→ **Hands down, we recommend Kauai Down Under for beginners, certification (all levels), and refresher dives.** One reason is that their instructor-to-student ratio never exceeds 1:4—that's true of all their dive groups. All dive gear included. ✉ *Sheraton Kauai Resort, 2440 Hoonani Rd., Koloa* ☎ *877/538–3483, 808/742–9534* ⊕ *www.kauaidownunderscuba.com* 💲 *From $149 for a 2-tank certified dive; $550 for certification.*

Fodor's Choice ★ **Ocean Quest Watersports/Fathom Five.** This operator offers it all: boat dives, shore dives, night dives, certification dives. They pretty much do what everyone else does with a few twists. First, they offer a three-tank premium charter for those really serious about diving. Second, they operate a Nitrox continuous-flow mixing system, so you can decide the mix rate. Third, they add on a twilight dive to the standard, one-tank night dive, making the outing worth the effort. Fourth, their shore diving isn't an afterthought. Finally, we think their dive masters are pretty darn good, too. They even dive Niihau in the summer aboard their 35-foot *Force*. In summer, book well in advance. ✉ *3450 Poipu Rd., Koloa* ☎ *808/742–6991, 800/972–3078* ⊕ *www.fathomfive.com* 💲 *From $155 for boat dives; from $100 for shore dives; $45 for gear rental, if needed.*

Seasport Divers. Rated highly by readers of *Scuba Diving* magazine, Seasport Divers' 48-foot *Anela Kai* tops the chart for dive-boat luxury. But owner Marvin Otsuji didn't stop with that. A second boat—a 32-foot catamaran—is outfitted for diving, but we like it as an all-around charter. The company does brisk business, which means it won't cancel at the last minute because of a lack of reservations, like some other companies, although they may book up to 18 people per boat. ■ TIP→ **There are slightly more challenging trips in the morning; mellower dive sites are in the afternoon.** The company runs a good-size dive shop for purchases and rentals, as well as a classroom for certification. Night dives are offered, and Niihau trips are available in summer. There's also an outlet in Kapaa. ⊠ *2827 Poipu Rd., look for yellow submarine in parking lot, Poipu* ☎ *808/742–9303, 808/742–9303* ⊕ *www.seasportdivers. com* ⊠ *From $140, includes gear; $100 1-tank shore dive.*

SNORKELING

Generally speaking, the calmest water and best snorkeling can be found on Kauai's North Shore in summer and South Shore in winter. The East Side, known as the windward side, has year-round, prevalent northeast trade winds that make snorkeling unpredictable, although there are some good pockets. The best snorkeling on the West Side is accessible only by boat.

A word on feeding fish: don't. As Captain Ted with HoloHolo Charters says, fish have survived and populated reefs for much longer than we have been donning goggles and staring at them. They will continue to do so without our intervention. Besides, fish food messes up the reef and—one thing always leads to another—can eliminate a once-pristine reef environment. As for gear, if you're snorkeling with one of the Napali boat-tour outfitters, they'll provide it; however, depending on the company, it might not be the latest or greatest. If you have your own, bring it. On the other hand, if you're going out with SeaFun or Z-Tourz, the gear is top-notch. If you need to rent, hit one of the "snorkel-and-surf" shops such as Snorkel Bob's in Koloa and Kapaa, Nukumoi in Poipu, or Seasport in Poipu and Kapaa, or shop Walmart or Kmart if you want to drag it home. Typically, though, rental gear will be better quality than that found at Walmart or Kmart. ■ TIP→ **If you wear glasses, you can rent prescription masks at the rental shops—just don't expect them to match your prescription exactly.**

BEST SPOTS

Just because we say these are good places to snorkel doesn't mean that the exact moment you arrive, the fish will flock—they are wild, after all.

Beach House (Lawai Beach). Don't pack the beach umbrella, beach mats, or cooler for snorkeling at Beach House. Just bring your snorkeling gear. The beach—named after its neighbor the Beach House restaurant—is on the road to Spouting Horn. It's a small slip of sand during low tide and a rocky shoreline during high tide; however, it's right by the road's edge, and its rocky coastline and somewhat rocky bottom make it great for snorkeling. Enter and exit in the sand channel (not over the rocky reef) that lines up with the Lawai Beach Resort's center atrium. Stay within the rocky points anchoring each end of the beach. The current

Continued on page 172

SNORKELING IN HAWAII

Molokini Crater

The waters surrounding the Hawaiian Islands are filled with life—from giant manta rays cruising off the Big Island's Kona Coast to humpback whales giving birth in the waters around Maui. Dip your head beneath the surface to experience a spectacularly colorful world: pairs of milletseed butterflyfish dart back and forth, redlipped parrotfish snack on coral algae, and spotted eagle rays flap past like silent spaceships. Sea turtles bask at the surface while tiny wrasses give them the equivalent of a shave and a haircut. The water quality is typically outstanding; many sites afford 30-foot-plus visibility. On snorkel cruises, you can often stare from the boat rail right down to the bottom.

Certainly few destinations are as accommodating to every level of snorkeler as Hawaii. Beginners can tromp in from sandy beaches while more advanced divers descend to shipwrecks, reefs, craters, and sea arches just offshore. Because of Hawaii's extreme isolation, the island chain has fewer fish species than Fiji or the Caribbean—but many of the fish that live here exist nowhere else. The Hawaiian waters are home to the highest percentage of endemic fish in the world.

The key to enjoying the underwater world is slowing down. Look carefully. Listen. You might hear the strange crackling sound of shrimp tunneling through coral, or you may hear whales singing to one another during winter. A shy octopus may drift along the ocean's floor beneath you. If you're hooked, pick up a waterproof fishkey from Long's Drugs. You can brag later that you've looked the Hawaiian turkeyfish in the eye.

Picasso Triggerfish

Milletseed Butterflyfish*

Yellow Tang

Moorish Idol

Hawaiian Whitespotted Toby*

Saddleback Wrasse*

Redlip Parrotfish

Hawaiian Turkeyfish*

Zebra Moray Eel

Stocky Hawkfish

Green Sea Turtle (Honu)

Spotted Eagle Ray

*endemic to Hawaii

POLYNESIA'S FIRST CELESTIAL NAVIGATORS: HONU

Honu is the Hawaiian name for two native sea turtles, the hawksbill and the green sea turtle. Little is known about these dinosaur-age marine reptiles, though snorkelers regularly see them foraging for *limu* (seaweed) and the occasional jellyfish in Hawaiian waters. Most female honu nest in the uninhabited Northwestern Hawaiian Islands, but a few sociable ladies nest on Maui and Big Island beaches. Scientists suspect that they navigate the seas via magnetism—sensing the earth's poles. Amazingly, they will journey up to 800 miles to nest—it's believed that they return to their own birth sites. After about 60 days of incubation, nestlings emerge from the sand at night and find their way back to the sea by the light of the stars.

SNORKELING

Many of Hawaii's reefs are accessible from shore.

The basics: Sure, you can take a deep breath, hold your nose, squint your eyes, and stick your face in the water in an attempt to view submerged habitats . . . but why not protect your eyes, retain your ability to breathe, and keep your hands free to paddle about when exploring underwater? That's what snorkeling is all about.

Equipment needed: A mask, snorkel (the tube attached to the mask), and fins. In deeper waters (any depth over your head), life jackets are advised.

Steps to success: If you've never snorkeled before, it's natural to feel a bit awkward at first, so don't sweat it. Breathing through a mask and tube, and wearing a pair of fins take getting used to. Like any activity, you build confidence and comfort through practice.

If you're new to snorkeling, begin by submerging your face in shallow water or a swimming pool and breathing calmly through the snorkel while gazing through the mask.

Next you need to learn how to clear water out of your mask and snorkel, an essential skill since splashes can send water into tube openings and masks can leak. Some snorkels have built-in drainage valves, but if a tube clogs, you can force water up and out by exhaling through your mouth. Clearing a mask is similar: lift your head from water while pulling forward on mask to drain. Some masks have built-in purge valves, but those without can be cleared underwater by pressing the top to the forehead and blowing out your nose (charming, isn't it?), allowing air to bubble into the mask, pushing water out the bottom. If it sounds hard, it really isn't. Just try it a few times and you'll soon feel like a pro.

Now your goal is to get friendly with

fins—you want them to be snug but not too tight—and learn how to propel yourself with them. Fins won't help you float, but they will give you a leg up, so to speak, on smoothly moving through the water or treading water (even when upright) with less effort.

Flutter stroking is the most efficient underwater kick, and the farther your foot bends forward the more leg power you'll be able to transfer to the water and the farther you'll travel with each stroke. Flutter kicking movements involve alternately separating the legs and then drawing them back together. When your legs separate, the leg surface encounters drag from the water, slowing you down. When your legs are drawn back together, they produce a force pushing you forward. If your kick creates more forward force than it causes drag, you'll move ahead.

Submerge your fins to avoid fatigue rather than having them flailing above the water when you kick, and keep your arms at your side to reduce drag. You are in the water—stretched out, face down, and snorkeling happily away—but that doesn't mean you can't hold your breath and go deeper in the water for a closer look at some fish or whatever catches your attention. Just remember that when you do this, your snorkel will be submerged, too, so you won't be breathing (you'll be holding your breath). You can dive head-first, but going feet-first is easier and less scary for most folks, taking less momentum. Before full immersion, take several long, deep breaths to clear carbon dioxide from your lungs.

If your legs tire, flip onto your back and tread water with inverted fin motions while resting. If your mask fogs, wash condensation from lens and clear water from mask.

TIPS FOR SAFE SNORKELING

- Snorkel with a buddy and stay together.
- Plan your entry and exit points prior to getting in the water.
- Swim into the current on entering and then ride the current back to your exit point.
- Carry your flippers into the water and then put them on, as it's difficult to walk in them, and rocks may be slippery.
- Make sure your mask fits properly and is not too loose.
- Pop your head above the water periodically to ensure you aren't drifting too far out, or too close to rocks.
- Think of the water as someone else's home—don't take anything that doesn't belong to you, or leave any trash behind.
- Don't touch any sea creatures; they may sting.
- Wear a T-shirt over your swimsuit to help protect you from being fried by the sun.
- When in doubt, don't go without a snorkeling professional; try a guided tour.
- Don't go in if the ocean seems rough.

Green sea turtle (Honu)

Kauai's calmest water and best snorkeling is on the North Shore in summer and South Shore in winter. Many of the best dive spots are on the South Shore.

runs east to west. ✉ *5017 Lawai Rd., makai (ocean) side of Lawai Rd., park on road in front of Lawai Beach Resort, Koloa.*

Kee Beach. Although it can get quite crowded, Kee Beach is quite often a good snorkeling destination if the water conditions are right. Just be sure to come during the off-hours, say early in the morning or later in the afternoon, or you will have difficulty finding a parking spot. ■ TIP→ **Snorkeling here in winter can be hazardous. Summer is the best and safest time, although you should never swim beyond the reef.** During peak times, a parking lot is available back down the road away from the beach. ✉ *At end of Rte. 560, Haena.*

Lydgate Beach Park. Lydgate Beach Park is typically the safest place to snorkel on Kauai, though not the most exciting. With its lava-rock wall creating a protected swimming pool, it's a good spot for beginners, young and old. The fish are so tame here it's almost like swimming in a saltwater aquarium. There is also a lifeguard, a playground for children, plenty of parking, and full-service restrooms with showers. ✉ *4470 Nalu Rd.* ⊕ *Just south of Wailua River, turn makai (towards ocean) off Rte. 56 onto Lehu Dr. and left onto Nalu Rd., Kapaa.*

FodorśChoice
★

Niihau. With little river runoff and hardly any boat traffic, the waters off the island of Niihau are some of the clearest in all Hawaii, and that's good for snorkeling and excellent for scuba diving. Like Nualolo Kai, the only way to snorkel here is to sign on with one of the tour boats venturing across a sometimes rough open-ocean channel: Blue Dolphin Charters and HoloHolo.

Nualolo Kai. Nualolo Kai was once an ancient Hawaiian fishpond and is now home to the best snorkeling along Napali Coast (and perhaps on all of Kauai). The only way to access it is by boat, including kayak. Though many boats stop offshore, only a few Napali snorkeling-tour operators are permitted to come ashore. We recommend Napali Explorer and Kauai Sea Tours.

Poipu Beach Park. You'll generally find good year-round snorkeling at Poipu Beach Park, except during summer's south swells (which are not nearly as frequent as winter's north swells). The best snorkeling fronts the Marriott Waiohai Beach Club. Stay inside the crescent created by the sandbar and rocky point, and within sight of the lifeguard tower. The current runs east to west. ⊠ *Hoone Rd.* ✛ *From Poipu Rd., turn right onto Hoone Rd.*

Tunnels (Makua). The search for Tunnels (Makua) is as tricky as the snorkeling. Park at Haena Beach Park and walk east—away from Napali Coast—until you see a sand channel entrance in the water, almost at the point. Once you get here, the reward is fantastic. The name of this beach comes from the many underwater lava tubes, which always attract marine life. The shore is mostly beach rock interrupted by three sand channels. You'll want to enter and exit at one of these channels (or risk stepping on a sea urchin or scraping your stomach on the reef). Follow the sand channel to a drop-off; the snorkeling along here is always full of nice surprises. Expect a current running east to west. Snorkeling here in winter can be hazardous; summer is the best and safest time for snorkeling. ⊠ *Haena Beach Park* ✛ *Near end of Rte. 560, across from lava-tube sea caves, after stream crossing.*

TOURS

FAMILY
Fodor's Choice
★

SeaFun Kauai. This guided snorkeling tour, for beginners and intermediates alike, is led by a marine expert, so there's instruction plus the guide actually gets into the water with you and identifies marine life. You're guaranteed to spot tons of critters you'd never see on your own. This is a land-based operation and the only one of its kind on Kauai. (Don't think those snorkeling cruises are guided snorkeling tours—they rarely are. A member of the boat's crew serves as lifeguard, not a marine life *guide*.) A morning or afternoon tour includes all your snorkeling gear—and a wet suit to keep you warm—and stops at one or two snorkeling locations, chosen based on ocean conditions. They will pick up customers at some of the resorts, depending on locale and destination. ⊠ *3477A Weliweli Rd., Koloa* ☎ *808/245–6400, 800/452–1113* ⊕ *www.alohakauaitours.com* ✉ *$85.*

8

STAND-UP PADDLING

Unlike kiteboarding, this is an increasingly popular sport that even a novice can pick up—*and* have fun doing. Technically, it's not really a new sport but a reinvigorated one from the 1950s. Beginners start with a heftier surfboard and a longer-than-normal canoe paddle. And, just as the name implies, stand-up paddlers stand on their surfboards and paddle out from the beach—no timing a wave and doing a push-up to stand. The perfect place to learn is a river (think **Hanalei** or **Wailua**) or a calm lagoon (try **Anini** or **Kalapaki**). But this sport isn't just for beginners. Tried-and-true surfers turn to it when the waves are not quite right for their preferred sport, because it gives them another reason to be on the water. Stand-up paddlers catch waves earlier and ride them longer than longboard surfers. In the past couple of years, professional stand-up paddling competitions have popped up, and surf shops and instructors have adapted to its quick rise in popularity.

EQUIPMENT AND LESSONS

Not all surf instructors teach stand-up paddling, but more and more are, like Blue Seas Surfing School and Titus Kinimaka Hawaiian School of Surfing *(see Surfing)*.

Back Door Surf Co. Along with its sister store across the street—Hanalei Surf Shop—Back Door Surf Co. provides just about all the rentals necessary for a fun day at Hanalei Bay, along with clothing and new boards. ✉ *Ching Young Village, 5-5190 Kuhio Hwy., Hanalei* ☎ *808/826–9000* ⊕ *www.hanaleisurf.com/backdoor.htm.*

Hawaiian Surfing Adventures. This Hanalei location has a wide variety of stand-up boards and paddles for rent, with a few options depending on your schedule. Check in at the storefront and then head down to the beach, where your gear will be waiting. Lessons are also available on the scenic Hanalei River or in Hanalei Bay, and include 30 minutes of ocean safety, paddling, and wave-reading instruction and an hour in the water to practice with the board. This Native Hawaiian–owned company also offers surfboard and kayak rentals and surfing lessons. ✉ *5134 Kuhio Hwy., Hanalei* ☎ *808/482–0749* ⊕ *www.hawaiiansurfingadventures.com* ✑ *Paddleboard rental from $30; surfboard rentals from $20; lessons from $65.*

Kauai Beach Boys. This outfitter is right on the beach at Kalapaki, so there's no hauling your gear on your car. Classes are also held at Poipu Beach, at the Marriott Waiohai. In addition to stand-up paddle lessons, they offer sailing and surfing lessons, too. ✉ *3610 Rice St., Lihue* ☎ *808/246–6333, 808/742–4442* ⊕ *www.kauaibeachboys.com* ✑ *$82 for 1½-hr surf or SUP lesson.*

Winter brings big surf to Kauai's North Shore. You can see some of the sport's biggest celebrities catching waves at Haena and Hanalei Bay.

SURFING

Good ol' stand-up surfing is alive and well on Kauai, especially in winter's high-surf season on the North Shore. If you're new to the sport, we highly recommend taking a lesson. Not only will this ensure you're up and riding waves in no time, but instructors will provide the right board for your experience and size, help you time a wave, and give you a push to get your momentum going. ■ TIP→ **You don't need to be in top physical shape to take a lesson. Because your instructor helps push you into the wave, you won't wear yourself out paddling.** If you're experienced and want to hit the waves on your own, most surf shops rent boards for all levels, from beginners to advanced.

BEST SPOTS

Perennial-favorite beginning surf spots include **Poipu Beach** (the area fronting the Marriott Waiohai Beach Club), **Hanalei Bay,** and the stream end of **Kalapaki Beach.** More advanced surfers move down the beach in Hanalei to an area fronting a grove of pine trees known as **Pine Trees,** or paddle out past the pier. When the trade winds die, the north ends of **Wailua** and **Kealia** beaches are teeming with surfers. Breaks off **Poipu** and **Beach House/Lawai Beach** attract intermediates year-round. During high surf, the break on the cliff side of **Kalihiwai** is for experts only. Advanced riders will head to Polihale to face the heavy West Side waves when conditions are right.

QUESTIONS FOR A SURF INSTRUCTOR

Thinking about taking surf lessons? These are a few good questions to ask your potential surf instructor:

■ Are you legally permitted to operate on the beach?

■ What equipment do you provide? (If you're a beginner, you'll want to hear about their soft-top beginner boards. You'll also want to know if they'll provide rash guards and aqua socks.)

■ Who will be my instructor? (It's not always the name on the company logo. Ask about your instructor's qualifications.)

■ How do you select the location? (Ideally, you'll be assured that they pick the location because of its gentle waves, sandy beach bottom, and good year-round conditions.)

■ What if the waves are too big? (Under the best circumstances, they'll select another location or reschedule for another day.)

■ How many students do you take at a time? (Don't book if it's more than four students per instructor. You'll definitely want some personal attention.)

■ Are you CPR- and lifeguard-certified? (It's good to know your instructor will be able to help if you get into trouble.)

EQUIPMENT AND LESSONS

FAMILY **Blue Seas Surfing School.** Surfer and instructor Charlie Smith specializes in beginners (especially children), and though he operates primarily at Poipu Beach, lessons are offered elsewhere on the island. His soft-top longboards are very stable, making it easier to stand up. He specializes in one-on-one or family lessons, so personal interaction is a priority. He has also added stand-up paddling to his operation. Transportation is provided, if needed. ✉ *1959 Hoone Rd., Koloa* ☎ *808/634–6979* ⊕ *www.blueseassurfingschool.com* ✑ *From $75 for a 1½-hr lesson.*

Hanalei Surf Company. You can rent boards here and shop for rash guards, wet suits, and some hip surf-inspired apparel. ✉ *Hanalei Center, 5-5161 Kuhio Hwy., Hanalei* ☎ *808/826–9000* ⊕ *www.hanaleisurf.com.*

Nukumoi Surf Co. Owned by the same folks who own Brennecke's restaurant, this shop offers surfing lessons, board (surfing, body, and stand-up paddle), snorkel, and beach-gear rental, as well as casual clothing. Their primary surf spot is the beach fronting the Sheraton. ✉ *2100 Hoone Rd., across from Poipu Beach Park, Koloa* ☎ *808/742–8019* ⊕ *www.nukumoi.com* ✑ *$75 for groups for 1½ hrs; $250 for private sessions.*

Progressive Expressions. This full-service shop has a choice of rental boards and a whole lotta shopping for clothes, swimsuits, and casual beach wear. ✉ *5428 Koloa Rd., Koloa* ☎ *808/742–6041* ⊕ *www.progressiveexpressions.com.*

Tamba Surf Company. This is Kauai's homegrown surf shop, and your best bet for surfboard and snorkel gear rentals, new boards, and surfing lessons on the East Side. Tamba is a big name in local surf apparel. ✉ *4-1543 Kuhio Hwy., Kapaa* ☎ *808/823–6942* ⊕ *www.tamba.com.*

Humpback whales arrive at Kauai in November and stick around until early April. You can see these majestic creatures breach and spout from shore, or take a boat tour.

Titus Kinimaka Hawaiian School of Surfing. Famed as a pioneer of big-wave surfing, this Hawaiian believes in giving back to his sport. Beginning, intermediate, and advanced lessons are available at Hanalei, with a maximum of three students. If you want to learn to surf from a living legend, this is the man. Advanced surfers can also take a tow-in lesson with a Jet Ski. ■TIP→ **He employs other instructors, so if you want Titus, be sure to ask for him. (And good luck, because if the waves are going off, he'll be surfing, not teaching.)** Customers are able to use the board for a while after the lesson is complete. ⊠ *Quicksilver, 5-5088 Kuhio Hwy., Hanalei* ☎ *808/652–1116* ⊕ *www.hawaiianschoolofsurfing.com* ⊠ *$65, 90-min group; $250 Jet Ski surf; $65, 90-min group stand-up paddle.*

WHALE-WATCHING

Every winter North Pacific humpback whales swim some 3,000 miles over 30 days, give or take a few, from Alaska to Hawaii. Whales arrive as early as November and sometimes stay through April, though they seem to be most populous in February and March. They come to Hawaii to breed, calve, and nurse their young.

TOURS

Of course, nothing beats seeing a whale up close. During the season, any boat on the water is looking for whales; they're hard to avoid, whether the tour is labeled "whale-watching" or not. Consider the

WHAT'S THAT WHALE DOING?

Although humpbacks spend more than 90% of their lives underwater, they can be very active above water while they're in Hawaii. Here are a few maneuvers you may see:

■ Blow: the expulsion of air that looks like a geyser of water.

■ Spy hop: the raising of just the whale's head out of the water, as if to take a look around.

■ Tail slap: the repetitive slap of the tail, or fluke, on the surface of the water.

■ Pec slap: the repetitive slap of one or both fins on the surface of the water.

■ Fluke up dive: the waving of the tail above water as the whale slowly rolls underwater to dive.

■ Breach: the launching of the entire whale's body out of the water.

whales a benefit to any boating event that may interest you. If whales are definitely your thing, though, you can narrow down your tour-boat decision by asking a few whale-related questions, like whether there's a hydrophone on board, how long the captain has been running tours in Hawaii, and if anyone on the crew is a marine biologist or trained naturalist.

Several boat operators will add two-hour afternoon whale-watching tours during the season that run on the South Shore (not Napali). Operators include **Blue Dolphin, Catamaran Kahanu, HoloHolo,** and **Napali Explorer** *(see Boat Tours)*. Trying one of these excursions is a good option for those who have no interest in snorkeling or sightseeing along Napali Coast, although keep in mind, the longer you're on the water, the more likely you'll be to see the humpbacks.

One of the more unique ways to (possibly) see some whales is atop a kayak. For such an encounter, try **Outfitters Kauai**'s South Shore kayak trip *(see Kayaking Tours)*. There are a few lookout spots around the island with good land-based viewing: Kilauea Lighthouse on the North Shore, the Kapaa Scenic Overlook just north of Kapaa town on the East Side, and the cliffs to the east of Keoniloa (Shipwreck) Beach on the South Shore.

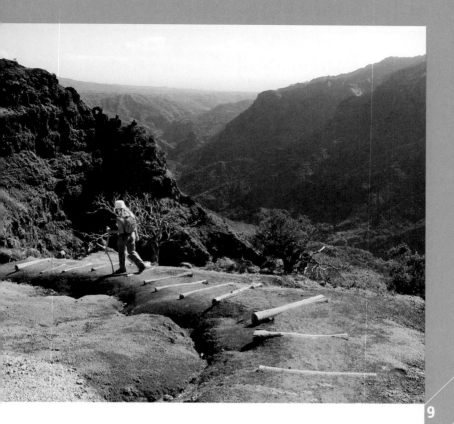

GOLF, HIKING, AND OUTDOOR ACTIVITIES

Updated
by Charles
Roessler

Kaui's outdoor recreation options extend well beyond the sand and surf, with plenty of activities to keep you busy on the ground and even in the air. You can hike the island's many trails, or consider taking your vacation into flight with a treetop zip line. You can have a backcountry adventure in a four-wheel drive, or relax in an inner tube floating down the cane-field irrigation canals.

Before booking tours, check with your concierge to find out what the forecast is for water and weather conditions. ■TIP➜ **Don't rely on the Weather Channel for accurate weather reports, as they're often reporting Oahu weather.** If you happen to arrive during a North Shore lull in the surf, you'll want to plan to be on the ocean in a kayak or snorkeling on the reef. If it's raining, ATV tours are the activity of choice.

For the golfer in the family, Kauai's spectacular courses are rated among the most scenic, as well as the most technical. Princeville Golf Course has garnered accolades from numerous national publications, and Poipu Bay Golf Course hosted the prestigious season-end PGA Grand Slam of Golf for 13 years, although Tiger (he won a record five-straight tournaments) and company, unfortunately, now head to Bermuda for this tourney.

One of the most popular Kauai experiences is to see the island from the air. In an hour or so, you can see waterfalls, craters, and other places that are inaccessible even by hiking trails (some say that 70% or more of the island is inaccessible). The majority of flights depart from the Lihue airport and follow a clockwise pattern around the island. ■TIP➜ **If you plan to take an aerial tour, it's a good idea to fly when you first arrive, rather than saving it for the end of your trip. It will help you visualize what's where on the island, and it may help you decide what you want to see from a closer vantage point during your stay.** Be prepared to relive your flight in dreams for the rest of your life. The most popular flight is 60 minutes long.

AERIAL TOURS

If you only drive around Kauai in your rental car, you will not see *all* of Kauai. There is truly only one way to see it all, and that's by air. Helicopter tours are the favorite way to get a bird's-eye view of Kauai—they fly at lower altitudes, hover above waterfalls, and wiggle their way into areas that a fixed-wing aircraft cannot. That said, if you've already tried the helitour, how about flying in the open cockpit of a biplane—à la the Red Baron?

Air Tour Kauai. This company, which is operated by the same group that runs Skydive Kauai, can hold up to six people in its Cessna 207 plane. The flights take off from the less crowded Port Allen Airport and will last 65 to 70 minutes. ✉ *Port Allen Airport, 3441 Kuiloko Rd., Hanapepe* ☎ *808/639–3446* ⊕ *www.airtourkauai.com* 🎫 *$99 per person.*

Blue Hawaiian Helicopters. This multiisland operator flies the latest in helicopter technology, the Eco-Star, costing $1.8 million. It has 23% more interior space for its six passengers, has unparalleled viewing, and offers a few extra safety features. As the name implies, the helicopter is also a bit more environmentally friendly, with a 50% noise-reduction rate. Even though flights run a tad shorter than others (50 to 55 minutes instead of the 55 to 65 minutes that other companies tout), they feel complete. A DVD of your tour is available for an additional $25. ✉ *3651 Ahukini Rd., Heliport 8, Lihue* ☎ *808/245–5800, 800/745–2583* ⊕ *www.bluehawaiian.com* 🎫 *$239.*

Fodor's Choice
★ **Jack Harter Helicopters.** Jack Harter was the first company to offer helicopter tours on Kauai. The company flies the six-passenger ASTAR helicopter with floor-to-ceiling windows, and the four-person Hughes 500, which is flown with no doors. The doorless ride can get windy, but it's the best bet for taking reflection-free photos. Pilots provide information on the Garden Island's history and geography through two-way intercoms. The company flies out of Lihue. Tours are 60 to 65 minutes and 90 to 95 minutes. Receive a $30 discount when you book through their website. ✉ *4231 Ahukini Rd.* ☎ *808/245–3774, 888/245–2001* ⊕ *www.helicopters-kauai.com* 🎫 *From $289.*

Safari Helicopters. This company flies the "Super" ASTAR helicopter, which offers floor-to-ceiling windows on its doors, four roof windows, and Bose X-Generation headphones. Two-way microphones allow passengers to converse with the pilot. There's a 60-minute waterfall tour and a 90-minute "eco-tour," which adds a landing in Olokele Canyon. Passengers are often met by Keith Robinson of *the* Robinson family, who provides a brief tour of the Kauai Wildlife Refuge, with endangered, endemic plants. A DVD is available for $26. ✉ *3225 Akahi St., Lihue* ☎ *808/246–0136, 800/326–3356* ⊕ *www.safarihelicopters.com* 🎫 *$239; eco-tour $314.*

Sunshine Helicopter Tours. If the name of this company sounds familiar, it may be because its pilots fly on all the main Hawaiian Islands except Oahu. On Kauai, Sunshine Helicopters departs out of two different locations: Lihue and Princeville. They fly the six-passenger FX STAR from Lihue and superroomy six-passenger WhisperSTAR birds from

9

Princeville. ■ TIP→ Discounts can be substantial by booking online and taking advantage of the "early-bird" seating during off-hours. ⊠ *3416 Rice St., Suite 203, Lihue* ☎ *808/240–2577, 866/501–7738* ⊕ *www. sunshinehelicopters.com* ✉ *From $244, Princeville $289.*

ATV TOURS

Although all the beaches on the island are public, much of the interior land—once sugar and pineapple plantations—is privately owned. This is really a shame, because the valleys and mountains that make up the vast interior of the island easily rival the beaches in sheer beauty. The good news is some tour operators have agreements with landowners that make exploration possible, albeit a bit bumpy, and unless you have back troubles, that's half the fun. ■ TIP→ If it looks like rain, book an ATV tour ASAP. That's the thing about these tours: the muddier, the better.

Fodor's Choice ★ **Kauai ATV Tours.** This is *the* thing to do when it rains on Kauai. Consider it an extreme mud bath. Kauai ATV in Koloa is the originator of the island's all-terrain-vehicle tours. The three-hour Koloa tour takes you through a private sugar plantation and historic cane-haul tunnel. The four-hour waterfall tour visits secluded waterfalls and includes a picnic lunch. This popular option includes a hike to secret WWII bunkers and a swim in a freshwater pool at the base of the falls—to rinse off all that mud. You must be 16 or older to operate your own ATV, but Kauai ATV also offers its four-passenger "Ohana Bug" and two-passenger "Mud Bugs" to accommodate families with kids ages five and older. ⊠ *3477A Weliweli Rd., Koloa* ☎ *808/742–2734, 877/707–7088* ⊕ *www.kauaiatv. com* ✉ *From $252 for 2 people.*

Kipu Ranch Adventures. This 3,000-acre property extends from the Huleia River to the top of Mt. Haupu. *Jurassic Park* and *Indiana Jones* were filmed here, and you'll see the locations for them on the three-hour Ranch Tour. The four-hour Waterfall Tour includes a visit to two waterfalls and a picnic lunch. Once a sugar plantation, Kipu Ranch today is a working cattle ranch, so you'll be in the company of bovines as well as pheasants, wild boars, and peacocks. If you're not an experienced ATV driver, they also offer guide-driven tour options. ⊠ *235 Kipu Rd., off Hwy. 50, Lihue* ☎ *808/246–9288* ⊕ *www.kipu-tours.com* ✉ *From $104.*

BIKING

Kauai is a labyrinth of cane-haul roads, which are fun for exploring on two wheels. The challenge is finding roads where biking is allowed and then not getting lost in the maze. Maybe that explains why Kauai is not a hub for the sport—yet. Still, there are some epic rides for those who are interested—both the adrenaline-rush and the mellower beach-cruiser kind. If you want to grind out some mileage, you could take the main highway that skirts the coastal area, but be careful: there are only a few designated bike lanes, and the terrain is hilly. You may find that keeping your eyes on the road rather than the scenery is your biggest challenge. "Cruisers" should head to Kapaa. A new section of Ke Ala Hele Makalae, a pedestrian and bicycle trail that runs along the East Side of Kauai, was completed in the summer of 2013, extending the multiuse path to about 8 miles. You can rent bikes (with helmets) from the activities desks of certain hotels, but these are not the best quality. You're better off renting from Kauai Cycle in Kapaa, Outfitters Kauai in Poipu, or Pedal 'n' Paddle in Hanalei. Ask for the "Go Green Kauai" map for a full description of Kauai biking options. △ **Following extensive flooding in early 2018, areas of Haena and along the Wailua River are undergoing repairs. Please check before visiting to make sure places are open.**

BEST SPOTS

Fodor's Choice
★

Ke Ala Hele Makalae (*coastal path*). This county beach park path follows the coastline on Kauai's East Side and is perfect for cruisers. Eventually, the path is projected to run some 20 miles, but an existing 6½-mile-long stretch already offers scenic views, picnic pavilions, and restroom facilities along the way—all in compliance with the Americans with Disabilities Act. The path runs from Lydgate Beach Park to secluded Kuna Bay (aka Donkey Beach). An easy way to access the longest completed section of the path is from Kealia Beach. Park here and head north into rural lands with spectacular coastline vistas, or head south into Kapaa for a more immersive experience. ⊠ *Kealia Beach, Kapaa* ⊕ *Trailhead: 1 mile north of Kapaa; park at north end of Kealia Beach* ⊕ *www. kauaipath.org/kauaicoastalpath*.

Moalepe Trail. This trail is perfect for intermediate to advanced trail-bike riders. The first 2 miles of this 5-mile double-track road wind steeply through pastureland. The real challenge begins when you reach the steep and rutted switchbacks, which during a rainy spell can be hazardous. Moalepe intersects the Kuilau Trail, which you can follow to its end at the Keahua Arboretum stream. ⊠ *Wailua (Kauai County)* ⊕ *From Kuhio Hwy. in Kapaa drive mauka (toward mountains) on Kuamoo Rd. for 3 miles and turn right on Kamalu Rd., which dead-ends at Olohena Rd. Turn left and follow until road veers sharply to right.*

Powerline Trail. Advanced riders are challenged by this trail. It's actually an abandoned electric-company service road that splits the island. It's 13 miles long; the first 5 miles go from 620 feet in elevation to almost 2,000. The remaining 8 miles descend gradually over a variety of terrain, some technical. You'll have to carry your bike through some sections, but the views will stay with you forever. ■ **TIP→ When it's wet—in summer or winter—this trail is a mess. Check with a knowledgeable bike shop for trail conditions first and be prepared to improvise.** ⊠ *Powerline Rd., Kilauea* ⊕ *The trailhead is mauka (upland), just past stream crossing at Keahua Arboretum, or at end of Powerline Rd. in Princeville, past Princeville Ranch Stables.*

Spalding Monument. For the novice rider, this ride offers a good workout and a summit ocean view that's not overly strenuous to reach. If you pick up a bike at Kauai Cycle in Kapaa, you can pedal a mile up Ke Ala

9

Bikers who prefer a leisurely cruise can pedal along the Ke Ala Hele Makalae Trail, an 8-mile, multiuse path in Kapaa.

Hele Makalae to reach the start of the ride, and even make a snack stop at the corner food truck without a detour. From near the end of Kealia Beach, ride up a gradual incline 2 miles through horse pastures to Spalding Monument, named for a former plantation owner, although there is no longer any signage. Palms circle the lava-rock wall, where you can picnic while enjoying a 180-degree ocean view. Behind you is the glorious mountain backdrop of Kalalea. Coasting back down the road offers an almost hands-free, continual ocean view along with a peek into rural Kauai most visitors miss. ⊠ *The loop begins at end of Kealia Beach, past mile marker 10 on mauka (mountain) side of road, Kealia.*

Wailua Forest Management Road. For the novice mountain biker, this is an easy ride, and it's also easy to find. From Route 56 in Wailua, turn *mauka* (toward the mountains) on Kuamoo Road and continue 6 miles to the picnic area known as Keahua Arboretum; park here. The pot-holed four-wheel-drive road includes some stream crossings—△ **stay away during heavy rains, because the streams flood**—and continues for 2 miles to a T-stop, where you should turn right. Stay on the road for about 3 miles until you reach a gate; this is the spot where the gates in the movie *Jurassic Park* were filmed, though it looks nothing like the movie. Go around the gate and down the road for another mile to a confluence of streams at the base of Mt. Waialeale. Be sure to bring your camera. ⊠ *Kuamoo Rd., Kapaa.*

Waimea Canyon Road. For those wanting a very challenging road work-out, climb this road, also known as Route 550. After a 3,000-foot climb, the road tops out at mile 12, adjacent to Waimea Canyon, which will pop in and out of view on your right as you ascend. From here it continues several miles (mostly level) past the Kokee Museum and ends at the Kalalau Lookout. It's paved the entire way, uphill 100%, and curvy. ⚠ There's not much of a shoulder on either road—sometimes none—so be extra cautious. The road gets busier as the day wears on, so you may want to consider a sunrise ride. A slightly more moderate uphill climb is Kokee Road, Route 552, from Kekaha, which intersects with Route 550. Bikes aren't allowed on the hiking trails in and around Waimea Canyon and Kokee State Park, but there are miles of wonderful four-wheel-drive roads perfect for mountain biking. Check at Kokee Natural History Museum for a map and conditions. ⊠ *Off Rte. 50, near grocery store, Waimea (Kauai County).*

EQUIPMENT AND TOURS

Kauai Cycle. This reliable, full-service bike shop rents, sells, and repairs bikes. Cruisers, mountain bikes (front and full suspension), and road bikes are available, with directions to trails. The Ke Ala Hele Makalae coastal path is right out the back door. ⊠ *4-934 Kuhio Hwy., across from Taco Bell, Kapaa* ☎ *808/821–2115* ⊕ *www.kauaicycle.com* ⊠ *Rentals from $20 per day and $110 per wk.*

Outfitters Kauai. Hybrid "comfort" and mountain bikes (both full suspension and hardtails) as well as road bikes are available at this shop in Poipu. You can ride right out the door to tour Poipu, or get information on how to do a self-guided tour of Kokee State Park and Waimea Canyon. The company also leads sunrise and evening coasting tours (under the name **Bicycle Downhill**) from Waimea Canyon past the island's West Side beaches. Stand-up paddle tours are also available. ⊠ *2827-A Poipu Rd., near turnoff to Spouting Horn, Poipu* ☎ *808/742–9667, 888/742–9887* ⊕ *www.outfitterskauai.com* ⊠ *Rentals from $25; tours $109.*

Pedal 'n' Paddle. This company rents old-fashioned, single-speed beach cruisers and hybrid road bikes. In the heart of Hanalei, this is a great way to cruise the town; the more adventuresome cyclist can head to the end of the road. Be careful, though, because there are no bike lanes on the twisting-and-turning road to Kee Beach. ⊠ *Ching Young Village, 5-5190 Kuhio Hwy., Hanalei* ☎ *808/826–9069* ⊕ *www.pedalnpaddle. com* ⊠ *Rentals from $15 per day and $60 per wk.*

GOLF

For golfers, the Garden Isle might as well be known as the Robert Trent Jones Jr. Isle. Four of the island's eight courses, including Poipu Bay—onetime home of the PGA Grand Slam of Golf—are the work of Jones, who maintains a home at Princeville. Combine these four courses with those from Jack Nicklaus, Robin Nelson, and local legend Toyo Shirai, and you'll see that golf sets Kauai apart from the other Islands as much as the Pacific Ocean does. ■TIP→ Afternoon tee times at most courses can save you big bucks.

The Makai course at Princeville Makai Golf Club has consistently been ranked a top course in the United States.

Kiahuna Plantation Golf Course. A meandering creek, lava outcrops, and thickets of trees give Kiahuna its character. Robert Trent Jones Jr. was given a smallish piece of land just inland at Poipu, and defends par with smaller targets, awkward stances, and optical illusions. In 2003 a group of homeowners bought the club and brought Jones back to renovate the course (it was originally built in 1983), adding tees and revamping bunkers. The pro here boasts his course has the best putting greens on the island. This is the only course on Kauai with a complete set of junior's tee boxes. ⊠ *2545 Kiahuna Plantation Dr., Koloa* ☎ *808/742–9595* ⊕ *www.kiahunagolf.com* ✉ *$96, including cart* ⅃ *18 holes, 6787 yards, par 70.*

Ocean Course Hokuala Golf Club. The Jack Nicklaus–designed Ocean Course Hokuala completed its latest renovation in November 2016 creating not only a superb golf experience, but a visual treat and a Hawaii educational experience as well. With an assortment of plants and tropical birds adding to the atmosphere, this course wends through dark ravines and over picturesque landscape. The 5th hole is particularly striking as it requires a drive over a valley populated by mango and guava trees. The final holes hold unmatched views of Nawiliwili Bay, including the harbor, a lighthouse, and secluded beaches. ⊠ *3351 Hoolaulea Way, Lihue* ☎ *808/241–6000, 800/634–6400* ⊕ *www. hokualakauai.com/golf* ✉ *From $160; after 2 pm $126* ⅃ *18 holes, 7156 yards, par 72.*

Poipu Bay Golf Course. Poipu Bay has been called the Pebble Beach of Hawaii, and the comparison is apt. Like Pebble Beach, Poipu is a links course built on headlands, not true links land. There's wildlife galore. It's not unusual for golfers to see monk seals sunning on the beach below, sea turtles bobbing outside the shore break, and humpback whales leaping offshore. From 1994 to 2006, the course (designed by Robert Trent Jones Jr.) hosted the annual PGA Grand Slam of Golf. Tiger Woods was a frequent winner here. Call ahead to take advantage of varying prices for tee times. ✉ *2250 Ainako St., Koloa* ☎ *808/742–8711* ⊕ *www. poipubaygolf.com* 💲 *$209 before noon, $189 after* 🏌 *18 holes, 6127 yards, par 72.*

> **LILIKOI ALERT**
>
> If you're hiking in May and June, you may come across *lilikoi*—often referred to as passion fruit— scattered like yellow eggs among the ferns. It tastes as sweet and floral as it smells—bite the tip of the rind off and you'll see speckled jelly with tiny black seeds; then slurp it right out of the skin. If you miss lilikoi season, scout out delicious lilikoi mustards and jams sold by local grocers. Lilikoi pie is also served at a few Hawaiian eateries.

Fodor's Choice ★ **Princeville Makai Golf Club.** The 27-hole Princeville Makai Golf Club was named for its five ocean-hugging front holes. Designed by golf-course architect Robert Trent Jones Jr. in 1971, the 18-hole championship Makai Course underwent extensive renovations from 2008 to 2010, including new turf throughout, reshaped greens and bunkers, refurbished cart paths and comfort stations, and an extensive practice facility. Since the renovation the Makai Course has consistently been ranked a top golf course in the United States. ■TIP→ **Check the website for varying rates as well as other nongolf activities at the facility like the Sunset Golf Cart Tour, where you ride the course, sans clubs, and take in the spectacular ocean views.** ✉ *4080 Lei O Papa Rd., Princeville* ⊕ *www.makaigolf.com* 💲 *$295* 🏌 *18 holes, 7223 yards, par 72; Woods Course: 9 holes, 3445 yards, par 36.*

Wailua Municipal Golf Course. Considered by many to be one of Hawaii's best public golf courses, this seaside course provides an affordable game with minimal water hazards, but it is challenging enough to have been chosen to host three USGA Amateur Public Links Championships. It was first built as a nine-holer in the 1930s. The second nine holes were added in 1961. Course designer Toyo Shirai created a course that is fun but not punishing. The trade winds blow steadily on the East Side of the island and provide a game with challenges. An ocean view and affordability make this one of the most popular courses on the island. Tee times are accepted up to seven days in advance and can be paid in cash, traveler's checks, and some credit cards. ✉ *3-5350 Kuhio Hwy., Lihue* ☎ *808/241–6666* ⊕ *www.kauai.gov/Golf* 💲 *$48 weekdays, $60 weekends; cart rental $20* 🏌 *18 holes, 6585 yards, par 72.*

HIKING

The best way to experience the *aina*—the land—on Kauai is to step off the beach and hike into the remote interior. You'll find waterfalls so tall you'll strain your neck looking, pools of crystal-clear water for swimming, tropical forests teeming with plant life, and ocean vistas that will make you wish you could stay forever.

■ TIP→ **For your safety wear sturdy shoes—preferably water-resistant ones.** All hiking trails on Kauai are free, so far. There's a development plan in the works that could turn the Waimea Canyon and Kokee state parks into admission-charging destinations. Whatever it may be, it will be worth it. ⚠ **Following extensive flooding in early 2018, areas of the Napali Coast, including the Kalalau Trail, are undergoing repairs. Please check before visiting to make sure places are open.**

BEST SPOTS

Hanalei-Okolehao Trail. *Okolehao* basically translates to "moonshine" in Hawaiian. This trail follows the Hihimanu Ridge, which was established in the days of Prohibition, when this backyard liquor was distilled from the roots of ti plants. The 2-mile hike climbs 1,200 feet and offers a 360-degree view of Hanalei Bay and Waioli Valley. Your ascent begins at the China Ditch off the Hanalei River. Follow the trail through a lightly forested grove and then climb up a steep embankment. From here the trail is well marked. Most of the climb is lined with hala, ti, wild orchid, and eucalyptus. You'll get your first of many ocean views at mile marker 1. ⊠ *Hanalei ✛ Follow Ohiki Rd. (north of Hanalei Bridge) 5 miles to U.S. Fish and Wildlife Service parking area. Directly across street is small bridge that marks trailhead.*

Ho'opi'i Falls. Tucked among the winding roads and grassy pastures of Kapahi, 3 miles inland from Kapaa town, is an easy hike to two waterfalls. A 10-minute walk will deliver you to the creek. Follow it around to see the first set of falls. The more impressive second falls are a mere 25 minutes away. The swimming hole alone is worth the journey. Just climb the rooted path next to the first falls and turn left on the trail above. Turn left on the very next trail to descend back into the canyon and follow the leafy path that zigzags along the creek—the falls and the swimming hole lie below. ⊠ *Kapaa ✛ On north end of Kapaa, ¼ mile past last lookout, is side road called Kawaihau. Follow road up 3 miles, then turn right on Kapahi Rd. into residential neighborhood. Kapahi Rd. dead-ends near trailhead. Look for yellow gate on your left.*

Fodor's Choice
★
Kalalau Trail. Of all the hikes on the island, Kalalau Trail is by far the most famous and in many regards the most strenuous. A moderate hiker can handle the 2-mile trek to Hanakapiai Beach, and for the seasoned outdoorsman, the additional 2 miles up to the falls is manageable. But be prepared to rock-hop along a creek and ford waters that can get waist high during the rain. Round-trip to Hanakapiai Falls is 8 miles. This steep and often muddy trail is best approached with a walking stick. If there has been any steady rain, wait for drier days for a more enjoyable trek. The narrow Kalalau Trail delivers one startling ocean view after another along a path that is alternately shady and sunny. Wear hiking shoes or sandals, and bring drinking water since the creeks on the trail are not potable. Plenty of food is always encouraged on a strenuous hike such as this one. If you plan to venture the full 11 miles into Kalalau, you need to acquire a camping permit, either online or at

Continued on page 192

HAWAII'S PLANTS 101

Tropical Hibiscus

Hawaii is a bounty of rainbow-colored flowers and plants. The evening air is scented with their fragrance. Just look at the front yard of almost any home, travel any road, or visit any local park and you'll see a spectacular array of colored blossoms and leaves. What most visitors don't know is that many of the plants they are seeing are not native to Hawaii; rather, they were introduced during the last two centuries as ornamental plants, or for timber, shade, or fruit.

Hawaii boasts nearly every climate on the planet, excluding the two most extreme: arctic tundra and arid desert. The Islands have wine-growing regions, cactus-speckled ranchlands, icy mountaintops, and the rainiest forests on earth.

Plants introduced from around the world thrive here. The lush lowland valleys along the windward coasts are predominantly populated by non-native trees including yellow- and red-fruited **guava**, silvery-leafed **kukui**, and orange-flowered **tulip trees**.

The colorful **plumeria flower**, very fragrant and commonly used in lei making, and

the giant multicolored **hibiscus flower** are both used by many women as hair adornments, and are two of the most common plants found around homes and hotels. The umbrella-like **monkeypod tree** from Central America provides shade in many of Hawaii's parks including Kapiolani Park in Honolulu. Hawaii's largest tree, found in Lahaina, Maui, is a giant **banyan tree**. Its canopy and massive support roots cover about two-thirds of an acre. The native **ohia tree**, with its brilliant red brush-like flowers, and the **hapuu**, a giant tree fern, are common in Hawaii's forests and are also used ornamentally in gardens.

Naupaka, Limahuli Garden

9

Bougainvillea | Guava | Monkeypod
Banyan | Ohia Lehua* | Tulip Tree
Plumeria | Pandanus | Hibiscus
Anthurium | Kukui | Hapuu

*endemic to Hawaii

DID YOU KNOW?

More than 2,200 plant species are found in the Hawaiian Islands, but only about 1,000 are native. Of these, 320 are so rare, they are endangered. Hawaii's endemic plants evolved from ancestral seeds arriving in the Islands over thousands of years as baggage with birds, floating on ocean currents, or drifting on winds from continents thousands of miles away. Once here, these plants evolved in isolation, creating many new species known nowhere else in the world.

the State Building in Lihue, for $20 per person per night. You should secure a permit well in advance of your trip. ⚠ **Following extensive flooding in early 2018, call to make sure that the trail is open and accessible.** ✛ *Drive north past Hanalei to end of road. Trailhead is directly across from Kee Beach* ⊕ *www.kalalautrail.com* ✉ *$20 per person per night.*

Mahaulepu Heritage Trail. This trail offers the novice hiker an accessible way to appreciate the rugged southern coast of Kauai. A cross-country trail wends its way along the water, high above the ocean, through a lava field, and past a sacred *heiau* (stone structure) . Walk all the way to Mahaulepu, 2 miles north, for a two-hour round-trip. ✛ *Drive north on Poipu Rd., turn right at Poipu Bay Golf Course sign. The street name is Ainako, but sign is hard to see. Drive down to beach and park in lot* ⊕ *www.hikemahaulepu.org.*

WATERFALL WARNING
The many waterfalls on Kauai can be quite alluring; however, it's important to:
■ Evaluate water conditions before entering—do not enter a waterfall pool during or after heavy rains.
■ Never dive into the pool.
■ Remember that the leptospirosis bacteria may be present in freshwater streams and pools.
■ Wear water-friendly shoes; the rocks can be quite slippery as you're entering and exiting the pool.

Sleeping Giant Trail. An easily accessible trail practically in the heart of Kapaa, the moderately strenuous Sleeping Giant Trail—or simply Sleeping Giant—gains 1,000 feet over 2 miles. We prefer an early-morning—say, sunrise—hike, with sparkling blue-water vistas, up the east-side trailhead, but there are other back-side approaches. At the top you can see a grassy grove with a picnic table. It is a local favorite, with many East Siders meeting here to exercise. ✉ *Haleilio Rd., off Rte. 56, Wailua (Kauai County).*

Waimea Canyon and Kokee State Park. This park contains a 50-mile network of hiking trails of varying difficulty that take you through acres of native forests, across the highest-elevation swamp in the world, to the river at the base of the canyon, and onto pinnacles of land sticking their necks out over Napali Coast. All hikers should register at Kokee Natural History Museum, where you can find trail maps, current trail information, and specific directions.

The **Kukui Trail** descends 2½ miles and 2,200 feet into Waimea Canyon to the edge of the Waimea River—it's a steep climb. The **Awaawapuhi Trail**, with 1,600 feet of elevation gains and losses over 3¼ miles, feels more gentle than the Kukui Trail, but it offers its own huffing-and-puffing sections in its descent along a spiny ridge to a perch overlooking the ocean.

The 3½-mile **Alakai Swamp Trail** is accessed via the **Pihea Trail** or a four-wheel-drive road. There's one strenuous valley section, but otherwise it's a pretty level trail—once you access it. This trail is a bird-watcher's delight and includes a painterly view of Wainiha and Hanalei valleys at the trail's end. The trail traverses the purported

LEPTOSPIROSIS

Leptospirosis is a bacterial disease that is transmitted from animals to humans. It can survive for long periods of time in freshwater and mud contaminated by the urine of infected animals, such as pigs, rats, and goats.

The bacteria enter the body through the eyes, ears, nose, mouth, and broken skin. To avoid infection, don't drink untreated water from the Kauai's streams; don't wade in waters above the chest or submerge skin with cuts and abrasions in island streams or rivers.

Symptoms are often mild and resemble the flu—fever, diarrhea, chills, nausea, headache, vomiting, and body pains—and may occur 2 to 20 days after exposure. If you think you have these symptoms, see a doctor right away.

highest-elevation swamp in the world via a boardwalk so as not to disturb the fragile plant and wildlife. It is typically the coolest of the hikes due to the tree canopy, elevation, and cloud coverage.

The **Canyon Trail** offers much in its short trek: spectacular vistas of the canyon and the only dependable waterfall in Waimea Canyon. The easy 2-mile hike can be cut in half if you have a four-wheel-drive vehicle. The late-afternoon sun sets the canyon walls ablaze in color. ⊠ *Kokee Natural History Museum, 3600 Kokee Rd., Kekaha* ☎ *808/335–9975 for trail conditions* ⊕ *www.kokee.org.*

EQUIPMENT AND TOURS

Fodor'sChoice
★
Kauai Nature Tours. Father-and-son scientists started this hiking tour business. As such, their emphasis is on education and the environment. If you're interested in flora, fauna, volcanology, geology, oceanography, and the like, this is the company for you. They offer daylong hikes along coastal areas, beaches, and in the mountains. ■TIP→ **If you have a desire to see a specific location, just ask. They will do custom hikes to spots they don't normally hit if there is interest.** Hikes range from easy to strenuous. Transportation is often provided from your hotel. ⊠ *5162 Lawai Rd., Koloa* ☎ *808/742–8305, 888/233–8365* ⊕ *www. kauainaturetours.com* ✐ *From $155.*

Princeville Ranch Adventures. This 4-mile hike traverses Princeville Ranch, crossing through a rain forest and to a five-tier waterfall for lunch and swimming. Moderately strenuous hiking is required. ⊠ *Rte. 56, between mile markers 27 and 28, Princeville* ☎ *808/826–7669, 888/955–7669* ⊕ *www.princevilleranch.com* ✐ *$129.*

HORSEBACK RIDING

Most of the horseback-riding tours on Kauai are primarily walking tours with little trotting and no cantering or galloping, so no experience is required. Zip. Zilch. Nada. If you're interested, most of the stables offer private lessons. The most popular tours are the ones including a picnic lunch by the water. Your only dilemma may be deciding what kind of water you want—waterfalls or ocean. You may want to make your decision based on where you're staying. The "waterfall picnic" tours are on the wetter North Shore, and the "beach picnic" tours take place on the South Side.

CJM Country Stables. Just past the Hyatt in Poipu, CJM Stables offers a three-hour picnic ride with noshing on the beach, as well as their more popular two-hour trail ride without the picnic break. The landscape here is rugged and beautiful, featuring sand dunes and limestone bluffs. CJM can get you as close as anyone to the secluded Mahaulepu Bay. They sponsor seasonal rodeos that are free and open to the public, and participate in other popular community events. ⊠ *Poipu Rd., Koloa* ✛ *1½ miles from Grand Hyatt Kauai* ☎ *808/742–6096* ⊕ *www.cjm-stables.com* ✍ *From $110.*

Fodor'sChoice   **Princeville Ranch Adventures.** A longtime *kamaaina* (resident) family oper-
★   ates Princeville Ranch. They originated the waterfall picnic tour, which runs 3½ hours and includes a short but steep hike down to Kalihiwai Falls, a dramatic three-tier waterfall, for swimming and picnicking. Princeville also has shorter, straight riding tours and private rides. A popular option is the three-hour combination Ride N' Glide tour with three zip lines. ⊠ *Kuhio Hwy., off Kapaka Rd., between mile markers 27 and 28, Princeville* ☎ *808/826–7669* ⊕ *www.princevilleranch.com* ✍ *Ride only from $119; private tours from $189.*

MOUNTAIN TUBING

For the past 40 years, Hawaii's sugarcane plantations have closed one by one. In the fall of 2009, Gay & Robinson announced the closure of Kauai's last plantation, leaving only one in Maui, the last in the state. The sugarcane irrigation ditches remain, striating these Islands like spokes in a wheel. Inspired by the Hawaiian *auwai*, which diverted water from streams to taro fields, these engineering feats harnessed the rain. One ingenious tour company on Kauai has figured out a way to make exploring them an adventure: float inflatable tubes down the route.

FAMILY   **Kauai Backcountry Adventures.** Both zip-line and tubing tours are offered. Popular with all ages, the tubing adventure can book up two weeks in advance in busy summer months. Here's how it works: you recline in an inner tube and float down fern-lined irrigation ditches that were built more than a century ago—the engineering is impressive—to divert water from Mt. Waialeale to sugar and pineapple fields around the island. They'll even give you a headlamp so you can see as you float through five covered tunnels. The scenery from the island's interior at the base of Mt. Waialeale on Lihue Plantation land is superb. Ages five and up are welcome. The tour takes about three hours and includes a picnic lunch and a swim in a swimming hole. ■ TIP➔ **You'll definitely want to pack water-friendly shoes (or rent some from the outfitter), sunscreen, a hat, bug repellent, and a beach towel.** Tours are offered up to a dozen times daily. ⊠ *3-4131 Kuhio Hwy., across from gas station, Hanamaulu* ☎ *808/245–2506, 888/270–0555* ⊕ *www.kauaibackcountry.com* ✍ *$114 per person.*

On the North Shore, adventure seekers will find a nine-zip-line course run by Princeville Ranch Adventures.

SKYDIVING

If you're a thrill seeker, it doesn't get any better than jumping out of an airplane over an island—oh, the views—and floating peacefully back down to earth tethered to a parachute.

Skydive Kauai. Ten thousand feet over Kauai and falling at a rate of 120 mph is probably as thrilling as it gets while airborne. First, there's the 25-minute plane ride to altitude in a Cessna 182, then the exhilaration of the first step into sky, the sensation of sailing weightless in the air over Kauai, and finally the peaceful buoyancy beneath the canopy of your parachute. A tandem free-fall rates among the most unforgettable experiences of a lifetime. Wed that to the aerial view over Kauai and you've got a winning marriage that you can relive with an HD video memory. ⊠ *Port Allen Airport, 3666 Kuiloko Rd., Hanapepe* ☎ *808/335–5859* ⊕ *www.skydivekauai.com* ☞ *$239.*

ZIP-LINE TOURS

The latest adventure on Kauai is "zipping," or "zip-lining." Regardless of what you call it, chances are you'll scream like a rock star while trying it. Strap on a harness, clip onto a cable running from one side of a river or valley to the other, and zip across. The step off is the scariest part. ■ TIP→ **Pack knee-length shorts or pants, athletic shoes, and courage for this adventure.**

Fodor's Choice ★ **Just Live.** When Nichol Baier and Julie Lester started Just Live in 2003, their market was exclusively school-age children, but soon they added visitor tours. Experiential education through adventure is how they describe it. Whatever you call it, sailing 70 feet above the ground for three-plus hours will take your vacation to another level. This is the only treetop zip line on Kauai where your feet never touch ground once you're in the air: seven zips and four canopy bridges make the Tree Top Tour their most popular one. For the heroic at heart, there's the Zipline Eco Adventure, which includes three zip lines, two canopy bridges, a climbing wall, a 100-foot rappelling tower, and a "Monster Swing." If you're short on time—or courage—you can opt for the Wikiwiki Zipline Tour, which includes three zip lines and two canopy bridges in about two hours. They now have a shop with outdoor gear specifically for the island's activities, although their primary focus remains community programming. Enjoy knowing that money spent here serves Kauai's children. ⊠ *Harbor Mall Shopping Center, 3501 Rice St., Lihue* ☎ *808/482–1295* ⊕ *www.zipkauai.com* ⊠ *From $79.*

Outfitters Kauai. This outfitter's most popular adventure, the Kipu Zipline Safari Tour, features an 1,800-foot tandem zip—that's right, you don't have to go it alone. You can also paddle the Wailua River or take the downhill bike ride along the Waimea Canyon road. They also offer The Flyline, the state's longest zip line, which has a "run" of 4,000 feet. ⊠ *2827-A Poipu Rd., Poipu* ☎ *808/742–9667, 888/742–9887* ⊕ *www. outfitterskauai.com* ⊠ *From $116.*

Princeville Ranch Adventures. The North Shore's answer to zip-lining is a nine-zip-line course with a bit of hiking, and suspension-bridge crossing thrown in for a half-day adventure. The 4½-hour Zip N' Dip tour includes a picnic and swimming at a waterfall pool, while the Zip Express whizzes you through the entire course in 3 hours. Both excursions conclude with a 1,200-foot tandem zip across a valley. Guides are energetic and fun. This is as close as it gets to flying; just watch out for the albatross. ⊠ *Rte. 56, between mile markers 27 and 28, Princeville* ☎ *808/826–7669, 888/955–7669* ⊕ *www.princevilleranch. com* ⊠ *From $139.*

UNDERSTANDING KAUAI

HAWAIIAN VOCABULARY

HAWAIIAN VOCABULARY

Although an understanding of Hawaiian is by no means required on a trip to the Aloha State, a *malihini*, or newcomer, will find plenty of opportunities to pick up a few of the local words and phrases. Traditional names and expressions are widely used in the Islands. You're likely to read or hear at least a few words.

With a basic understanding and some uninhibited practice, anyone can have enough command of the local tongue to ask for directions and to order from a restaurant menu. One visitor announced she would not leave until she could pronounce the name of the state fish, the *humuhumunukunukuāpua'a*.

Simplifying the learning process is the fact that the Hawaiian language contains only eight consonants—H, K, L, M, N, P, W, and the silent *'okina,* or glottal stop, written '—plus the five vowels. All syllables end in a vowel. Each vowel, with the exception of a few diphthongized double vowels such as *au* (pronounced "ow") or *ai* (pronounced "eye"), is pronounced separately. Thus *'Iolani* is four syllables (ee-oh-la-nee), not three (yo-la-nee). Although some Hawaiian words have only vowels, most contain consonants, but consonants are never doubled.

Pronunciation is simple. Pronounce *A* "ah" as in *father*; *E* "ay" as in *weigh*; *I* "ee" as in *marine*; *O* "oh" as in *no*; *U* "oo" as in *true*.

Consonants mirror their English equivalents, with the exception of *W*. When the letter begins any syllable other than the first one in a word, it is usually pronounced as a *V*. *'Awa,* the Polynesian drink, is pronounced "ava," *'ewa* is pronounced "eva."

Almost all long Hawaiian words are combinations of shorter words; they are not difficult to pronounce if you segment them. *Kalaniana'ole,* the highway running east from Honolulu, is easily understood as *Kalani ana 'ole.* Apply the standard pronunciation rules—the stress falls on the next-to-last syllable of most two- or three-syllable Hawaiian words—and Kalaniana'ole Highway is as easy to say as Main Street.

Now about that fish. Try *humu-humu nuku-nuku āpu a'a.*

The other unusual element in Hawaiian language is the *kahakō,* or macron, written as a short line (ˉ) placed over a vowel. The kahakō puts emphasis on a syllable that would normally not be stressed. The most familiar example is probably *Waikīkī.* With no macrons, the stress would fall on the middle syllable; with only one macron, on the last syllable, the stress would fall on the first and last syllables. Some words become plural with the addition of a macron, often on a syllable that would have been stressed anyway. No Hawaiian word becomes plural with the addition of an *S,* since that letter does not exist in the language.

The Hawaiian diacritical marks are not printed in this guide.

Pidgin

You may hear pidgin, the unofficial language of Hawaii. It is a Creole language, with its own grammar, evolved from the mixture of English, Hawaiian, Japanese, Portuguese, and other languages spoken in 19th-century Hawaii.

Glossary

What follows is a glossary of some of the most commonly used Hawaiian words. Hawaiian residents appreciate visitors who at least try to pick up the local language.

'a'ā: rough, crumbling lava, contrasting with *pāhoehoe,* which is smooth.

'ae: yes.

aikane: friend.

āina: land.

akamai: smart, clever, possessing savoir faire.

akua: god.

ala: a road, path, or trail.

ali'i: a Hawaiian chief, a member of the chiefly class.

aloha: love, affection, kindness; also a salutation meaning both greetings and farewell.

'ānuenue: rainbow.

'a'ole: no.

'apōpō: tomorrow.

'auwai: a ditch.

auwē: alas, woe is me!

'ehu: a red-haired Hawaiian.

'ewa: in the direction of 'Ewa plantation, west of Honolulu.

hala: the pandanus tree, whose leaves (*lau hala*) are used to make baskets and plaited mats.

hālau: school.

hale: a house.

hale pule: church, house of worship.

ha mea iki or **ha mea 'ole:** you're welcome.

hana: to work.

haole: ghost. Since the first foreigners were Caucasian, *haole* now means a Caucasian person.

hapa: a part, sometimes a half; often used as a short form of *hapa haole*, to mean a person who is part-Caucasian.

hau'oli: to rejoice. *Hau'oli Makahiki Hou* means Happy New Year. *Hau'oli lā hānau* means Happy Birthday.

heiau: an outdoor stone platform; an ancient Hawaiian place of worship.

holo: to run.

holoholo: to go for a walk, ride, or sail.

holokū: a long Hawaiian dress, somewhat fitted, with a yoke and a train. It was worn at court, and at least one local translates the word as "expensive mu'umu'u."

holomū: a post–World War II cross between a *holokū* and a mu'umu'u, less fitted than the former but less voluminous than the latter, and having no train.

honi: to kiss; a kiss. A phrase that some tourists may find useful, quoted from a popular hula, is *Honi Ka'ua Wikiwiki:* Kiss me quick!

honu: turtle.

ho'omalimali: flattery, a deceptive "line," bunk, baloney, hooey.

huhū: angry.

hui: a group, club, or assembly. A church may refer to its congregation as a *hui* and a social club may be called a *hui*.

hukilau: a seine; a communal fishing party in which everyone helps to drive the fish into a huge net, pull it in, and divide the catch.

hula: the dance of Hawai'i.

iki: little.

ipo: sweetheart.

ka: the. This is the definite article for most singular words; for plural nouns, the definite article is usually *nā*.

kahuna: a priest, doctor, or other trained person of old Hawai'i, endowed with special professional skills that often included prophecy or other supernatural powers; the plural form is kāhuna.

kai: the sea, saltwater.

kalo: the taro plant from whose root *poi* (paste) is made.

kamā'aina: literally, a child of the soil; it refers to people who were born in the Islands or have lived there for a long time.

kanaka: originally a man or humanity, it is now used to denote a male Hawaiian or part-Hawaiian, but is occasionally taken as a slur when used by non-Hawaiians. *Kanaka maoli,* is used by some Native Hawaiian rights activists to embrace part-Hawaiians as well.

kāne: a man, a husband. If you see this word on a door, it's the men's room. If you see *kane* on a door, it's probably a misspelling; that is the Hawaiian name for the skin fungus tinea.

kapa: also called by its Tahitian name, *tapa,* a cloth made of beaten bark dyed and stamped with a repeat design.

kapakahi: crooked, cockeyed, uneven. You've got your hat on *kapakahi*.

kapu: keep out, prohibited. This is the Hawaiian version of the more widely known Tongan word *tabu* (taboo).

kapuna: grandparent; elder.

kēia lā: today.

keiki: a child; *keikikāne* is a boy, *keikiwahine* a girl.

kona: the leeward side of the Islands, the direction (south) from which the *kona* wind and *kona* rain come.

kula: upland.

kuleana: a homestead or small plot of ground on which a family has been installed for some generations without necessarily owning it. By extension, *kuleana* is used to denote any area or department in which one has a special interest or prerogative. You'll hear it used this way: If you want to hire a surfboard, see Moki; that's his *kuleana.*

lā: sun.

lamalama: to fish with a torch.

lānai: a porch, a balcony, an outdoor living room. Don't confuse this two-syllable word with the three-syllable name of the island, Lāna'i.

lani: heaven, the sky.

lau hala: the leaf of the *hala,* or pandanus tree, widely used in handicrafts.

lei: a garland of flowers.

limu: sun.

lolo: stupid.

luna: a plantation overseer or foreman.

mahalo: thank you.

makai: toward the ocean.

malihini: a newcomer to the Islands.

mana: the spiritual power that the Hawaiian believed inhabited all things and creatures.

manō: shark.

manuwahi: free, gratis.

mauka: toward the mountains.

mauna: mountain.

mele: a Hawaiian song or chant, often of epic proportions.

Mele Kalikimaka: Merry Christmas (a transliteration from the English phrase).

Menehune: a Hawaiian pixie.

moana: the ocean.

mu'umu'u: the voluminous dress in which the missionaries enveloped Hawaiian women. Culturally sensitive locals have embraced the Hawaiian spelling but often shorten the spoken word to "mu'u." Most English dictionaries include the spelling "muumuu."

nani: beautiful.

nui: big.

ohana: family.

'ono: delicious.

pāhoehoe: smooth, unbroken, satiny lava.

Pākē: Chinese. This *Pākē* carver makes beautiful things.

palapala: document, printed matter.

pali: a cliff, precipice.

pānini: prickly pear cactus.

paniolo: a Hawaiian cowboy, a rough transliteration of *español,* the language of the Islands' earliest cowboys.

pau: finished, done.

pilikia: trouble. The Hawaiian word is much more widely used here than its English equivalent.

puka: a hole.

pupule: crazy, like the celebrated Princess Pupule. This word has replaced its English equivalent in local usage.

pu'u: volcanic cinder cone.

waha: mouth.

wahine: a female, a woman, a wife, and a sign on the ladies' room door; the plural form is *wāhine.*

wai: freshwater, as opposed to saltwater, which is *kai.*

wailele: waterfall.

wikiwiki: to hurry, hurry up (since this is a reduplication of *wiki,* quick, neither *W* is pronounced as a *V*).

TRAVEL SMART
KAUAI

GETTING HERE AND AROUND

▌ AIR TRAVEL

Flying time is about 10 hours from New York, 8 hours from Chicago, and 5 hours from Los Angeles.

Some of the major airline carriers serving Hawaii fly directly from the U.S. mainland to Kauai, allowing you to bypass connecting flights out of Honolulu. Although Lihue Airport is smaller and more casual than Honolulu International, it can also be quite busy during peak times. Allot extra travel time during morning and afternoon rush-hour traffic periods to avoid stressing over missing a flight.

Plan to arrive at the airport approximately 60 minutes before departure for interisland flights and slightly longer than that for flights to the mainland.

Plants and plant products are subject to regulation by the Department of Agriculture, both on entering and leaving Hawaii. Upon leaving the Islands, you'll have to have your bags x-rayed and tagged at one of the airport's agricultural inspection stations before you proceed to check-in. Pineapples and coconuts with the packer's agricultural inspection stamp pass freely; papayas must be treated, inspected, and stamped. All other fruits are banned for export to the U.S. mainland. Flowers pass—except for gardenias, rose leaves, jade vine, and mauna loa. Also banned are insects, snails, soil, cotton, cacti, sugarcane, and all berry plants.

You'll have to leave dogs and other pets at home. A 120-day quarantine is imposed to keep out rabies, which is nonexistent in Hawaii. If specific pre- and post-arrival requirements are met, animals may qualify for a 30-day or 5-day-or-less quarantine.

Air Travel Resources in Hawaii State of Hawaii Airports Division Offices. ☏ *808/836–6413* ⊕ *www.hawaii.gov/dot/airports.*

AIRPORTS

On Kauai, visitors fly into Lihue Airport, on the East Side of the island. Visitor information booths are outside each baggage-claim area. Visitors will also find news- and lei stands, an HMS Host restaurant, and a Travel Traders gift shop at the airport.

For most domestic and international flights however, Honolulu International Airport (HNL) is the main stopover. From Honolulu, there are interisland flights to Kauai departing regularly from early morning until evening. In addition, some carriers offer nonstop service directly from the U.S. mainland to Lihue Airport (LIH).

To travel interisland from Honolulu on Hawaiian Air you will depart from the connected interisland terminal. For other airlines you will leave from the commuter-airline terminal, located in a separate structure adjacent to the main terminal building. A free bus service, the Wiki Wiki Shuttle, operates between terminals.

Contacts Honolulu International Airport (HNL). ☏ *808/836–6413* ⊕ *www.hawaii.gov/dot/airports.* **Lihue Airport (LIH).** ☏ *808/274–3800* ⊕ *www.hawaii.gov/dot/airports.*

GROUND TRANSPORTATION

Marriott Kauai and Kauai Beach Resort provide airport shuttles to and from the Lihue Airport. In addition, travelers who've booked a tour with Kauai Island Tours, Roberts Hawaii, or Polynesian Adventure Tours will be picked up at the airport.

SpeediShuttle offers transportation between the airport and hotels, resorts, and time-share complexes on the island. There is an online reservation and fare quote system for information and bookings. Or, you can hire a taxi or limousine. Cabs are available curbside at baggage claim. Cab fares to locations around the island are estimated as follows: Poipu

$35–$41, Wailua–Waipouli $17–$20, Lihue–Kukui Grove $10, Princeville–Haena $72–$95. Kauai North Shore Limo offers service to Lihue Airport.

Uber and Lyft are somewhat recent arrivals on island, but you can still expect to pay around $75–$80 for a ride from the Airport to Princeville (approximately 30 miles).

Contacts Kauai North Shore Limo.
☎ 808/634–7260 ⊕ kauainorthshorelimo.com.
SpeediShuttle. ☎ 877/242–5777 ⊕ www.speedishuttle.com.

FLIGHTS

Alaska Airlines has a daily Seattle–Lihue flight. American Airlines offers a daily, nonstop Los Angeles–Kauai flight, in addition to its service into Honolulu, Maui, and the Big Island. Delta has a Los Angeles–Lihue flight and also serves Oahu (Honolulu) and Maui. United Airlines provides direct service to Lihue Airport from Denver, Los Angeles, and San Francisco. The carrier also flies into Honolulu, Maui, and the Big Island. Hawaiian offers a daily, nonstop Los Angeles–Kauai flight; all other Mainland flights require a connection in Honolulu.

INTERISLAND FLIGHTS

Interisland flight travel has become expensive in recent years, so be ready to pay should you wish to visit neighboring islands. Hawaiian Airlines services Kauai. In addition to offering a discount for booking online, all have free frequent-flier programs that will entitle you to rewards and upgrades the more you fly. Be sure to compare prices offered by all the interisland carriers. If you are somewhat flexible with your days and times for island-hopping, you should have no problem getting a round-trip ticket.

▌ BUS TRAVEL

On Kauai, the County Transportation Agency operates the Kauai Bus, which provides service between Hanalei and Kekaha. It also provides limited service

to the airport and to Koloa and Poipu. The fare is $2 for adults, and frequent-rider passes are available.

Information Kauai Bus. ☎ 808/246–8110 ⊕ www.kauai.com/kauai-bus.

▌ CAR TRAVEL

The best way to experience all of Kauai's stunning beauty is to get in a car and explore. The 15-mile stretch of Napali Coast, with its breathtaking, verdant-green sheer cliffs, is the only part of the island that's not accessible by car. Otherwise, one main road can get you from Barking Sands Beach on the West Side to Haena on the North Shore.

Asking for directions will almost always produce a helpful explanation from the locals, but you should be prepared for an island term or two. Instead of using compass directions, remember that Hawaii residents refer to places as being either *mauka* (toward the mountains) or *makai* (toward the ocean) from one another. Hawaii has a strict seat-belt law. All those riding in the vehicle must wear a seat belt. The fine for not wearing a seat belt is $112. There is also a law forbidding the use of handheld devices while driving. Jaywalking is also common in the Islands, so please pay careful attention to the roads. It also is considered rude to honk your horn, so be patient if someone is turning or proceeding through an intersection.

While driving on Kauai, you will come across several one-lane bridges. If you are the first to approach a bridge, the car on the other side will wait while you cross. If a car on the other side is closer to the bridge, then you should wait while the driver crosses. If you're enjoying the island's dramatic views, pull over to the shoulder so you don't block traffic.

GASOLINE

You can count on having to pay more at the pump for gasoline on Kauai than on the U.S. mainland. There are no gas stations past Princeville on the North Shore, and no stations past Waimea on the West Side, so if you're running low, fuel up before heading out to the end of the road.

PARKING

On Kauai there are no parking meters, parking garages, parking tags, or paid parking. If there's room on the side of the road, you can park there. A good rule of thumb is if there are other cars parked in that area, it's safe to do the same.

ROAD CONDITIONS

Kauai has a relatively well-maintained highway running south from Lihue to Barking Sands Beach; a spur at Waimea takes you along Waimea Canyon Drive to Kokee State Park. A northern route also winds its way from Lihue to the end of the road at Haena, the beginning of the rugged and roadless Napali Coast. Opt for a four-wheel-drive vehicle if dirt-road exploration holds any appeal.

ROADSIDE EMERGENCIES

If you find yourself in an emergency or accident while driving on Kauai, pull over if you can. If you have a cell phone with you, call the roadside assistance number on your rental-car contract or AAA Help. If you find that your car has been broken into or stolen, report it immediately to your rental-car company and an agent can assist you. If it's an emergency and someone is hurt, call 911 immediately and stay there until medical personnel arrive.

CAR RENTAL

Should you plan to do any sightseeing on Kauai, it is best to rent a car. Even if all you want to do is relax at your resort, you may want to hop in the car to check out one of the island's popular restaurants.

While on Kauai, you can rent anything from an econobox to a Ferrari. Rates are usually better if you reserve through a rental agency's website. It's wise to make reservations far in advance and make sure that a confirmed reservation guarantees you a car, especially if you're visiting during peak seasons or for major conventions

or sporting events. Rates begin at about $25 to $35 a day for an economy car with air-conditioning, automatic transmission, and unlimited mileage, depending on your pickup location. This does not include the airport concession fee, general excise tax, rental-vehicle surcharge, or vehicle license fee. When you reserve a car, ask about cancellation penalties. Many rental companies in Hawaii offer coupons for discounts at various attractions that could save you money later on in your trip.

In Hawaii you must be 21 years of age to rent a car, and you must have a valid driver's license and a major credit card. Those under 25 will pay a daily surcharge of $15–$25. Request car seats and extras such as GPS when you book. Hawaii's Child Restraint Law requires that all children three years and younger be in an approved child safety seat in the backseat of a vehicle. Children ages four to seven must be seated in a rear booster seat or child restraint such as a lap and shoulder belt. Car seats and boosters range from $5 to $8 per day.

Your unexpired driver's license is valid for rental for up to 90 days.

Since the road circling the island is usually two lanes, allow plenty of time to return your vehicle so that you can make your flight. Traffic can be bad during morning and afternoon rush hour. Give yourself about two hours before departure time to return your vehicle.

LOCAL DO'S AND TABOOS

GREETINGS

Hawaii is a very friendly place, and this is reflected in the day-to-day encounters with friends, family, and even business associates. Women often hug and kiss one another on the cheek, and men shake hands and sometimes combine that with a friendly hug. When a man and a woman are greeting each other and are good friends, it is not unusual for them to hug and kiss on the cheek. Children are taught to call any elders "auntie" or "uncle," even if they aren't related. It's a way to show respect and can result in a local Hawaiian child having dozens of aunties or uncles. It's also reflective of the strong sense of *ohana* (family) that exists in the Islands.

When you walk off a long flight, perhaps a bit groggy and stiff, nothing quite compares with a Hawaiian lei greeting. The casual ceremony ranks as one of the fastest ways to make the transition from the worries of home to the joys of your vacation. Though the tradition has created an expectation that everyone receives this floral garland when he or she steps off the plane, the State of Hawaii cannot greet each of its nearly 7 million annual visitors.

If you've booked a vacation with a wholesaler or tour company, a lei greeting might be included in your package, so check before you leave. If not, it's easy to arrange a lei greeting for yourself or your companions before you arrive into Lihue Airport. Kamaaina Leis, Flowers & Greeters has been providing lei greetings for visitors to the Islands since 1983. To be really wowed by the experience, request a lei of plumeria, some of the most divine-smelling blossoms on the planet. A plumeria or dendrobium orchid lei is considered standard and costs approximately $25 per person.

Kamaaina Leis, Flowers & Greeters.
☎ *808/836–3246.*

LANGUAGE

Hawaii was admitted to the Union in 1959, so residents can be sensitive when visitors refer to their own hometowns as "back in the States." Remember, when in Hawaii, refer to the contiguous 48 states as "the mainland" and not as "the United States." When you do, you won't appear to be such a *malahini* (newcomer).

English is the primary language on the Islands. Making the effort to learn some Hawaiian words can be rewarding, however. Despite the length of many Hawaiian words, the Hawaiian alphabet is actually one of the world's shortest, with only 12 letters: the five vowels, *a, e, i, o, u,* and seven consonants, *h, k, l, m, n, p, w.* Hawaiian words you're most likely to encounter during your visit to the Islands are *aloha, mahalo* (thank you), *keiki* (child), *haole* (Caucasian or foreigner, often a derogatory term), *mauka* (toward the mountains), *makai* (toward the ocean), and *pau* (finished, all done). Hawaiian history includes waves of immigrants, each bringing its own language. To communicate with each other, they developed a sort of slang known as "pidgin." If you listen closely, you'll know what is being said by the inflections and by the extensive use of body language. For example, when you know what you want to say but don't know how to say it, just say, "You know, da kine." For an informative and somewhat hilarious view of things Hawaiian, check out Jerry Hopkins's series of books titled *Pidgin to the Max* and *Fax to the Max,* available at most local bookstores in the Hawaiiana sections.

ESSENTIALS

■ COMMUNICATIONS

With cell-phone service spotty in many of the remote areas, you can't always rely on Internet capability no matter the data plan. With that being said, most of the major hotels and resorts offer high-speed access in rooms and/or lobbies. You should check with your hotel in advance to confirm that access is wireless. If you're staying at a small inn or B&B without Internet access, ask the proprietor for the nearest café or coffee shop with wireless access.

■ HEALTH

In addition to being the Aloha State, Hawaii is known as the Health State. The life expectancy here is 79 years, the longest in the nation. Balmy weather makes it easy to remain active year-round, and the low-stress aloha attitude certainly contributes to general well-being. When you are visiting the Islands, however, there are a few health issues to keep in mind.

The Hawaii State Department of Health recommends that you drink 16 ounces of water per hour to avoid dehydration when hiking or spending time in the sun. Use sunblock, wear UV-reflective sunglasses, and protect your head with a visor or hat for shade. If you're not acclimated to warm, humid weather, you should allow plenty of time for rest stops and refreshments. When visiting freshwater streams, be aware of the tropical disease leptospirosis, which is spread by animal urine and carried into streams and mud. Symptoms include fever, headache, nausea, and red eyes and may not appear immediately. If left untreated, it can cause liver and kidney damage, respiratory failure, internal bleeding, and even death. To avoid this, don't swim or wade in freshwater streams or ponds if you have open sores, and don't drink from any freshwater streams or ponds, especially after heavy rains.

On the Islands, fog is a rare occurrence, but there can often be "vog," an airborne haze of gases released from volcanic vents on the Big Island. During certain weather conditions such as "Kona Winds," the vog can settle over the Islands and wreak havoc with respiratory and other health conditions, especially asthma or emphysema. If susceptible, stay indoors and get emergency assistance if needed.

The Islands have their share of bugs and insects that enjoy the tropical climate as much as visitors do. Most are harmless but annoying. When planning to spend time outdoors in hiking areas, wear long-sleeved clothing and pants and use mosquito repellent containing DEET. In very damp places you may encounter the dreaded local centipede. On the Islands they usually come in one of three colors: brown, blue, or bright orange. They range from the size of a worm to an 8-inch cigar. Their sting is very painful, and the reaction is similar to bee- and wasp-sting reactions. If stung, immediately run very hot water over the wound for 20 minutes or so. When camping, shake out your sleeping bag before climbing in, and check your shoes in the morning, as the centipedes like cozy places. If planning on hiking or traveling in remote areas, always carry a first-aid kit and appropriate medications for sting reactions.

■ HOURS OF OPERATION

Even people in paradise have to work. Generally, local business hours are weekdays 8–5. Banks are usually open Monday–Thursday 8:30–4 and until 6 on Friday. Some banks have Saturday-morning hours.

Many self-serve gas stations stay open around the clock, with full-service stations usually open from around 7 am until 9 pm. The larger U.S. post offices are open weekdays 8:30 am–4:30 pm and Saturday

8:30–noon. Check operating hours for smaller post offices.

Most museums generally open their doors between 9 am and 10 am and stay open until 5 pm Tuesday–Saturday. Many museums operate with afternoon hours only on Sunday and close on Monday. Visitor-attraction hours vary throughout the state, but most sights are open daily, with the exception of major holidays such as Christmas. Check local publications upon arrival for attraction hours and schedules if visiting over holiday periods. The local dailies carry a listing of local cultural events for those time periods.

Stores in resort areas sometimes open as early as 8, with shopping-center opening hours varying from 9:30 to 10 on weekdays and Saturday, a bit later on Sunday. Bigger malls stay open until 9 weekdays and Saturday and close at 5 on Sunday. Boutiques in resort areas may stay open as late as 11.

PACKING

Hawaii is casual: sandals, bathing suits, and comfortable, informal clothing are the norm. In summer, synthetic slacks and shirts, although easy to care for, can be uncomfortably warm.

One of the most important things to tuck into your suitcase is sunscreen, though it is readily available at most stores.

As for clothing in the Hawaiian Islands, there's a saying that when a man wears a suit during the day, he's either going for a loan or he's a lawyer trying a case. Only a few upscale restaurants require a jacket for dinner. The aloha shirt is accepted dress in Hawaii for business and most social occasions. Shorts are acceptable daytime attire, along with a T-shirt or polo shirt. There's no need to buy expensive sandals on the mainland—here you can get flip-flops for a couple of dollars and off-brand sandals for $20. Golfers should remember that many courses have dress codes requiring a collared shirt; call courses you're interested in for details.

If you're not prepared, you can pick up appropriate clothing at resort pro shops. If you're visiting in winter, bring a sweater or light- to medium-weight jacket. A polar fleece pullover is ideal and makes a great impromptu travel pillow.

SAFETY

Hawaii is generally a safe tourist destination, but it's still wise to follow the same common-sense safety precautions you would normally follow in your own hometown.

Be wary of those hawking "too good to be true" prices on everything from car rentals to attractions. Many of these offers are just a lure to get you in the door for time-share presentations. When handed a flier, read the fine print before you make your decision to participate.

Safety Transportation Security Administration. ⊕ *www.tsa.gov.*

TAXES

There's a 4.16% state sales tax on all purchases, including food. The state sales tax plus the hotel room tax add approximately 14% to your hotel bill. A $3-per-day road tax is also assessed on each rental vehicle.

TIME

Hawaii is on Hawaiian standard time, five hours behind New York and two hours behind Los Angeles for the winter months.

While the U.S. mainland uses daylight saving time from March until November, Hawaii does not, so add an extra hour of time difference between the Islands and U.S. mainland destinations during that part of the year. You may also find that things generally move more slowly here. That has nothing to do with your watch—it's just the laid-back way called Hawaiian time.

▌ TIPPING

Tip cabdrivers 15% of the fare. Standard tips for restaurants and bar tabs run from 15% to 20% of the bill, depending on the standard of service. Bellhops at hotels usually receive $1 per bag, more if you have bulky items such as bicycles and surfboards. Tip the hotel room maid $1 per night, paid daily. Tip doormen $1 for assistance with taxis; tips for concierges vary depending on the service. For example, tip more for "hard-to-get" event tickets or dining reservations.

For single-day guided activities like a boat trip to Napali, a zip-lining tour, or surf lessons, you should tip each guide at least $10–$20 if you feel he or she enhanced your experience. Often, the tour company takes the bulk of your booking price, and the locals who are sharing their alohas with you are depending on your tips.

▌ TOURS

Globus has two Hawaii itineraries that include Kauai, one of which is an escorted cruise on Norwegian Cruise Lines' *Pride of America* that includes two days on the Garden Island. Tauck Travel offers an 11-night *Best of Hawaii* tour that includes two nights on Kauai with leisure time for either relaxation or exploration.

EscortedHawaiiTours.com, owned and operated by Atlas Cruises & Tours, sells more than a dozen Hawaii trips ranging from 7 to 12 nights operated by various guided-tour companies including Globus and Tauck. Several of these trips include two to three nights on Kauai.

Recommended Companies Atlas Cruises & Tours. ☎ 800/942–3301 ⊕ www.atlas-travelweb.com. **Globus.** ☎ 866/755–8581 ⊕ www.globusjourneys.com. **Tauck Travel.** ☎ 800/788–7885 ⊕ www.tauck.com.

SPECIAL-INTEREST TOURS

BIRD-WATCHING

Hawaii has more than 150 species of birds that live in the Hawaiian Islands. Field Guides has a three-island (Oahu, Kauai,

FODORS.COM CONNECTION

Before your trip, be sure to check out what other travelers are saying in Travel Ratings and Talk Forums on ⊕ *www.fodors.com*.

and the Big Island), 10-day guided bird-watching trip for 14 birding enthusiasts that focuses on endemic land birds and specialty seabirds. While on Kauai, birders will visit Kokee State Park, Alakai Wilderness Preserve, and Kilauea Point. The trip costs about $4,950 per person and includes accommodations, meals, ground transportation, interisland air, an eight-hour pelagic boat trip, and guided bird-watching excursions. Travelers must purchase their own airfare to and from their gateway city. Field Guides has been offering worldwide birding tours since 1984.

Victor Emanuel Nature Tours, the largest company in the world specializing in birding tours, has two nine-day trips that include Kauai. The guide for both tours is Bob Sundstrom, a skilled birder with a special interest in birdsong who has been leading birding tours in Hawaii and other destinations since 1989. *Spring Hawaii* is the theme of the late February/early March birding trip, when seabird diversity on the island is at its peak. Birders will see the *koloa* (Hawaiian duck), one of Hawaii's most endangered wetland birds, as well as Laysan albatrosses, red- and white-tailed tropic birds, red-footed boobies, wedge-tailed shearwaters, great frigate birds, brown boobies, and possibly even red-billed tropic birds. Participants in the *Fall Hawaii* birding trip will visit Oahu, Kauai, and the Big Island in October. Birders will see Kauai honeycreepers and Hawaiian short-eared owls at Kokee State Park and Alakai Swamp and seabirds at the National Wildlife Refuges at Kilauea and Hanalei. Both the *Spring Hawaii* and *Fall Hawaii* tours cost about $4,295 per person. Both trips include accommodations, meals, interisland air, ground transportation, and guided excursions. Travelers must purchase their own airline ticket to and from their gateway city. Tours begin in Honolulu and end up in Hilo.

Contacts Field Guides. ☎ 800/728–4953 ⊕ www.fieldguides.com. **Victor Emanuel Nature Tours.** ☎ 800/328–8368 ⊕ www.ventbird.com.

CULTURE

RoadScholar (formerly Elderhostel), a nonprofit educational travel organization, offers several guided tours for older adults that focus on Hawaiian culture. With all the tours listed, travelers must purchase their own airline tickets to Hawaii. We've chosen a few of our favorite tours here, but more information on tour subjects can be found on the organization's website.

Best of Kauai's Natural and Cultural Wonders is a six-night tour presented in association with the Kauai Historical Consortium. You'll visit Hanalei, Kilauea Point National Wildlife Refuge, Grove Farm Homestead Museum, Kauai Museum, and Kokee Natural History Museum. You'll learn *lauhala* weaving and other traditional arts and crafts and discover why the island truly is like no other. The cost of this tour starts at $1,725 per person and includes accommodations, meals, ground transportation, admission fees, as well as tipping charges and a travel assistance plan.

The Best of Hawaii and Kauai is a 10-night tour, split up by 5 nights on the Big Island of Hawaii and 5 nights on Kauai. Exploring the natural beauty of these two islands, you'll visit Volcanoes National Park and the Hamakua Coast on Hawaii, then explore the Kilauea Point National Wildlife Refuge and the National Tropical Botanical Gardens on Kauai, learning about these two islands' diverse birdlife, marine life, forests, volcanoes, and more. Prices start at $2,748 per person and include accommodations, meals, ground transportation, admission fees, and interisland air travel between Kauai and the Big Island.

Contact Road Scholar. ☎ 800/454–5768 ⊕ www.roadscholar.org.

ECO-TOURS

Want to spend a week in Kauai hiking, snorkeling, surfing, and paddling? Kayak Kauai has a seven-day *Discovery Tour* where you will explore Kauai's peaks and canyons, rivers and coastlines, and discover lagoons with crystal-clear water and breathtaking waterfalls, sacred trails, and miles of ivory-white sand beaches. Tours are offered every month and include accommodations, airport shuttles, van support during the week, communal gear, linens, all meals, guides, day tours, and activities. *Discovery Tour* is rated moderate but can be challenging at times, and participants should be in good physical condition. With a group of four or more, it is priced at $1,750 per person. Travelers must purchase their own airline tickets between their gateway cities and Kauai.

Contact Kayak Kauai. ☎ 808/826–9844, 888/596–3853 ⊕ www.kayakkauai.com.

HIKING

Hiking the Garden Island is the theme of a weeklong trip to Kauai sponsored by Sierra Club Outings. In addition to daylong hikes of 5 to 9 miles through many of the rain forests in Kokee State Park, participants will have opportunities for snorkeling and swimming at secluded beaches, as well as bird-watching. Hikers also will help in the maintenance of some of the trails. Accommodations are in shared cabins and, as with all Sierra Club Outings, participants are expected to help prepare some of the meals using only local, fresh ingredients. The trip costs about $1,695 per person and includes accommodations, meals, and ground transportation.

Timberline Adventures offers periodic trips to the Garden Island, including its *Kauai: Waimea Canyon and the NaPali Coast*, a six-day journey into the rain forests of Kokee State Park and Waimea Canyon. With miles of hiking trails, it's an opportunity to explore Kauai's inner beauty, including rare birds, waterfalls, and spectacular scenery. Other day trips have you hiking Sleeping Giant and kayaking the Wailua River. Perhaps the best hike is along the Kalalau Trail up into Hanakapiai Falls, with a payoff of tropical tranquility. Cost is $3,495/person for a double booking or $4,395 for a single.

Travelers must purchase their own tickets to and from their gateway city.

Contacts Sierra Club Outings. ☎ 415/977–5500 ⊕ sierraclouboutings.org. **Timberline Adventures.** ☎ 800/417–2453 ⊕ www.timberline-adventures.com.

■ VISITOR INFORMATION

Before you go, contact the Kauai Visitors Bureau for a free travel planner that has information on accommodations, transportation, sports and activities, dining, arts and entertainment, and culture. You can also take a virtual tour of the island that includes great photos and helpful planning information.

The Hawaii Tourism Authority's Travel Smart Hawaii site offers tips on everything from packing to flying. Also visit the Hawaii State Vacation Planner for all information on the destination, including camping.

ONLINE TRAVEL TOOLS
The Hawaii Department of Land and Natural Resources has information on hiking, fishing, and camping permits and licenses; online brochures on hiking safety and mountain and ocean preservation; and details on volunteer programs. The Kauai Visitors Bureau has Kauai-specific information on everything from activities to lodging options and organizes it by geographic regions on the island.

Contacts Hawaii Department of Land and Natural Resources. ✉ *Kalanimoku Bldg., 1151 Punchbowl St., Honolulu* ☎ *808/587–0400* ⊕ *dlnr.hawaii.gov.* **Hawaii Tourism Authority.** ✉ *1801 Kalakaua Ave., 1st fl., Honolulu* ☎ *808/973–2255* ⊕ *www.hawaiitourismauthority.org.*

ALL ABOUT KAUAI
Resources Hawaii Beach Safety. ⊕ *hawaiibeachsafety.com.* **Hawaii Department of Land and Natural Resources.** ⊕ *dlnr.hawaii.gov.* **Kauai Vacation Explorer.** ⊕ *www.kauaiexplorer.com.* **Kauai Visitors Bureau.** ⊕ *www.gohawaii.com/kauai.*

INDEX

PHOTO CREDITS

NOTES

NOTES

NOTES

NOTES

NOTES

NOTES

NOTES

NOTES

ABOUT OUR WRITERS

 Charles E. Roessler is a longtime Kauai resident who was an editor for the *Japan Times* and the *Buffalo News* after teaching English and journalism for 10 years. He contributes to the *New York Times* as a stringer/freelancer and loves Kauai, especially playing tennis and swimming at Anini Beach. Charles updated the Experience, Exploring, and Golf, Hiking, and Outdoor Activities sections of this guide.

 Joan Conrow is an independent journalist who splits her time between Kauai and New Mexico. She has written about Hawaii politics, culture, environment, and lifestyles for many regional and national publications. She helped write the original Fodor's guide to Kauai and updated the Shops and Spas, Where to Eat, Where to Stay, Water Sports and Tours, Beaches, and Nightlife and Performing Arts sections of this guide.